THE RETURN OF
THE BENEDICTINES
TO LONDON

by the same author

WESTMINSTER CATHEDRAL: FROM DREAM TO REALITY

THE RETURN OF THE BENEDICTINES TO LONDON

A History of Ealing Abbey from 1896 to Independence

RENE KOLLAR

BURNS & OATES

First published in 1989

Burns and Oates Ltd
Wellwood, North Farm Road,
Tunbridge Wells, Kent TN2 3DR,
England

ISBN 0 86012 175 5

Laserset by Scribe Design, Gillingham, Kent
Printed and bound in Great Britain by
Biddles Ltd, Guildford and King's Lynn

CONTENTS

LIST OF ILLUSTRATIONS

Title page: The Arms of Ealing Abbey, granted by the College of Arms in 1956. The design is by the late Dom Aelred Barnes who used heraldic symbols to trace Ealing's history and tradition.

The photographs are reproduced by John Ross

INTRODUCTION

Benedictine monasticism has played an influential role in the social, political, and religious development of England. Statesmen, pastors, and educators can be counted among the followers of St Benedict. Moreover, Benedictine monasteries have provided schools to educate the youth of England and inns to welcome the weary pilgrim or traveller. Human frailty was recorded in visitation reports and thrived in popular legends and stores, but by the sixteenth century the monasteries were clearly in need of reform. They had grown fat and were no match for the designs of Henry VIII.

Determined to have his divorce and resolved to sever ties to papal claims of authority, Henry believed that the wealth and the number of the monasteries might threaten the royal reformation. A dissolution was in order, and an eager Parliament provided the legal justification which gave a veneer of lawfulness to monastic suppression and spoliation. Henry's Roman Catholic daughter Mary eventually brought the monks back to London, but Elizabeth dismissed them during her reign. Monks, therefore, did not grace the environs of the capital for nearly three centuries. At the end of the nineteenth century, however, the Benedictines of Downside responded to Cardinal Herbert Vaughan's invitation to settle in Ealing so that they might provide monastic voices to sing the Divine Office at his new cathedral (a new Westminster) in nearby central London.

Vaughan's romantic dream never materialized. His flirtations with the French monks of Solesmes, whom he also invited to London, drew angry protests from the English Benedictines. The native monks demanded the privilege of staffing the new English Roman Catholic cathedral. And moreover, Vaughan's preference for the monks piqued and angered some of his secular clergy. They wondered why their Cardinal did not approach them, and some raised a storm against his monastic plans. Suspicion, jealousy, and rivalry eventually wrecked the original design: liturgical duties at Westminster Cathedral were entrusted to the secular clergy. But the Downside monks at Ealing did not disperse back to Somerset.

This history of Ealing Abbey traces the slow and steady growth of the monastic community from 1896 to 1947, when it became an independent priory. The experience of this suburban monastery reflects the struggles of the larger Roman Catholic community in England: tension between the secular clergy and religious orders; the purpose and future of Roman Catholic education; the strain put upon traditional parish structures by an increase in population and changes in class structure; the question of religious authority; and the trials and difficulties associated with two world wars. Nor is it a cold institutional saga: men of vision and fortitude brought with them into the capital a firm determination to succeed and a fierce loyalty to Benedictine principles. The history of Ealing Abbey also offers something to both the professional and amateur student of monasticism. If a common thread runs through the story of these monks, it is their struggle to reconcile the precepts of traditional English monasticism to the demands and challenges of an unfamiliar, urban setting. The Ealing monks have succeeded in this task.

This work is another contribution by the author to the study of modern English Benedictine history. An earlier book, *Westminster Cathedral: From Dream to Reality*, describes Cardinal Vaughan's early vision for a monastic foundation at Westminster Cathedral, his overtures to the French and English Benedictines, and the eventual abandonment of his romantic and impractical plan. Sections of this book have appeared earlier in print. 'Bishops and Benedictines: The Case of Father Richard O'Halloran' published in the *Journal of Ecclesiastical History*, July 1987 (Cambridge University Press), sketches the stormy relations between this cleric and the Ealing monks. 'The Return of the Benedictines to London,' published in *Tjurunga* (September 1987) emphasizes the motives behind the English Benedictines' desire to return to London. 'Ealing: The Proper and Respectable London Suburb' was published in *Local History* (April/May 1986).

This project was undertaken at the request of Abbot Francis Rossiter, superior at Ealing and at present Abbot President of the English Benedictine Congregation, and the Ealing community. The archives at Ealing Abbey supplied a treasure trove for monastic history. The encouragement and support of the Ealing community was invaluable. Founding members of the 1947 independent priory, along with the late Dom Adrian Morey, agreed to be interviewed. Their comments contributed greatly to the last two chapters. Doms Philip Jebb, Daniel Rees and Aidan Bellenger of Downside, the founding abbey, assisted me on my several research trips there and made my stays enjoyable. Miss Elizabeth Poyser, Archivist of the Archdiocese of Westminster, helped me to find information about Ealing's early history among the Vaughan and Bourne papers. Father William Mol of Mill Hill made the O'Halloran file available to me. And the friendly staff of the local history section of the London Borough of Ealing Library supplied valuable assistance dealing with the borough's history. In America, three research grants from St Vincent

College made my trips across the Atlantic possible. John Elliott, the History Department of St Vincent College, St Vincent Seminary, and Archabbot Paul Maher have supported me in my research. And my thanks to special students.

Lastly, a note about money matters in the text. I have not tried to render any modern equivalents and have expressed all sums as they were expressed at the time in pounds, shillings and pence, and occasionally, as with school fees, in guineas (£1.1s.0d.). In general terms, though, one can say that a sum from the period of the 1940s has to be multiplied by eleven times to reach the equivalent money of the late 1980s.

June 1989 R.K.

CHAPTER I

A New Westminster Cathedral and Benedictine Monks

cathedral in central London, many English Catholics agreed, was
needed not only to provide a place of worship for the faithful of
the metropolis, but would also provide a visible monument to the
respectability and achievements of their religion. 'The outward
symbol of this ability to build well and expensively was Westminster
Cathedral.'[1] Moreover, some proud Roman Catholics wanted a permanent
monument to their first Archbishop of the industrial age, Nicholas Wiseman,
who had died in 1865. His successor, Cardinal Henry Manning, saw other
priorities, and his dedication to the eradication of poverty in London meant
that a new cathedral might have to be sacrificed. Manning believed that 'the
work of saving these children was his first duty, the first duty of the Catholics
in London'.[2] 'Could I leave 20,000 children without education and train my
friends to pile up stone and bricks?'[3] Cathedral building represented an
expensive relic associated with medieval civilizations: 'I have been content
with my Old Sarum and Selsey. The days of Salisbury and Chichester are to
come'.[4] E. S. Purcell, in his life of Manning, captured the archbishop's
thoughts on a new cathedral:

> A memorial church to Cardinal Wiseman belonged to the past, but the saving of
> Catholic children from the Protestant workhouse or reformatories, where their faith
> would be lost, belonged to the present and the future, and he made this saving work
> the primary end and aim of his labours.[5]

Nevertheless, zealous Catholics continued to dream, and even purchased the
site for the future London cathedral. Manning's successor, Cardinal Herbert
Vaughan, eventually emerged as the individual who pushed the plans for this
new church to fruition.

Vaughan[6] became the Archbishop of Westminster in 1893 and he brought
to his large urban archdiocese a sense of triumphalism, loyalty to Rome, and
a commitment to educational and financial reforms. But dedication to the
construction of a new cathedral also coloured his tenure in office. 'When
Vaughan became Archbishop, he immediately decided as his major project, to
build a cathedral which would be a liturgical, pastoral and intellectual centre

1

for English Catholicism.'[7] Long overdue recognition of the progress of Roman Catholics in Britain became the motivation behind Cardinal Vaughan's desire, and the 'building of Westminster Cathedral was both symbolic of his general attitude as well as an example of his administrative ability'.[8] According to his biographer, Vaughan wanted a 'Cathedral which should be the heart of the Church in England, and the vivifying centre of its spirit and worship'.[9] Moreover, 'it was to be the home of a companionship of priests, the example of whose lives should colour all the ideals and activities of the diocese'. This new church must necessarily become the spiritual centre of England. Lecturers would address the faithful, meeting space would be available for clubs, and dedicated clergy would minister to the spiritual needs of the London area. Because of his untiring efforts and the financial contributions of numerous eager Roman Catholics, Westminster Cathedral emerged from a dream into a reality.

With pomp and grandeur, Cardinal Herbert Vaughan solemnly blessed the foundation stone of his new cathedral in June 1895. At a celebration following the impressive ceremony, Vaughan sketched his plans for the future of his metropolitan church. This was to be no ordinary place of worship. Vaughan pointed out 'that the Catholic body must have a cathedral in which the sacred liturgy of the church should be carried out in all its fullness day by day, and many times a day, as it was of old in Westminster and in Canterbury'.[10] The dignitaries present, ecclesiastical and lay, greeted this vision with applause. If Vaughan wanted to bring back the glories of the pre-Reformation Roman Catholic Church to Britain, then he could not ignore the English Benedictine Congregation. As in the days before the destruction of the Henrician reforms, monks must breathe life into this new Westminster. And the English monks were eager to accommodate the Archbishop's wish. Vaughan, whose brother Jerome was a monk of St Gregory's, Downside, revealed that this 'anxiety with regard to the Cathedral was allayed by the readiness with which he found the English Benedictine Fathers, full of life and energy and numbers, ready to come back to Westminster'.[11] The monks of St Gregory's, whom the Cardinal admired, would supply the manpower. The London suburb of Ealing would be a suitable location for the Benedictines who would take charge of the liturgy at Vaughan's cathedral.

Located approximately ten miles west of Hyde Park Corner, Ealing always enjoyed a reputation for rusticity, respectability, and country life. During the eighteenth century, Ealing and Little Ealing, 'described merely as very pleasant villages near Brentford',[12] attracted numerous royal and noble residents before evolving into the proper middle-class suburb of the 1860s. The population of Ealing parish, including Old Brentford, climbed slowly from an estimated 5,000 in 1801 to 7,800 in 1831, and then close to 10,000 in 1851. This growth in population and the reputation of a community with 'the solid respectable residences of the nineteenth century' coincided with advances in technology, especially the expansion of the Great Western Railway which opened its local station in 1838.[13] By 1864, consequently, individuals were already speculating about land development in Ealing, and the solid character of Victorian Ealing was 'illustrated by the fact that in 1868 houses at Castle Hill were being advertised at rentals from £150 to £250 per annum'. Many houses were both grand and impressive: 'semi-detached houses along Kent Gardens and villas in Cleveland Road each contained eight and ten bedrooms respectively'.[14]

If the railway contributed to the expansion of Ealing, it also accounted for its class-consciousness. The timetable and fares of the various railways after the middle of the century illustrate that these companies catered to the needs of a prosperous middle class. Moreover, the local boards of Ealing fought against the introduction of cheap fares and actively opposed any expansion of the tramway down the Uxbridge Road until 1885. The working class, therefore, was excluded, and Ealing retained its special character. 'The virtual absence of early morning trains and the relatively high fares did not encourage the development of the working-class suburbs to any extent comparable with the growth of the middle-class railway suburbs during the same period.'[15] The *Middlesex County Times* commented in 1872 that it was 'almost incredible that a company like the Great Western, with a suburb district at its command, should . . . not run a single train to the metropolis before 8am'.[16] The same paper seven years later noted that 'working people such as mechanics, laundry assistants, and daily labourers . . . certainly have not the means to afford extravagant railways fares.'[17] Only at the turn of the century did early morning trains at low return rates appear.

Consequently, Ealing rapidly developed into a purely residential area with a proud class prejudice. In 1878, for example, new houses in the suburb tripled from the previous years, and this increase was six times the total number of houses constructed in 1876.[18] Twenty years later, the population had expanded to over 35,000, and potential residents of Ealing were told that one could relax and enjoy life in Ealing. 'Promotional literature, often financed by tradesmen, presented Ealing as more of a separate town in its own right than any other outlying suburb.'[19] During the 1890s, Ealing offered 'every advantage of modern civilization' with a gentle touch of 'charming rusticity'. During the same decade, a contemporary account described Ealing as progressing quietly and steadily, 'keeping a "step in advance" of the majority of the surrounding districts with a lower yearly death rate and a lower yearly rate than any district of a corresponding character and population can boast of'.[20] The author could not foresee any change in the fibre and complexion of Ealing. The area 'has grown into one of the most properous and best known of the western districts', he noted with pride, and 'if the Ealing of the future is true to the tradition of the past thirty years . . . [it] will still enable it to occupy the foremost places amongst the western suburbs of London'.[21]

The residents of Edwardian Ealing took as much pride in their suburb as their Victorian ancestors. According to *The Victorian History of the Counties of England*, during the first years of the new century 'Ealing . . . claimed to be the Queen of the Suburbs'.[22] With a census which topped 33,000, Ealing was chartered as a borough in 1901, the first of the modern Middlesex boroughs.[23] The Ealing citizen valued its open spaces and country-like simplicity.

A contemporary history literally canonized its subject: 'and it is no small qualification to know that the once comparatively unknown village is recognized as the Queen of the Suburbs, with a name that stands out, far and near, for its advance in sanitary work and its retention to the fullest extent of its floriculture and sylvan beauty'.[24] Another Edwardian description commented that Ealing enjoyed all the conveniences of town life, 'while its tree-bordered streets, its finely-wooded public parks and other open spaces and the magnificent stretch of open country to the north, stamp it as a country town, or, in the phrase of the moment, a "garden city."'[25] Ealing's success and popularity would continue. On 3 June 1911, the Lord Mayor proudly described his borough as a 'garden suburb'.[26] And he produced the statistics to substantiate this boast: 'Since 1873 . . . the District Council had planted 12,000 trees; there were fifty miles of avenues, a record for any suburb; and 160 acres of open space and recreation grounds'.

Consequently, Ealing attracted respectable and established families. In 1901, the largest industries were the building trade and transport, which employed 1,458 and 99 respectively. The jobs held by working women reflected the character of the area. Domestic servants numbered 4,616 in 1901, but the number of increased to 5,545 a decade later.[27] At the turn of the century, Ealing employed a higher proportion of women servants than any section of London with the exception of Hampstead and Kensington.[28] The rates of 'female domestic servants to the total number of separate occupiers was 60 per cent in 1901. . ..'[29] In contrast, the figure for nearby Acton was only 25 per cent.

Although cheaper housing became more available after 1904, the prosperous areas retained their identity, and consequently the middle class still dominated the London suburb. Civic pride and a class-consciousness continued to characterize the attitude and spirit of Ealing. A local paper boasted that 'few of the shops were mere branches of London stores . . . and there were many fashionable promenades, clubs, hostels and entertainments'.[30] Another publication supported this contention: 'Ealing is, by general consent, one of the best shopping centres out of London'.[31]

Later Victorian and Edwardian Ealing, therefore, enjoyed all the cosmopolitan allurements, but did not suffer the drawbacks and harshness of urban life. A low death rate was repeatedly stressed, and the reason behind this phenomenon was attributed to Ealing's gravel subsoil. Residents were also assured that they had escaped other problems associated with the capital. 'It has no cemeteries except its own, no workhouse within its borders, no poor Law Schools, [and] no lunatic asylums.'[32] Criminals were sent to neighbouring towns for trials. Consequently, Ealing told its inhabitants that it had 'successfully resisted all attempts to make it a dumping-ground for London's nuisances'.[33] But Ealing did not oppose progress. Commenting on advances in health and sanitation, a local writer noted with pride that 'Ealing was the first place in the Thames valley where a systematic and successful attempt was made to prevent the sewage passing into the River Thames'.[34]

In addition to its gentrified character, Ealing's long tradition of outstanding educational facilities greatly contributed to its image of respectability. Excellent private shools had flourished in Ealing since the eighteenth century. One can measure the standards of these institutions by some of their students: Henry Addington, Viscount Sidmouth; Thomas Bruce, Earl of Elgin; Edward Bulwer-Lytton; and the Oxford theologian John Henry Newman. Louis-Philippe, future King of the French, taught geography and mathematics at Great Ealing School. 'The village of Ealing has been for many years noted for its schools,' a turn-of-the-century local historian pointed out, the most famous being the Great Ealing School, which was 'second only to the great public schools of Eton and Harrow'.[35] From nine schools in 1826, the number grew to twenty-nine early in the twentieth century. Ealing's commitment to educational quality and excellence, therefore, mirrored the community's boast of respectability, propriety and comfort.

The Roman Catholics of this growing and prosperous suburb of the capital had already enjoyed the services of Benedictine monks before Cardinal Vaughan's dreams to establish them there. According to Dom Gilbert Dolan, OSB, an historian of the Benedictines in England and later parish priest at the Ealing mission, 'Ealing was under the spiritual care of the Benedictines from AD 1825 to AD 1850'.[36] 'The register of baptisms of the Acton Mission during that period,' he pointed out, 'contains several entries relating to Ealing . . . The first entry is of date 16 July 1825, about which time the Benedictine Fathers seem to have come to Acton'. He also identified Dom William Scott, a monk of Downside, as the first monk to reside at Acton. 'The Acton mission covered a wide area; beside Acton itself, the following places were served by it: Ealing, Turnham Green, Hanwell, Brentford and Shepherd's Bush.' Dom Gilbert discovered at least one dozen Ealing residents who were baptized by the Benedictines from the Acton mission. Moreover, the 1850 parish census list contained the names of fourteen parishioners who lived in Ealing.[37]

In the mind of Cardinal Vaughan, Ealing seemed an ideal place, and his plan for a Benedictine foundation there seemed simple: 'while safeguarding the position and rights of the chapter, to hand over the whole working and management of the cathedral to the monks'.[38] As in the Middle Ages, therefore, a cathedral would be staffed by the Black Monks. A Prior would be the immediate superior, but Vaughan hoped to enjoy the privileges and jurisdiction of an Abbot. According to his biographer, this vision 'at one time certainly represented what the Cardinal meant when he spoke of the Benedictines coming back to Westminster'. Moreover, Vaughan wanted to hand over 'to the Benedictines the two missions in Westminster, which would ultimately be incorporated in the Cathedral parish, so that they might become familiar with the district they would have to work in when the Cathedral was opened'.[39] Vaughan maintained that 'there could be no higher or holier work any body of men could be called upon to undertake, and he still unhesitatingly counted on the co-operation of the monks'.[40]

To bring the Benedictine monks to London was the first step. The Benedictines had settled at Downside near Bath in 1814, and by the 1890s the community had grown in membership. These monks were committed to missionary work and the conversion of England to Roman Catholicism, and London would become the centre for this activity.[41] On 5 May 1896, therefore, Cardinal Vaughan wrote to the superior at Downside, Prior Hugh Edmund Ford[42] and suggested that a piece of property in Ealing 'would make an excellent gift for the community'.[43] Moreover, the Cardinal stated, he was 'disposed to give' to the monks 'the Ealing mission'. Vaughan remarked that the property was currently owned by the Visitation Sisters, but it could be purchased for 'something under £4,000'. Ford responded and told Vaughan that he would soon be attending a headmasters' conference near London, and 'could look at the property then'.[44] But the Downside Prior also indicated that he was developing his own plans about a possible Benedictine presence in London: 'Your Eminence would I suppose wish us to try and do more than merely take charge of the mission, but when I see the property I will call'. On the same day that Ford responded to Cardinal Vaughan, he wrote to Abbot Benedict Snow,[45] then living in East Dulwich, and informed him of the invitation to start a foundation in London. Prior Ford sent him a copy of the Cardinal's letter of 5 May and asked if he could 'go and look at Ealing with a view to the enclosed'.[46] 'If you have an opportunity,' Ford continued, 'you might call at Archbishop's House and learn . . . all the details of the mission . . . We could then decide on the answer to the Cardinal.'

Through the energy and foresight of Prior Ford, the dream of a Benedictine presence in Ealing began to take shape. Born on 23 March 1851 at Clarence Villa, Clifton Park, Hugh Ford was sent to Downside in 1861 to begin his education. Believing that he had a Benedictine vocation, he entered Downside, and made his solemn profession as a monk on 10 February 1873. Four years later he was ordained a priest by the Bishop of Clifton. In 1885, he was elected as Prior of Downside, 'being chosen, practically unanimously, at the first scrutiny'.[47] He held the post until 1888. After a stay at Beccles 1889–94, the community again chose him as their superior. Near the turn of the century, the bull *Diu Quidem* raised the English Benedictine priories to the rank and status of abbeys to be governed by Abbots, and on 26 September 1900, Hugh

Edmund Ford was elected the first Abbot at Downside. During his entire monastic life Ford laboured to imprint his interpretation of English Benedictinism on the Ealing foundation. He believed, for example, 'that the education and training of Catholic youth was an apostolic and monastic work',[48] and Ealing must not abandon this sacred mission. As one of the leading spokesmen of the so-called 'monastic movement' at Downside, Ford championed a vision of monastic life which would soon materialize at Ealing:

> the means whereby we are to work for the conversion of our country, now that the monasteries are in England, are, besides our external missionary work, those works which especially characterize the traditional action of our Order ... the liturgy, teaching, solid studies, theological, historical, and philosophical, the need of which is felt in England, but which can only be pursued with success by monks living in Community.[49]

During this early and sensitive period of negotiations about Ealing, Ford relied heavily on the experience and expertise of Abbot Benedict Snow.

Abbot Snow's role in the settlement of Ealing, consequently, cannot be underestimated. As Prior Ford's advisor, Snow showed himself an enthusiastic supporter of the new Benedictine foundation. Born in London on 23 September 1838, Dom Terence Benedict Snow entered Downside and took solemn vows on 24 June 1857, and was later ordained as priest in 1865. While stationed at St Peter's Liverpool, his fellow monks soon recognized his skills as a shrewd, intelligent and prudent administrator. In 1888, he was elected Provincial of York, and during the same year was honoured with the title of titular Abbot of Glastonbury. East Dulwich became his home from 1894 until his death in 1905, and from this London mission he gave Ford invaluable counsel on Ealing. Pragmatism and shrewdness characterized his approach to problems. His contemporaries believed that he 'was suspicious of anything which savoured of sensation, and disliked profoundly advertisement of overdue publicity'.[50] 'He was conservative in his methods to the last, and did not really encourage new experiment in parochial administration.'[51] His approach to the difficulties and the problems which faced the new mission at Ealing reflected his cautious manner, but when Ford explained that Cardinal Vaughan had offered the Benedictines a foundation there, Abbot Snow sprang into action.

A week later Snow visited Ealing. His report to Ford was positive and glowing. 'I went to Ealing today,' he wrote, 'it is a very pleasant place, beautifully wooded and thoroughly suburban.'[52] Snow pointed out that there were two railway stations nearby and emphasized that the area was a strictly residential neighbourhood. He described the prospective site for the new foundation, Castle Hill House, as 'beautiful', a 'good substantial house'. Snow then explained that a group of nuns from Westbury occupied the house. They 'have only been there a month,' he continued, 'but find the place too small for them and too near the road . . . so they are only there temporarily and looking for a larger place.'

The Abbot apologized that he could not offer much information on the local Roman Catholic population or its priest, Fr Richard O'Halloran.[53] 'I thought it best not to call on him as I gather from the Cardinal's letter that he might not know anything about the offer.' No chapel existed, and mass was celebrated in Fr O'Halloran's house. He estimated that the congregation averaged around one hundred. Concerning the legal aspects of any possible sale, Abbot Snow admitted that he did not approach the solicitors who were handling the matter, Blount, Lynch, and Petre, since it might be premature to discuss concrete proposals for the purchase. Because many individuals believed that 'Benedictines are so rich', Snow suggested that 'it would be better done through a third party if there is any idea of purchase'. Abbot Snow ended his report to Prior Ford with a glimmer of guarded optimism: 'I think it is a promising place in a rising neighbourhood but the difficulty is to get a return for the £4,000 purchase money – a deal and no church'.

Because of this encouragement and his own vision of an urban monastic foundation, Prior Ford approached the Visitation Sisters in May 1896 about the sale of Castle Hill House. Sister Mary Frances, the Mother Superior, told the Prior that the community planned to leave Ealing in June for larger accommodation in Harrow. She explained that Castle Hill House 'was bought when we only proposed to make a foundation', but eventually a much larger community of sisters moved to Ealing.[54] The Superior then told Prior Ford that the property 'became unsuitable because there are only two and a half acres of ground'. 'We shall be very pleased,' she continued, 'to let you see the whole place any day you like to call.' As for price, she informed Ford that the sisters were advised to ask for £4,100. It became apparent, therefore, that the nuns wanted the monks to purchase their property, and later explained that 'it will be very nice to think it will fall into Catholic hands'.[55] 'We could sell it tomorrow if we would sell to Protestants,' Sister Mary Frances wrote in June. With the Visitation Sisters anxious to conclude a bargain with the Benedictines, negotiations with Cardinal Vaughan presented the next step on the road to a settlement at Ealing.

Abbot Snow now advised Prior Ford on how to deal with the Cardinal, and sent him a draft letter for consideration. Snow urged Ford to be cautious and pointed out the dangers and difficulties which might face the monks once they settled in Ealing: the occupation of the monks; 'uncertain prospects of [a] school; uncertainty of means of support; burden of interest; and the erection of a church'.[56] A foundation in London had clearly captured the imagination of both Benedictines. Moreover, additional work, activity, and a source of funds must supplement any choir duty in Westminster Cathedral. If Benedictines from Downside were to settle in the environs of London, Snow believed they must be involved in parish work in addition to their ceremonial duties at the cathedral. Ford had already recognized this problem. Early in his correspondence with Cardinal Vaughan, for example, he had expressed his own vision for the future of Benedictine monks in London.[57] He believed that rendering the liturgy exclusively at Westminster Cathedral was inappropriate.[58]

Even though Ford believed that a Benedictine foundation in the capital was imperative, he also understood that any rash or unplanned action would be destructive. A man of prudence, he was not mesmerized by the imagination and idealism of Cardinal Vaughan. Consequently, Prior Ford's reply to Cardinal Vaughan's invitation, which was essentially the draft that Snow had sent him, reflected his pragmatic considerations. 'I cannot but express to Your Eminence our grateful acknowledgement for offering us the work that you suggest at Ealing,' he informed the Cardinal, 'and our appreciation of the confidence placed in us by entrusting it to us.'[59] Ford admitted that he wanted more time to explore all avenues for success at Ealing. Secure and stable work for his monks, however, must be secured immediately. 'Your Eminence will recognized the dangers of establishing a religious community without sufficient occupation for its members and the consequent difficulty in maintaining a religious spirit . . . Hence I feel,' he continued, 'a scruple in sending a religious anywhere without assigning a definite work that he could and would do.' In the future, Ford suggested, a Benedictine school associated with the Ealing mission should become a real possibility. Moreover, 'the prospects of a school can only be tested by further acquaintance with the existing neighbourhood, and some data to forecast its future development'.

Ford's business acumen also surfaced in this reply to the Cardinal. He argued, for example, that parochial work in Ealing must definitely form a part of any bargain. A five-year trial period would test the feasibility of this idea. Ford, therefore, suggested that Cardinal Vaughan grant him permission to send a monk to Ealing 'at once to get things together and attend to the spiritual wants of the people shortly after . . . I have little doubt that I could give him a companion to attend to the convent'. With a congregation entrusted to the monks and the possibility of a Benedictine school, Ford saw a bright future for Ealing. 'If this meets with Your Eminence's approval I should be willing to take the risk of purchasing the property, which will be a substantial earnest of our intention to carry out your wishes.' Ford concluded his letter to Cardinal Vaughan by pointing out that pastoral work in the London area would not detract from any liturgical duties at the cathedral. 'I would add that the establishment of a house at Ealing would not render it more difficult to find men for the Cathedral, on the contrary it would I think render it easier by providing another community from which to draw when the time comes.' Ford had made his position clear. He would gladly assign monks for work at Westminster Cathedral only if there were some pastoral duties and the possibility of a school, both of which would supply additional income for the London venture.

Along with this formal response, Prior Ford also enclosed a more personal note. In it, he revealed that the question of the future relationship between the monks working at the cathedral, those living at Ealing, and the community at Downside had already surfaced, but he thought it 'would be better to let these work themselves out as time goes on'.[60] The Prior also hinted that the interest of Downside might be harmed if definite conditions were stipulated at this stage of the talks. Ealing, for example, could become an independent monastery within a decade. Ford also admitted that he was a novice in such undertakings as the establishment of new foundations, and confessed that he had sought more experienced counsel. Nonetheless, he professed his desire to continue to explore the Ealing venture and asked for an interview between himself and the Cardinal.

Vaughan responded that he also wanted a meeting and suggested 11 June. The Cardinal, however, quickly drew attention to a serious problem with Prior Ford's plans or designs for an Ealing foundation. According to Cardinal Vaughan, the existence of a Benedictine school in the suburb created a serious problem: Vaughan noted 'that certain difficulties have arisen as to a college at Ealing'.[61] 'Not that there is no need of one and the need will become greater each year in the neighbourhood,' Cardinal Vaughan pointed out, 'but Wanstead presents many advantages and would be a better place than Ealing in several respects.' With this note of caution or apprehension about the possibility of a monastic educational apostolate, the future of the monks in Ealing rested on the outcome of the meeting between Cardinal Vaughan and Prior Ford in London.

The interview took place on 11 June at Archbishop's House, but no records or notes of the meeting survive. Both clerics, however, finally reached a series of agreements after much discussion, and Vaughan later enumerated these in a subsequent letter to Prior Ford. Vaughan clearly and forcefully announced his position: 'In reference to our conversation on the proposal that you should open a house at Ealing and take charge of the mission I make the following conditions.'[62] The Cardinal promised to authorize a Benedictine foundation at Ealing 'provided the consent of the Holy See can be obtained'. But in respect to a school operated by the monks, Cardinal Vaughan stipulated that an Ealing foundation 'is not to include the opening of any School other than a Public Elementary School'. Moreover, permission had to be obtained from the ordinary of the archdiocese for the Benedictines to alter this requirement in the future. The Cardinal did, however, make some concessions to Prior Ford's requests. According to the Cardinal's letter, two elements must constitute the life and work of this new urban monastery: 'the serving of the mission in the usual way', and the 'establishment of a Religious Community of your Order and the observance of Common Life according to your rule, within five years of your going to Ealing'. Pastoral work, therefore, would supplement work at the cathedral, but Vaughan placed another stipulation on the Benedictines. If after the five-year period a community of six monks had failed to materialize or prosper, Vaughan claimed the prerogative to repay the Benedictine Order for the money expended on the purchase of the property, and he could then insist on his right to take possession of the Ealing property. But Cardinal Vaughan's ultimate purpose for proposing a Benedictine foundation near London could be found in the conclusion of his letter to Prior Ford: 'one of the principle reasons inducing the Cardinal Archbishop to invite the Benedictines to open a house at Ealing is that they may be sufficiently near to Westminster to contribute to the Choral service of the Cathedral'.

Cardinal Vaughan had presented his terms in a clear and straightforward manner. To Ford, however, they were too narrow, too restrictive; a compromise must be reached before he could commit his monks to this new venture. The Prior's notes, for example, make it clear that the necessary application to Rome would be for permission to establish 'a *domus* [i.e. a monastery] at Ealing with the care of the mission attached'.[63] In other words, Ford wanted it clearly understood that, when a sufficient number of monks resided at Ealing, the community could then apply to seek 'the full ecclesiastical position, rights and privileges of a Benedictine monastery'. Moreover, Ford believed that the Cardinal's limitation on an education apostolate run by the Benedictines 'would not prevent us . . . from having private pupils, as it is permitted to any mission'. The ban on a secondary school, however, did not seriously upset Prior Ford. 'He anticipated that when the parish at Ealing began to grow there would be many parents desirous of having a Catholic day school for their boys, which would secure their not having to attend non-Catholic establishments.'[64] Consequently, Ford reason-ed, Vaughan would eventually become anxious to have the monks operate a secondary school in Ealing. In general, Prior Ford also believed that Vaughan's regulations frustrated and hindered any future expansion for the Ealing foundation, and he believed that the monks 'ought to be free to deal with the land we buy for ourselvs in the way most advantageous'.[65]

In an attempt to soften Vaughan's conditions, Ford met again with the Cardinal at Belmont Priory on 29 June 1896. The Cardinal agreed to some amendments, which 'were read to . . .[him] and approved by him',[66] but the wording concerning the power of the Cardinal to appropriate the property at Ealing if certain conditions were not met was modified. The new wording of the agreement read:

> the Archbishop shall have the power to purchase from you the Benedictine Order at cost price the land now bought for the mission and to repay you any money your Order may have expended upon the land, for the benefit of the mission or upon buildings which the Archbishop shall not have considered unnecessary for the mission, and the Benedictines shall retire from Ealing.

After the Belmont meeting, Prior Ford again approached Abbot Snow, who from the beginning had never lost interest in the Ealing project, and sought his advice. Ford told his friend that the Cardinal 'would not modify the wording of his proposal' about a school at Ealing.[67] According to Prior Ford, the Cardinal had expressed a fear that even a dozen students at Ealing 'would take the cream of the neighbourhood and leave St Charles [in Bayswater] the rest . . .' Vaughan obviously wanted to protect the interests of St Charles, but did agree that if the monks wanted one or two students to help financially, he would not refuse permission. When asked by the Cardinal to comment on the extent of the responsibilities of the monks for singing the Divine Office at Westminster Cathedral, Ford told Abbot Snow that he remained silent. This letter to the Abbot, moreover, also contained a sense of urgency: Ford argued that the site in Ealing must be purchased immediately. 'The nuns will be getting impatient,' he wrote, and '. . . we shall have to be ready with a proposal for getting the money.' It again became apparent that the important point for Prior Ford was not the realization of Cardinal Vaughan's dream of monks chanting their psalms in London, but, on the other hand, the establishment of a community with 'the full ecclesiastical position, rights and privileges of a Benedictine monastery'. His argument to Snow was clear: 'We had better get this while we can; the time when it would take effect would depend on ourselves.' 'Another Archbishop,' Ford reasoned, 'might oppose us in this.'

Not surprisingly, Snow's response again indicated his optimism and strong commitment to the Ealing scheme. 'As far as I can judge I think Ealing a very desirable locality for a Settlement,' he wrote to Ford, and 'it is a growing place within easy distance of London and as good a situation as we are likely to get in the Suburbs in the Westminster Diocese.'[68] He urged Ford not to worry about finances. In the first place, 'a priest ought to be able to get a living of the Catholics that are now there'. Moreover the convent in Ealing could employ another monk as a chaplain. The price asked for the property, approximately £4,000, did not seem excessive, and Snow believed that 'as far as one can judge the value of the land will increase should we – after a trial – be inclined to give it up'. Finally, he told Prior Ford that the Benedictines should already begin to draw up plans for the construction of a church and begin to think about the organization of the parish.

Snow could not restrain himself from commenting on Cardinal Vaughan's stipulations governing the establishment of the Benedictine colony in Ealing. A school would certainly ensure the success of the enterprise, and Snow believed the Cardinal's prohibition was unrealistic and unworkable. According to the Abbot's logic:

> the neighbourhood seems to be such that a school somewhat higher than an elementary one will become a necessity to prevent children going to private Protestant schools, and as soon as this evil can be demonstrated it will be very difficult for the ecclesiastical authorites to refuse a higher grade school for boys to rescue them from Protestant hands.

Without a school of this character, Vaughan's demand that there be six priests within five years might be difficult to meet. Like Ford, Abbot Snow was not smitten by the Cardinal's romantic musings about monks, plainchant, and the metropolitan cathedral; the success of the monastic foundation took precedence. 'The Choral Service at the Cathedral might be a blunder,' Snow informed his friend, but 'this is so worded that it can scarcely be held to as a condition sine qua non.' Moreover, 'it ought to be paid for if it ever comes to pass'.

In addition to Abbot Snow, Prior Ford also sought the opinion and advice of other English Benedictines. Dom Benedict Tidmarsh, formerly Procurator of the Southern Province, informed Ford that he thought 'the Cardinal's offer should be favourably considered, and if possible accepted, with perhaps some modifications'.[69] In respect to problems concerning the school, he pointed out that 'the restriction as to a school seems rather unreasonable, as it is not likely to interfere with any existing schools in the Diocese'. Some doubts existed, however, concerning the extent of the monks' liturgical duties at Westminster Cathedral: 'I suppose it only means assisting on great occasions or great festivals, but even this [would] be depriving the Ealing House of its regular choir duties'. Agreeing with Snow and Ford, he believed that singing plainchant in central London was not at all primary or essential. This monk explained to Prior Ford that 'regular daily attendance at Westminster would be out of the question'. And then, he continued, the expenses of 'travelling to and fro frequently' would be prohibitive. Even with these objections, Dom Benedict urged Ford to accept the Cardinal's offer, and reminded him not to repeat the failure of the previous East Dulwich venture.

Another Benedictine, Dom Wulstan Richards, advised Ford to welcome the Cardinal's invitation even with the conditions he imposed on the Benedictines. 'I cordially approve of the purchase of the site at Ealing and also of accepting the terms of the Cardinal,' he urged Prior Ford.[70] Dom Wulstan pointed out that the Benedictine monks could no longer 'get into London with a free hand, and we must accept such a qualified gift. . . .' Moreover, there was no reason why the 'London house of studies [in Great Ormond Street] could not be transferred to Ealing, a more healthy and fitting home than where it is at the present.' He also told Ford that the mount of money asked for the house and land could not be considered unreasonable; such a dwelling could not be built for less. Unlike the reply of Dom Benedict Tidmarsh, Dom Wulstan's reply bubbled with enthusiasm. Ford would receive the 'congratulations of every Gregorian' if he could bring this negotiation to a successful issue'. The Cardinal's conditions or stipulations must be accepted. London represented the prize and a 'foothold at last' secured for the Benedictines.

Another important issue now suddenly resurfaced. By the end of June the Visitation Sisters had become increasingly anxious about the Castle Hill property. The Mother Superior explained to Prior Ford that the community was 'on the point of leaving . . . for Harrow and should be very grateful to know from you whether you are still entertaining thoughts of taking the place.'[71] Again, she played the religious card: 'We should be of course very pleased if we were succeeded here by a religious community, and we are anxious to have a line from you as several other persons have been enquiring about the house.' Throughout the summer, the Superior continued to woo the Benedictines. 'I was very glad to get [your] letter and to hear it is almost settled about Ealing,' she wrote Ford, and 'it will be very nice having your Fathers so near.'[72] Prior Ford's interest in Castle Hill House never wavered: he reassured the nuns that he remained optimistic that the Cardinal would approve of the Ealing settlement; and he emphasized that the Abbot President of the English Benedictine Congregation and his Council would be swayed by the reasonable price.[73] Before negotiations on the sale of the property or talks with Archbishop's House could proceed any farther, however, Prior Ford had to secure the necessary permission of Abbot President Anselm O'Gorman and his advisors for the settlement of the Benedictines in Ealing.

Now supported by Abbot Snow, Prior Ford wrote to Dom Anselm O'Gorman, President of the English Benedictine Congregation and his Council, the Regimen, and presented strong arguments in favour of sending English Benedictines from Downside to London.[74] On 17 August, therefore, Ford informed the President that 'the Cardinal has asked us to open a house at Ealing and offered us the Mission'.[75] Moreover, he continued, Cardinal Vaughan made the 'offer with the hope that we may later on have a community there'. Consequently, Ford asked the President to begin to explore the avenues for applying to the Holy See for the required permission to establish a foundation in Ealing. On the following day, Prior Ford sent copies of Vaughan's offer and conditions to the President and the Regimen. He also enclosed a summary of Abbot Snow's favourable opinion. In addition to these documents, Ford added his own arguments for accepting the Cardinal's invitation: monks could live a monastic life at Ealing, conduct an urban parish, and at the same time be close enough to Westminster Cathedral to conduct the liturgical duties. He explained that the Benedictines could easily take the fifteen-minute trip on the Great Western Railway to central London for their work at the cathedral. Ealing, moreover, 'is said to be one of the best districts near London still unoccupied as a parish', Ford told his confrères, and 'the district is rapidly developing and will have the character of a high class suburb'.[76] The fate and future of a Benedictine presence in Ealing now rested with the President and the Regimen.

President O'Gorman replied immediately and thanked Ford for the information concerning developments at Ealing. He also invited the Prior to attend a meeting of the council to present the matter in person. But Prior Ford hesitated; he claimed that he had already forwarded all the information concerning Ealing and the Cardinal's offer to the President and the Regimen. Moreover, it was President O'Gorman's responsibility to consult his council on matters of this magnitude.[77] If requested, however, he would visit O'Gorman at his convenience and clarify any problems or difficulties. After this response by Ford, President O'Gorman began to contact members of the Regimen. Dom Alphonsus Morrall responded quickly. He informed the Abbot President that Prior Ford had already presented the Ealing proposal to a meeting of his council at Downside, which he attended. The Downside Council accepted the plan, but he had several reservations, which he expressed to President O'Gorman. Dom Alphonsus stated that he could not wholeheartedly support the idea, but on the other hand, could not fully oppose it. According to his report, 'no one saw how the conditions as to the numbers of Priests to be there in a fixed numbr of years could be fulfilled'.[78] He also questioned how the 'means for their support [could] be provided by the people at Ealing, where everything – congregation included – has to be created'. Dom Alphonsus told the President that Prior Ford claimed he enjoyed the approval of influential members of the English Benedictine Congregation for the Ealing proposal. 'I submit my judgement to theirs,' he informed O'Gorman, 'although not without misgivings.'

The Abbot President next contacted Dom Romuald Wood at Hereford. The President informed him that Prior Ford wanted to open a house at Ealing at the request of Cardinal Vaughan, reminded him that the approval of the Regimen was required, and drew his attention to Abbot Snow's letter of support, which he enclosed. Moreover, the President also revealed that he, like Dom Alphonsus Morrall, did not share the optimism and enthusiasm generated by Snow and Ford. The President wrote that he told Ford that 'the establishment at Ealing [presented] some difficulty for Downside'.[79] O'Gorman then stated four problems which he saw with Ford's Ealing designs: an additional foundation would place a strain on the small and over-burdened community at Downside; two Benedictine communities or houses already existed in London at Great Ormond Street and Dulwich;[80] 'the drain made by Cambridge on [the] Gregorians'; and finally, 'the prospect of having to send many subjects to the new Cathedral'. Nonetheless, the President noted, 'all the Gregorian family wants it'. The President told Dom Romuald to read Dom Alphonsus Morrall's comments, which he included, and asked for an opinion. The letter ended with President O'Gorman's candid comments on the question:

> As for myself, I feel inclined to grant the permission. The money question seems safe and if they cannot carry Ealing on, they will have to drop *it*, or some other establishment in London. It will be extremely advantageous to have one or more sites near London for recruiting purposes and for a proper display of our life and liturgy.

By the end of August, therefore, Prior Ford and Abbot Snow were campaigning for the Ealing scheme. Both saw the establishment of a

Benedictine house in the fashionable suburb as a boon; however, they were not as enthusiastic about committing monks to singing plainchant in Westminster Cathedral as Cardinal Vaughan. The President of the English Benedictine Congregation and the Regimen had also considered the matter. One member had already expressed his doubts, but also stated that he would voice no strong objection to the plan. Becuase of the apparent manpower shortage at Downside, the Abbot President also had some serious questions. But other considerations outweighed these reservations. Responses from the other two members of the Regimen testified to the prestige and respect enjoyed by Ford and Abbot Snow. If they sincerely wanted to open a foundation in London, they should get their wish. Dom Romuald Wood's response to O'Gorman's letter captured this spirit: 'I do not make any objection to the project'.[81] The last member of the Regimen also reflected this deference. Dom Cuthbert Doyle admitted that 'St Gregory's ought to be very chary about venturing upon any new undertaking', and he warned the Abbot President that Downside might be asked to consider some other worthwhile project.[82] 'Nonetheless in view of the opinion of so shrewd a man as Abbot Snow and the unanimity of the Gregorian Familia,' he informed the Abbot President that he was 'quite ready to acquiesce in the generally expressed wish of its members and say, by all means let them take Ealing.'

With the approval and cautious support of the Regimen, Abbot President O'Gorman wrote Prior Ford: 'In a few words the whole Regimen consents to accept the new establishment at Ealing'.[83] O'Gorman told Ford that he would petition the Holy See as soon as possible. But his vision of the new London undertaking also went beyond the narrow boundaries set by Cardinal Vaughan. He also advised Ford to ask the Cardinal 'for permission . . . to erect a college and monastery' in addition to serving the mission. 'We must take every precaution,' President O'Gorman continued, 'for future development.' The President also warned Ford of the possibility of trouble from the priest who was currently ministering in Ealing, Father Richard O'Halloran, who had sent him a threatening letter protesting the intrusion of the monks into his mission. O'Gorman noted that 'the poor fellow is very sore about the matter', and with a touch of wit added that Father O'Halloran 'needs a good deal of Ealing!' In another letter, O'Gorman virtually gave Ford a free hand in his dealings with Cardinal Vaughan, and told the Prior that 'whatever modifications the Cardinal and yourself may make, I suppose they will at least be the *framework* for any future documents'.[84]

At the end of the month, Prior Ford received the official document from the office of the Abbot President of the English Benedictine Congregation which stated:

> According to our Constitution I have reported the question to the Reverend *Definitori* of the Regimen. After mature consideration, we decided unanimously to accept the foundation which was offered as well as the Monastery to be built

successively, and eventually the mission of the place called Ealing, subject to the conditions requested by the Bull *Romanos Pontifices* concerning the permission of the Ordinary and the Holy See.[85]

O'Gorman's concern for propriety and the minutiae of ecclesiastical protocol also surfaced in a final instruction to Ford: 'Notice the way of folding the Popes [*sic*] petition – Below the outward address, ought to appear the name of the person who presents the petition to Rome'.

When informed, Abbot Snow was overjoyed at the news concerning the future of monasticism in Ealing, and he wrote Prior Ford that he was 'glad there is no trouble on the part of the President'.[86] He expressed some anxiety, however, since it appeared to him that the Abbot President believed that the main object of the Benedictines living in London was staffing a mission and engaging in parochial work, and the establishment of a stable monastic community as 'quite subsidiary'. Consequently, he urged Ford to be clear and forceful in his petition to Rome and to emhasize the desire for permission to establish a proper Benedictine monastery in the suburb. Throughout September 1896, moreover, Abbot Snow continued to busy himself in the Ealing project. In addition to the purchase of Castle Hill House, Snow also explored other pieces of nearby property. He expressed some interest, for example, in some sites facing Montpelier Avenue. In addition to this, Snow began to dream about a future church for the monks, who had not yet arrived in Ealing. The vision was grand and majestic. A 'Church when placed on our site will be in a commanding position at the top of the new road and easy access to the bulk of the people.'[87] He also informed Ford that the negotiations with the nuns for the purchase of Castle Hills House were progressing smoothly; if both parties could agree on the price of £4,000, a contract for the purchase could be drawn up. Throughout late autumn, Snow enthusiastically continued to negotiate for the property in Ealing, and his optimism grew. In his mind, the area was increasing both in numbers and respectability, and the Benedictine monks would be a valuable addition.

But Prior Ford did not abandon his responsibilities for the Ealing foundation to Abbot Snow. At the end of September, the Prior informed Snow that he had received the necessary papers from President O'Gorman and that he would 'forward them to the Cardinal asking him to send them on to his agent in Rome to have them attended to'.[88] Ford then began to enter into the final stages of talks with Cardinal Vaughan concerning the establishment of the Benedictines in the Westminster Archdiocese. The blessing and permission of the Holy See presented the next hurdle.

On 1 October 1896, Prior Ford informed Cardinal Vaughan that the Benedictines of Downside were eager to take root in Ealing. Ford enclosed a packet of documents which included: the formal petition of the English Benedictine Congregation to the Holy See; the permission of Abbot President O'Gorman and the Regimen; and the list of agreements or conditions under which the Cardinal would welcome the Benedictines into his diocese. Ford pressed Vaughan to expedite matters as quickly as possible, for the nuns who owned the property at Ealing, he claimed, were pressing the Benedictines to complete the purchase of the property. He wrote: 'If Your Eminence would forward the papers to your agent in Rome for presentation and would accompany them with a letter expressing your wish to see the petition granted, the business would be attended to at once'.[89] Ford pointed out that he had enclosed several copies of the terms under which the Cardinal had invited the monks into London. He suggested he sign and date one, and return this to him at Downside. Ford also drew attention to the change of wording in respect to the Cardinal's right to purchase the Ealing property if the experiment failed, and reminded Vaughan that they had agreed to this at Hereford. On 8 October, the Cardinal sent Prior Ford a signed copy of the stipulations and authorized the Benedictine monks to begin a monastic foundation at Ealing.

The time was ripe to close the deal with the nuns for the purchase of Castle Hill House. In the event of the Holy See raising serious questions about the Ealing plan, Ford was still determined to push on with the deal: 'Even if Rome makes a difficulty we should not give up, but fight it out, and we cannot expect the nuns to wait'.[90] On 10 October, therefore, Ford signed and returned the contract for the Ealing property to the offices of Blount, Lynch and Petre. As agreed earlier, the price was £4,000. Almost immediately, Ford began to search for tenants who would lease some space in the house on a short-term basis.

Ford still needed canonical approval from Rome. Before the formal petition was sent, he had sought the advice and expertise of Abbot President O'Gorman, and asked O'Gorman to compose a draft letter in Italian which he could then forward to Rome.[91] After Ford received the requested letter, he thanked O'Gorman and told him he intended to suggest that Cardinal Vaughan send it directly to Rome. 'This will make the petition his business and will secure it attention,' Ford reasoned, 'and will at the same time keep me straight with his Eminence.'[92] The polished document which Ford sent Cardinal Vaughan for the Roman authorities stated:

> After obtaining the permission of the Superiors of our Congregation, as well as the assent of his Eminence the Cardinal Archbishop, [the petitioner] humbly implores of the Holy See the faculty of founding a new residence in Ealing as well as of building a monastery later on and eventually of accepting from the same Cardinal the mission of the same place, Ealing, under the following conditions stated by His Eminence the Cardinal Archbishop of Westminster.[93]

Following this state, the five conditions or stipulations were appended without comment.

On 20 October 1896, Propaganda Fide, the organisation in the Vatican which at this time oversaw the Roman Catholic Church in England and other 'missionary' countries, granted the request.[94] A week later, Cardinal Vaughan informed Prior Ford that he had received 'the necessary permission from the Holy See for you to take Ealing: the conditions being those we agreed upon'.[95] The Chapter of Westminster Cathedral was also informed of this in early November,[96] and Archbishop's House soon asked Downside for the names of the monks who would be assigned to Ealing for the new Diocesan *Directory*.[97] But an ominous sign appeared. In response to Prior Ford's request for a copy of the Roman rescript, Archbishop's House informed him that 'there is likely to be some delay in the execution of the Rescript' because of 'the opposition of the priest now at Ealing,' Father O'Halloran.[98]

Once armed with the authority of the papal rescript, however, and with the permission of Cardinal Vaughan, the English Benedictines quickly made plans to take possession of their recently purchased property in Ealing. Two monks were assigned to take up residence at Castle Hill House. The *Downside Review* told its readers that 'Dom Bernard Bulbeck and Dom Aidan Howlett have been selected to start our new mission at Ealing, which promises to become an important railway centre in the near future.'[99] At the age of seventy-one and plagued throughout his life by ill-health, Dom Bernard seemed an unlikely candidate to take charge of the new London mission. But one reason for his appointment was 'his quiet and genial disposition [which] seemed to render him the most fitting to be the first to take possession of the new mission which was offered to us at Ealing'.[100] Dom Aidan's main responsibilities consisted of ministering to a nearby convent of nuns.

Cardinal Vaughan's anxiety and urgency about the arrival of the Benedictines in the Archdiocese of Westminster surfaced early in 1897. 'How soon can you send a priest or two to take possession of the mission?' Vaughan asked the Prior in February, 'I should wish it to be done this month.'[101] But the Cardinal's letter also revealed a sense of caution. For the time being, he ruled out the possibility of the construction of any new church, and told Ford that the monks would have to conduct their services in Castle Hill House. Vaughan seemed rather hesitant to commission the Downside monks officially to begin their pastoral duties in Ealing: 'I do not wish you to take over the mission until I am able to convey it to you'. Still, the Cardinal wanted to know the name of the priest Prior Ford intended to send. Vaughan gave away the reason behind this request; the priest currently at Ealing had made some threatening noises. 'You must expect nothing, I fear, from O'Halloran,' he wrote. With this warning about the local cleric, who would soon plague the monks, the English Benedictines began to move to Ealing.

Dom Bernard arrived and, in the spring, faculties were granted to him by Archbishop's House and to any other priest assigned to assist him. This did not go unnoticed. The Catholic press greeted the Benedictines with enthusiasm. The *Catholic Times* announced that 'the Benedictine Fathers from Downside have . . . established themselves at Ealing and have taken over the mission . . . [and] it is intended before long to erect a spacious church and monastery'.[102] The *Universe* struck an historical chord: 'The Benedictines, whom His Eminence Cardinal Vaughan is re-establishing at Westminster and Ealing, were in pre-Reformation times the most numerous and widely distributed religious order in England . . .'[103] The local Ealing press also announced the arrival of the monks into their suburb, and emphasized their intention to construct a church, which seemed to contradict Vaughan's explicit instruction. 'An architect has inspected the proposed site, which is part of the grounds of the old mansion,' it reported, 'and when the edifice is raised it will be an interesting addition to the many fine buildings in and around this important suburb of London, which is growing to be one of the most popular places of resort.'[104]

And the monks quickly took advantage of this fine opportunity. Dom Bernard, despite his age and questionable health, exhibited a spirit of dogged determination in his new assignment. For example, in April he boasted that nearly twenty parishioners attended his Sunday morning mass. But the strain and the responsibility soon began to take its toll on his frail condition. Several months after this arrival, he reported to Downside that two masses were needed on Sunday, but he also confessed to Prior Ford that his health would not permit any additional work: 'I doubt if I shall be able to manage it [an increased Sunday mass schedule] . . . and it will be a sad affair if I fall and collapse'.[105] Consequently, he asked Ford for the assistance of an 'active priest' to help with the work he could not manage. Without this, Dom Bernard stated that he would get 'a bad name which would be a pity after all this fuss'.

The accomplishments of this elderly monk during his first year at Ealing seemed to support his plea for help. The 'spiritual' census of the Ealing mission, the *Spiritualia Ministeria*, recorded the following statistics for 1897: 100 parishioners, one convert, three baptisms, and 56 communicants.[106] Dom Bernard's first financial report was also remarkable. With no extensive building campaign and no lavish source of funds for any improvements, 1897 ended with a slight deficit. Dom Bernard reported a loss of only £146 for the year.[107] The major expenses were the house account (£116.19s.11d) and furniture and kitchen utensils (£4.7s.4d). Offertory collections (£47.3s.7d) and bench rates and stipends (£22.15s.6d) represented the chief source of income. An additional healthy and eager wage-earner might offset this negative financial condition at Ealing. Dom Bernard's drive to acquire the services of an 'active priest' met with success. In less than a year, Dom Aidan Howlett, who had charge of the Sisters of Nazareth convent, was transferred to Conventry, and Dom Benedict Weld-Blundell was appointd to assist Dom Bernard.

Dom Bernard's deteriorating health, however, did not escape the attention of Cardinal Vaughan. In December 1898 Vaughan wrote to Prior Ford and told him that he was 'much concerned about the condition of Ealing'.[108] The Cardinal's anxiety centred on the stamina of the Ealing priest. 'Father Bulbeck is a holy and venerable man,' Ford was informed, but 'he has not the physical and mental vigour to contend successfully against the difficulties of his position.' Dom Bernard must be replaced. Cardinal Vaughan's letter stated that he 'must insist upon your placing there, with as little delay as possible, a Father who will be fit for the position of Superior'. Some Benedictines had also noted a need for a change. Dom Aidan Gasquet, for example, realized that fresh blood was needed and told Prior Ford that 'what we want . . . at Ealing is the man'. 'The more I think of it,' he wrote, 'the more I fancy Fr Gilbert to look after things.' At the end of December, Ford sent Abbot President O'Gorman a copy of Vaughan's negative report on Dom Bernard and stated that 'the delay in Fr Dolan's being at Ealing is seriously harmful to us'.[110] Dom Bernard's health had also become a matter of public concern. The *Downside Review* later remarked that with 'health failing, he left Ealing and became chaplain . . . to a small community of nuns'.[111]

Finally in March 1899, it was officially announced that 'Dom Gilbert Dolan has been appointed to take charge of the Mission at Ealing'.[112] Dom Vincent Corney replaced Dom Benedict in September. But Dom Bernard's final year as the priest-in-charge at Ealing cannot be regarded as a failure. It witnessed a slight improvement in the young foundation's financial well-being: during 1898, the deficit had been cut to £63 as compared to £146 in the previous year; and more importantly, the offertory collection nearly doubled, as did the total income for the year.[113] Moreover, the mission continued to grow. The 1898 census revealed that the Catholic parish had doubled to approximately two hundred people.[114] But concerns about the growth and health of the mission were not the only things which concerned the Benedictines.

Cardinal Vaughan had forcefully stipulated that no school could be attached to the mission unless it was a public elementary school. Prior Ford and his advisors, however, had entertained other plans from the beginning; a proper school was essential for success. In the autumn of 1898, for example, Ford had commissioned Dom Benedict Weld-Blundell to write a 'statement in favour of a high school . . . send it to me and I will write to the Cardinal'.[118] Already in 1897, Ford had decided that a nearby piece of property, Orchard Dene, might not only be a good financial investment, but also house a future Benedictine school. Not until the following year, however, did Ford actively start a correspondence with his solicitors about the possibility of buying this property and its stately home. Abbot Snow again appeared. The Abbot warned that it was a 'considerable risk' to purchase the property: 'I should not hesitate if our affairs at Ealing were more developed or if there were not already a heavy liability with nothing at present really accomplished'.[116] Moreover, he did not think that the financial risk of purchasing Orchard Dene 'should fall on the place as a mission, or that the people of Ealing should be expected to pay capital or interest'. Ford's enthusiasm temporarily cooled.

In the following year, however, Abbot Snow began to modify his earlier cautious attitude. He admitted that he still felt a reluctance because of 'the uncertainty of what form the future development will take [and] to commit ourselves to so large an outlay'.[117] On the other hand, Snow admitted, 'supposing that at some future time more land were needed we might not be able to obtain it'. Consequently, Abbot Snow gave his blessing to the project on one condition: 'I think we might venture on the purchase, provided that it is distinctly understood that it is only to secure the land and not to using it'. Dom Aidan Gasquet also firmly supported Ford's vision and encouraged him to secure Orchard Dene. In the summer of 1897 Gasquet told his friend that he was 'strongly for securing the property [since] I do not think we could go wrong'.[118] In the following year, Gasquet still remained committed to the purchase: 'I have no doubt that we ought to secure the land in question'.[119] According to Gasquet, 'from all one hears there can be no reasonable doubt that the ground will retain its value'.

Ford then approached the Abbot President of the English Benedictine Congregation and the Regimen and asked for permission to purchase Orchard Dene. Prior Ford boldly stated his case: 'An opportunity is likely to occur of purchasing a plot of land adjoining the site we already possess at Ealing'.[120] Ford noted that the plot covered two and three-fourths acres, a stately house stood on the site, and the entire estate could become the property of the Benedictines for £6,000. Moreover, Ford related that the council at Downside was 'of the opinion that it would be wise under the conditions to purchase the land, and in course of time when the house at Ealing grows and if a school is opened there, the land would then be required'. He also enclosed the favourable recommendations of Abbot Snow and Aidan Gasquet. 'Having obtained their unanimous consent,' Ford asked President O'Gorman and the membership of the Regimen to borrow the money. This request was granted on 20 September 1898, and Ford purchased Orchard Dene on 17 January 1899 for £5,950. The Benedictines, therefore, had begun to plan for the school which Cardinal Vaughan had clearly forbidden. The optimism and initial successes of the Ealing Benedictines, however, were soon challenged by the words and actions of the local secular priest, Rev Richard O'Halloran.

CHAPTER II

Father O'Halloran and the Monks of Ealing Abbey

Richard Joseph O'Hallloran was born to Denis O'Halloran and Johanna Roach on 24 December 1856 at Ballyhindon, County Cork.[1] He received his early education at the French College, Dublin, and St Colman's in Fermoy. He felt called to Orders and, on 9 September 1875, O'Halloran entered St Joseph's College, Mill Hill in North London as a candidate for St Joseph's Society for Foreign Missions. He took the required Propaganda Vow before he was ordained Subdeacon in 1879, and he was ordained a Deacon during the following year. As a Deacon, he was appointed Master of Discipline at the Apostolic School, Caedongred, Wales, which was operated by the Mill Hill Fathers.

Controversy soon coloured his career; rumours soon caught the attention of the superior at Mill Hill which questioned his prudence and integrity. The superior, Father Benoit, wrote and pointed out allegations about his 'reckless' behaviour towards some of his students. O'Halloran answered this letter and wrote that he was 'very sorry to hear that I have done a considerable amount of damage in the minds of some of the students – and may lead to the loss of their vocation.'[2] Personality traits which later emerged during the troubles at Ealing were already present. He complained that he was misunderstood. He also exhibited symptoms of a martyr, and told this superior that he had 'None to consult and advise me . . . no one to whom I can look for solace in my difficulties'. In this response to Father Benoit, he openly criticized several members of the staff, especially two who were ex-religious. Concerning those students who might lose their vocations because of his actions, O'Halloran stated that they 'have none to lose'. As for the source of these rumours, he blamed a drunken woman whom he had publicly rebuked and then dismissed. Throughout this letter, he repeatedly begged his superior to believe that he had always acted in a prudent and proper manner at the college.

One of his students, however, took exception that no disciplinary action had been brought against O'Halloran. This individual wrote to Father Benoit and complained that he was 'not at all satisfied, much less edified, when I consider the way Mr O'Halloran has conducted himself since he came'.[3] This student alleged that whenever he had violated a rule he 'was censured by our Master of Discipline in words that went beyond the just bounds'. 'I mean,' he continued, 'that he was sometimes so intemperate in speaking as to offer insults to me and thereby transgressed the laws of justice.' O'Halloran, according to his account, mocked the student and accused him of living on the charity of the Mill Hill Fathers. Moreover, this letter continued, the Master of Discipline's conduct and words towards his ecclesiastical superiors 'has savoured and continues to savour of disrespect and arrogance'. Another student also complained that O'Halloran's 'conduct is anything but gentlemanly'.[4] 'His manner of repremanding [sic] students is beyond all bound,' the letter went on, and 'for the least violation of the rule he puts us on our knees and repremands [sic] us before the whole study.' According to this account, O'Halloran's arrogance had destroyed the character of the school, the self-confidence of the Rector, and the spirit of the students. For example, 'he told us that when we would be a priest he would expel us and get a new lot.

In spite of these serious allegations and criticisms of his work in Wales, Richard O'Halloran was ordained a priest by Bishop John Hedley, Auxiliary Bishop of Newport and Menevia, on 18 December 1880. Two weeks after his ordination, however, Father O'Halloran suddenly left the Mill Hill Missionary Society. The last entry in the Society's log book concerning his affiliation with Mill Hill stated: 'Jan. 3/81. Left Society immed't after Priesthood'.

One reason for O'Halloran's sudden departure might have been some criticisms voiced by his superior in London concerning his conduct as Master of Discipline. Prior to his ordination, for example, O'Halloran admitted that Father Benoit had accused him of acting imprudently and ignoring the rules and regulations the superior had drawn up to temper the young cleric's actions in Wales.[6] But O'Halloran later argued that the reason for leaving the Mill Hill Fathers was based solely on a lofty principle: his refusal to take the missionary oath, which would have bound him to work on the foreign missions of the society and which was required of all members of the society. Work of this nature was the *raison d'être* of the Mill Hill Fathers. Herbert Vaughan, the founder of the society, treasured the idea of priests labouring in Europe and among the Blacks in North America. According to his biographer, 'it was a high ideal and one difficult for flesh and blood . . . there was no room here for half measures, or for compromises between the world and God'.[7] The Mill Hill Father, in Vaughan's vision, dedicated his priestly vocation to this goal: 'the sentence was to be for life . . . the missioner who goes out from St Joseph College leaves England for ever . . .' Vaughan wanted 'men filled with the Apostolic spirit, who in a spirit of perfect detachment would consecrate themselves to the service of the Heathen, not for a term of years, but without reserve and for ever'.[8] O'Halloran refused to bend or compromise on the question of the oath, and this became the origin of the animosity between himself and Vaughan, which later exploded in Ealing. But friction between the two had already begun to develop during the early 1880s.

In 1881 Father O'Halloran approached the Bishop of Nottingham, Edward G. Bagshawe, and asked him for clerical employment. The Bishop entrusted him with a mission at Hucknall Larkard. Nottingham had become famous as a refuge for disgruntled or dissatisfied priests. Bagshawe, according to J. Derek Holmes in his *More Roman than Rome*, had expanded and increased his diocesan commitments without the necessary manpower, and consequently 'he increased the number of priests by hasty ordinations and by accepting clergy from other dioceses or religious orders'.[9] 'In his attempt to alleviate a desperate shortage of priests, the Bishop sacrificed quality to quantity.'

In the early months of the year, O'Halloran wrote to Vaughan, who had been consecrated Bishop of Salford in 1872 and later elected Superior General of the Mill Hill Fathers for life in 1875, and asked for permission to join the English diocese. 'Should your lordship not consider it well to keep me under the jurisdiction of the society,' O'Halloran petitioned his legal ecclesiastical superior, 'I humbly beg your lordship's sanction and that of Propaganda to obtain a transfer to some bishop who would think fit to accept my services,'[10] Since England was still under the jurisdiction of the Propaganda in Rome, O'Halloran, along with some other members of Mill Hill, argued that it was still technically a missionary country. This became the argument to seek admission into an English diocese. The Bishop of Salford's response to O'Halloran's request has not survived, but in light of Vaughan's view of the importance of the missionary oath and from fragments of O'Halloran's other letters, the Bishop did not treat this petition with magnanimity. In the first place, Vaughan felt cheated; O'Halloran was educated and ordained to serve in the foreign missions and not on native soil. Secondly, Vaughan had personally raised money by begging trips throughout America and England to educate and train the Mill Hill student. Like others who sought to join an English diocese, Bishop Vaughan demanded that Father O'Halloran repay what the Society had expended on his priestly education. The price of freedom for O'Halloran was estimated at £100.

Upon his arrival in this diocese, Father O'Halloran wrote to Father Benoit at Mill Hill and pleaded with him to 'put an end to the present question between the Bishop of Salford [Vaughan] and myself'.[11] The problem, O'Halloran related, grew out of his refusal to take the missionary oath. Father O'Halloran asked the Mill Hill superior the following question: 'How . . . a person taking orders on a missionary title from your Society is understood to bind himself to *join your Society* as well as *to go on your Missions?*' He drew Father Benoit's attention to 'a rule of the Propaganda that if they [priests] do not carry out the conditions of joining the Society they should either cease to be priests or engage themselves to some other bishop outside of Europe'. O'Halloran argued that 'the *Rule* of the Propaganda should be known to the students before admitting them to take Orders'. Ignorance became his defence; he had never understood the implications of the oath or the consequences of refusing to take it. He maintained, therefore, that he 'never heard of such a rule', and argued that he did 'not come under the operation of the Rule'. Father O'Halloran concluded his shaky defence by stating that Bishop Vaughan had only recently informed him that the missionary oath was a requirement, and if not taken, he must suffer the ecclesiastical consequences.

Although O'Halloran cast himself as a martyr unjustly punished by an archaic requirement, Father Benoit's notes paint another picture. Benoit informed Bishop Vaughan that 'the obligations of our missioners are explained publicly . . . . At the approach of the Subdeaconate, F. O'Halloran, like the others, had to copy the Propaganda Vow, which in itself is very clear.'[12] Father Benoit maintained that he interviewed O'Halloran, 'asked him whether he understood distinctly the obligations contained in it', and offered to clarify any questions or problems about the missionary vow. Benoit did not attempt to settle the tension which existed between O'Halloran and Bishop Vaughan. In the mind of the Mill Hill Superior, O'Halloran knew and understood the rules and obligations of the Society.

In January 1882, Father O'Halloran again approached Bishop Vaughan, and this time tried a new tactic: he complained of the unjust treatment that he had received at the hands of the Mill Hill authorities; and explained that the Bishop of Nottingham, 'who has been most charitable and kind to me,' needed a clarification on his priestly status since he could not leave 'the Mission in a state of uncertainty any longer'.[13] But even this lacked diplomacy. He accused Vaughan of being 'determined on my ruin', and expressed his resistance and strong opposition to the missionary oath: 'I *will* never *willingly* obey any Bishop under whose jurisdiction you intend to place me by force'. He then emphasized the 'harsh treatment and unheard of cruelties' which he suffered as a member of Vaughan's society. O'Halloran accused Father Benoit of the following atrocities: Benoit summoned a policeman to arrest him during a recent visit to Mill Hill; the superior 'cast me adrift in the world without testimonials or character references'; permission to celebrate mass was denied; and Father Benoit even refused to give him the address of the Bishop of Salford. O'Halloran ended this letter with an emotional appeal for Vaughan's sympathy. 'This letter will be my last,' he promised 'I am worn out and tired of this cruelty.'

The Bishop of Nottingham, Edward Bagshawe, soon entered this perplexed and confused situation. Vaughan contacted his fellow prelate and accused Father O'Halloran of acting under false pretences. He stated that the priest owed the Mill Hill Fathers a large sum of money for his education, and told Bishop Bagshawe that if he assumed the debt, O'Halloran would be free to enter the Diocese of Nottingham. Bagshawe, however, took this opportunity to voice his opinion of the case, and for the time being, became Father

O'Halloran's episcopal champion. The Bishop pointed out that 'the oath to the Society was at that time expressly and intentionally separated from the Propaganda oath'.[14] Moreover, he continued to lecture Vaughan, the guidelines drawn up by Propaganda Fide did not force one either to follow the rules of the Mill Hill Fathers in respect of missionary work or to seek a transfer to a foreign bishop. Bagshawe told Vaughan that this alternative was not clear in the minds of many who entered the Society. He also told Vaughan that bishops and religious superiors always took risks in providing an expensive education for their candidates; even after ordination or profession trained clerics often gave up or left their vocation. Bagshawe supported Father O'Halloran's arguments: '. . . the students in their educational course were . . . in a sort of novitiate trying their vocation for the Society, but free (until the time comes for taking its oath) to join it or do missionary work elsewhere'. He challenged Vaughan's demands for financial reimbursement, and stated that if a candidate left he did 'not think as a rule that either money is paid back or false pretenses supposed . . .' Bagshawe admitted that in cases of deliberate dishonesty, restitution was a matter of justice, but in respect to O'Halloran's dilemma, he could not 'see the evidence of it in the circumstances of . . . the case'.

Thus begun the long and bitter relationship between Vaughan and O'Halloran. Writing in 1901 about his early struggles and difficulties with the Mill Hill Fathers and their founder, Father O'Halloran described Vaughan's role in the bleakest and most derogatory terms. After he recounted the circumstances surrounding his refusal to take the oath, he attacked Vaughan and noted that 'every effort that fiendish ingenuity could invent was made to influence my young mind to go against my conscience; power, success in life, and honours were offered to me to win me to take this vow'.[15] 'I was then cast our penniless on the streets,' he related, 'and at once the Mill Hill authorities wrote letters to every bishop, defaming me and telling them not to give me employment anywhere.'[16] According to O'Halloran's account, 'this is the key to Dr. Vaughan's hatred of me. . . .'[17]

Father O'Halloran's provocative rhetoric, his suspicious nature, and the lack of important supporting documentation seriously diminished the objectivity and credibility of his narration of the origins of the battle with Bishop Vaughan. But the fact that O'Halloran had developed a fiery and pathological hatred of Vaughan soon after he left the Mill Hill Fathers is painfully clear. The resolution of this conflict over his status as a priest in the Diocese of Nottingham remained cloudy, but he did live and work in the diocese until the spring of 1882. At that time Bishop Bagshawe also experienced his behaviour. Complaints concerning the impropriety of some of Father O'Halloran's actions reached the episcopal ear during May. And the Bishop immediately sought an explanation of some serious charges from the visiting priest whom he had once defended to Bishop Vaughan. Bishop Bagshawe singled out three accusations: that O'Halloran had orally attacked a parishioner 'to the distress of her family' from his pulpit; 'that you have many times allowed the Schoolmistress to sleep in your house . . . in defiance of the public talk which has gone on and is going on about you and her'; and that the 'grossest charges of immorality are brought against you'.[19] The Bishop pointed out that the charges stem from the testimony of one person, and therefore 'are not adequately proved'. Bagshawe, however, continued: 'the second point – mentioned above – however seems for me a very serious corroboration'. The punishment was serious and harsh. 'Under the circumstances I cannot pass over what I consider to have been very grave and imprudent a disturbance – giving rise to grave scandal,' he informed O'Halloran. He ordered Father O'Halloran to 'give up the property and charge of your mission on or before 19 May on which day your faculties in this diocese and the charge of Hucknall Mission will expire.'

Surprisingly and paradoxically, Father O'Halloran appealed to his antagonist, Bishop Vaughan, for advice and assistance. He sent the Bishop of Salford a copy of Bagshawe's rebuke and demand that he must leave the diocese. In a letter, O'Halloran admitted that Vaughan still remained his 'recognized Superior – pending the decision of the Propaganda', and added that he needed help 'to vindicate my innocence'.[19] Again he donned the mantle of a martyr. 'This town is a most immoral place,' O'Halloran began his defence. 'The Mormons are numerous – and those who are not professed Mormons are practically as bad.' Consequently, he believed that it was his priestly obligation and duty 'to condemn and preach against this wickedness'. In addition to the wicked influence of this American religion, 'several Irish people . . . are living most infamous lives – and among the number I discovered the Mother and sisters of my servant'. O'Halloran declared that their lives were 'no better than public prostitutes', and therefore he fired his servant girl. 'Smarting under this dismissal,' he told Bishop Vaughan, 'the family proceeded to invent *crimes* against me . . . sacrilege, fornication and abortion – committed with my schoolmistress.' Father O'Halloran denied that he spoke specifically of his ex-servant's family 'from the altar or as an *individual* case: I condemn the bad houses in general'.

O'Halloran admitted to Vaughan that the schoolmistress had slept in his house, but then pleaded that he did not know of any ecclesiastical law forbidding it. 'My Schoolmistress is a most respectable young lady from York,' he continued, 'who was devoting her life to the welfare of the mission for a nominal salary'. Because she had worked long and hard hours, he confessed that he 'did not consider it prudent to allow her to go to her lodgings so late – knowing the badness of the inhabitants and fearing that she should meet with insults on the way'. He strongly denied any charges of sexual relations with the woman. Throughout this strange letter, O'Halloran's feelings of persecution and suspicion again emerged. He described the village as a 'savage mission' and argued that he did 'not deserve the dreadful punishment inflicted by his Lordship,' the Bishop of Nottingham. Father O'Halloran believed that the Bishop had orchestrated a campaign to drive him out of the diocese and led a movement to discredit and blacken his character.

O'Halloran continued to plead his innocence to Vaughan, and he associated his troubles at Nottingham with his problems with the Mill Hill Fathers and Bishop Vaughan. He pointed out that he was hemmed in by two great difficulties: 'your claims on the one hand – and leaving my mission under such sad and unjust circumstances . . .' O'Halloran worked to salvage his tainted reputation and begged Vaughan to believe that he had been 'conscientious in . . . refusing to join the Society'. His failure to repay the £100 to cover his education should not be interpreted as malicious. 'I am anxious to have that misunderstanding between you and myself settled,' he pleaded, 'since it is the root of all evil and is prejudicing my character.' With refreshing naïveté, he asked Bishop Vaughan to give him a mission in the Salford Diocese until the 'release from your jurisdiction comes from Rome'.

Not suprisingly, Bishop Vaughan refused to welcome this pugnacious cleric into the Manchester area, but he suggested instead another country. 'Having considered your proposal about Australia,' O'Halloran replied to Vaughan's offer, 'I am willing to go to either Sydney or Melbourne.'[20] Consequently, O'Halloran urged Bishop Vaughan to arrange matters, and reminded him that he had 'no means to pay the expense'. He ended this letter to Vaughan with a pious declaration that it was 'God's will that I should go there'. But O'Halloran failed to leave Britain. In December, a Canon of the Diocese of Nottingham informed Father Benoit at Mill Hill that Father O'Halloran had departed from the diocese: 'our Bishop could not put up with his manner of preaching and denouncing those who gave him offence from the Altar'.[21] The wandering cleric, however, had procured another appointment. 'It is said that the Bishop of Middlesbrough [Richard Lacy] has appointed him chaplain to Lady Sykes,' Canon Douglas reported, 'and our Bishop thinks the report is true though he would have thought it improbable.' Prophetically the Canon concluded his note: 'the Bishop of Middlesbrough has made a sad mistake and will have cause to regret it'.

Bishop Richard Lacy had indeed appointed Father O'Halloran as the chaplain to Lady Sykes, a convert to Roman Catholicism, and also entrusted to him the Yorkshire mission of Driffield. And from this northern post, O'Halloran continued to keep up his correspondence with Father Benoit in London. The themes or subjects had become familiar. O'Halloran described himself as 'a young priest longing to belong to some Bishop and to gain the merit of true obedience'.[22] He complained about the intransigent attitude of Bishop Vaughan: 'Not bound to my Bishop – and not incorporated in a diocese I feel like a star launched from its sphere – and in a certain sense hampered in my missionary work'. Father O'Halloran pleaded with Father

Benoit that he could not repay the Mill Hill Fathers for his education. After proclaiming his love, devotion, and dedication to the society, O'Halloran bluntly stated the purpose behind this letter. 'I now venture to ask your reverence to act as a *mediator* between the Bishop of Salford and myself – and to procure for me my *exeat* – that I may be free to bind myself for life in obedience to the Bishop of Middlesb[rough] and his successors.'

O'Halloran also described his parochial work in Yorkshire in terms of a pioneer. He related how he began and 'carried on in the greatest poverty and in the face of trying opposition'. O'Halloran boasted that he hoped 'to erect a school to accommodate 300 children – and to purchase another house and site of land for a convent of nuns'. And this signalled God's blessings on his work. The reason for this real or imaginary success, however, he credited to his training at Mill Hill. Consequently, he laboured to convince Father Benoit that it was not duplicity, but that his 'conscience obliged' him to leave the society. Moreover, his controversial departure 'was pleasing to Him and in accordance with His will.' Father O'Halloran promised to try to repay his education debt by donating a percentage from the Sunday collections each year and also by contributing an annual sum of £2 to Mill Hill. Having expressed his good intent and trying to clear his conscience, O'Halloran ended this letter with repeated plea to Father Benoit 'that you will speak to his Lordship the Bishop of Salford on my behalf to get my *exeat*'.

Father Benoit's reply angered O'Halloran who immediately and boldly corrected Benoit's impression that he was willing to negotiate a surrender. 'I offered *no conditions*,' Father O'Halloran informed the Mill Hill superior, 'I merely asked your reverence to act as mediator between his Lordship the Bishop of Salford and myself.'[23] 'The Bishop and myself will never understand each other,' he exclaimed, and he described the relationship between himself and Vaughan as an 'unchristian transaction', a 'scandal'. He ended his letter with another request that Father Benoit use his influence 'with the Bishop of Salford and explain *my side* of the question to him and get me my *exeat*'. O'Halloran also enclosed a note from Bishop Lacy of Middlesbrough which stated that he would welcome O'Halloran into his diocese.

On 5 March, Father Benoit informed Father O'Halloran that he had approached Bishop Vaughan to obtain the requested *exeat*, and he reported that the Bishop was 'willing to accept your proposal just as it stands'.[24] But Benoit failed to mention the procedure or course O'Halloran should pursue. By the end of March, therefore, Father O'Halloran's sense of urgency had become evident. He told Father Benoit that Bishop Lacy still wanted to welcome him into the diocese, but he needed the precious *exeat*. Close to finding a friendly haven where he could exercise his ministry, O'Halloran conceded one of the points which started the row: he promised to reimburse the Mill Hill Fathers for the money spent on his education. He told Father Benoit: 'I understand to pay St Joseph's Missionary College the sum of £100 in compensation for any losses [*sic*] it incurred through me'.[25] Consequently, the *exeat* was granted, and with the permission of Bishop Vaughan, Father O'Halloran became a priest of the Diocese of Middlesbrough.

The correspondence between Father O'Halloran and the Mill Hill authorities, therefore, ceased in March 1884. O'Halloran continued to labour at his Yorkshire mission at Driffield, where he acted as chaplain to Lady Sykes. This irenic atmosphere did not last; the question of Irish Home Rule became the catalyst which propelled O'Halloran again into a heated public controversy. During the 1886 General Election, which was fought over the Irish Question, the Conservative candidate, Christopher Sykes, was defeated by the Liberal candidate. In defiance of the Sykeses, Father O'Halloran backed the latter. According to an 1897 interview with O'Halloran, a 'complaint was made to the Bishop of Middlesbrough – whether by Lady Sykes or another is a matter of no consequence – that this young Irish priest had thrown in his lot with the Irish cause in defiance of his patrons'.[26] Sykes, however, contested the outcome of the election, accused McArthur, the Liberal candidate, of electoral mismanagement, and appealed to the recently enacted Corrupt Practices Act. The court dismissed charges of misspent money and fraudulent accounts, but after examining the ballots declared that Sykes had won by a slim majority of eleven votes, and awarded the seat to him.[27] During the hearing, according to O'Halloran, he was locked up in a monastery at the insistence of Bishop Lacy because he claimed that he possessed evidence which was crucial to the outcome.

To verify this story, the *Daily Chronicle* later contacted the Bishop of Middlesbrough and asked him to comment on Father O'Halloran's accusation. Lacy admitted that he had warned O'Halloran not to get involved with politics[28] but denied that he intimidated, punished or imprisoned O'Halloran for his support of Gladstone's Home Rule programme. It appeared, however, that the priest did possess some mysterious letters which might have had a bearing on the election and trial, and that Lacy did order O'Halloran to withdraw from the judicial proceedings. 'This is most deplorable, and must be stopped at all hazards,' the Bishop demanded. 'The injury to religion would be enormous by a priest appearing in a witness-box under such circumstances.'[28]

Still, the charges of inquisitorial imprisonment on the part of Bishop Lacy demanded an explanation. Because of his disregard of Bishop Lacy's order to avoid the publicity surrounding the disputed election, O'Halloran claimed that 'his lordship did then and there arbitrarily abuse his episcopal authority by withdrawing the faculties of Father O'Halloran' and 'by imprisoning him in a monastery at Bishop-Eton, Liverpool, during the period of eight days ... [during] the months of November and December'.[30] In the same statement, Father O'Halloran admitted that he had protested against this misuse of episcopal power, but agreed to go to the monastery in Liverpool provided the

Bishop pay the expenses, which Lacy did. Nonetheless O'Halloran also maintained that he 'was imprisoned under *pretext* of retreat'. The Rector of the Liverpool Redemptorist monastery, however, told the *Daily Chronicle* that Father O'Halloran had made a retreat there, but also that he 'was never locked up at Bishop-Eton'.[31] According to the Rector, 'our houses are never locked from the inside during the day, but they are locked at ten o'clock at night'. But Bishop Lacy did discipline Father O'Halloran because of his involvement in politics. The Bishop wrote and reminded O'Halloran that 'I have allowed you to remain ex-gratia at the presbytery', but he told the priest that he could 'no longer extend this favour to you'.[32] Consequently, Bishop Lacy ordered O'Halloran 'to retire peacefully and promptly, and you have no further connection with the mission'.

Father O'Halloran's fiery character, his sense of persecution, and a sneering contempt for ecclesiastical authority, clearly emerged from his stormy relationship with Bishop Lacy. Because of the episcopal reprimand and discipline, O'Halloran savagely turned on the Bishop who had welcomed him into Middlesbrough. In a fit of anger, Father O'Halloran described his encounter with Bishop Lacy as an example of the 'episcopal system of nagging'.[33] Lacy's object, he believed, 'was to goad me into the commission of some act of folly which might bring about my ruin and serve his ends'. The 'infamous' tactics of this Bishop, whom O'Halloran described as an 'irresponsible autocrat', had a single purpose: the punishment and humiliation of questioning clerics like himself. Not only the Bishop of Middlesbrough, but all prelates now became the object of Father O'Halloran's scathing attack. 'As a rule,' according to O'Halloran, 'the bishops light their cigars with the Pope's mandates when not in their own favour, [and] they set themselves up as irresponsible autocrats whilst pretending outwardly to be submissive to the Holy See.' 'It cannot be denied,' he also claimed, 'that the bishops manipulate and do what they like with the charitable bequests, the church endowments, and other sources of ecclesiastical revenues . . .' As in his past disagreements with his ecclesiastical superiors, O'Halloran's reactions to this real or imaginary persecution revealed an arrogance and paranoia which would plague him throughout his life. After this contretemps with the Bishop of Middlesbrough, Father O'Halloran began to search for another area of England in which to carry out his priestly missionary work.

The peripatetic cleric next appeared in the Archdiocese of Westminster. According to his version of the story, Cardinal Manning, 'my good friend, invited me to his diocese of Westminster', and 'I accepted'.[34] But his arrival in London had other ramifications; O'Halloran claimed that by this action he 'became a priest of Westminster'. Father O'Halloran also believed that Cardinal Manning had become his protector and champion of his cause against Bishop Vaughan, 'the accuser'.[35] O'Halloran later related how Manning told him that 'Bishop Vaughan and his agents have exceeded their

powers, and grossly wronged you in sending you adrift . . . [and] they certainly
have taken advantage of your youth, your inexperience . . .' And Manning
gave him charge of the mission of St Catherine-in-the-Bow, but this peaceful
condition did not last. In 1892, four years after his arrival in the capital, his
old superior and adversary, Herbert Vaughan, became the Archbishop of
Westminster on the death of Cardinal Manning. The past troubles flared up
again immediately. According to O'Halloran's story, 'Dr Vaughan had
scarcely placed the symbol of jurisdiction around his neck, when he sent me
a peremptory order to leave the diocese – that he did not want me under
him'.[36] Commenting on the translation of Vaughan to Westminster, O'Halloran described the ex-Bishop of Salford as 'an impulsive and head-strong
man, who never thinks before he acts, but acts first and thinks after'.
O'Halloran attempted to block this man's attempt to banish him from St
Catherine's and the archdiocese, and appealed directly to Rome. Father
O'Halloran argued that he was a priest of the Archdiocese of Westminster,
and therefore Vaughan could not dismiss him so 'flippantly'. Archbishop
Vaughan, on the other hand, contended that O'Halloran was a priest of the
Diocese of Middlesbrough and could be sent away at the whim of the ordinary.

According to Vaughan, 'in the year 1893, we felt bound to point out to the
Rev. Richard O'Halloran that he was not a subject of the Diocese of
Westminster, and that we desired to dispense with his services'.[37] Archbishop
Vaughan also took his case to Rome. At first Propaganda Fide asked Vaughan
'to be patient, since it seemed . . . that in the complaint sent by this priest there
was something favourable to him'.[38] 'But,' the Cardinal Prefect continued,
'seeing . . . [that] he is not affiliated to the diocese of Westminster and he has
no benefice in it, Your Eminence can do with the priest what you think more
suitable in the Lord'. Vaughan, however, did not take this opportunity to expel
O'Halloran. Clerics were needed in the sprawling capital and Father
O'Halloran might fill a gap. Rome also recognized the problem, and the
document from Propaganda declared that if O'Halloran wanted to remain
temporarily in London, he had to sign a statement that he did not 'belong to
the Archdiocese of Westminster and . . . shall be willing to leave whenever His
Eminence the Cardinal Archbishop shall desire. . .' Father O'Halloran was
informed of the decision taken by Rome, and in order to remain in the
Archdiocese of Westminster for the time being, he signed the document
required by Rome, the wording being exactly the same.[39] One could almost
predict Father O'Halloran's interpretation of this event. He considered the
document which he signed 'a fraud'.[40] Throughout his life, therefore, he
continued to argue that he was a priest of the Archdiocese of Westminster and
had no canonical connection with the Diocese of Middlesbrough. 'That
document,' he always maintained, 'is not only a fraud but it is foolishness; it
is childish. . .' He later told the Ealing Benedictines that the paper was 'a hoax'
and a 'forgery'.[41] Cardinal Vaughan, therefore, not only failed to order this

troublesome cleric to leave the Archdiocese of Westminster, but he gave him another mission. The fashionable western suburb of Ealing became O'Halloran's next vineyard.

Cardinal Vaughan explained this appointment. 'In order that the Rev. R. O'Halloran might not be inconvenienced by being suddenly thrown out of work,' Vaughan decided 'to offer him a temporary post so as to give him time to look for employment elsewhere.'[42] Because of O'Halloran's past history and his volatile relationship with Cardinal Vaughan, Vaughan made the priest agree to the following statement: 'I hereby declare that I undertake the mission at Ealing with the agreement that any debts which may be contracted by me without authority will be considered private debts, according to the regulations of the Diocese, and that there is no claim whatsoever on the Diocese for such debts'.[43] O'Halloran signed this document on 13 July 1894. Cardinal Vaughan had reason to believe, therefore, that he had the proper assurance and safeguard that Father O'Halloran's tenure at Ealing would be brief and at archiepiscopal pleasure.

The Ealing priest, however, saw things differently. This London mission needed a saviour, and O'Halloran had volunteered. The Ealing mission had been established in 1890, but the efforts of its first incumbent, Father Hedditch, had floundered. 'In point of fact, there was no school, and a considerable debt to undertake,'[44] Father O'Halloran later revealed in an interview with the press, and 'three of four other priests had timidly shrunk from the task'.[45] In spite of his earlier disclaimer, O'Halloran believed that this appointment gave additional proof to his contention that he enjoyed the status of a Roman Catholic priest incardinated in the Archdiocese of Westminster. Vaughan 'commissioned me to form and build up this mission, and cast the whole financial responsibility on my poor shoulders'.[46] Consequently, he enjoyed the rights and privileges of any Westminster priest: 'What right had he to do all this, if I belonged to another diocese and to another bishop?'

In spite of his earlier failures, Father O'Halloran laboured admirably and single-handedly to breathe life into the tired Ealing mission. Soon after his arrival, *The Tablet* reported that 'the new mission of SS Joseph and Peter had made great progress since its commencement about three years ago'.[47] Initially, this Roman Catholic weekly reported, 'Mass was said in a private house in Windsor Road'. When this proved too small and inadequate for the growing Ealing congregation, O'Halloran was forced to move 'to a beautiful spot in Mattock Lane off Ealing Green, where services were carried on in the large drawing-room of Mattock Lodge'. But Father O'Halloran had to expand and build. Although Cardinal Vaughan had placed certain restrictions on the priest concerning the construction of a church, O'Halloran had collected enough funds and disregarded Vaughan's prohibition. In 1896, therefore, he could boast that 'a spacious church' now welcomed the worshippers.

By 1897 Father O'Halloran's Ealing mission appeared to be thriving. Circulars announced the times of masses, a schedule of confessions, and even the subject-matter of the priest's homilies. The church, however, symbolized O'Halloran's apparent success. 'The Church of SS Joseph and Peter is a modest iron structure,' a newspaper noted, 'admirably and even beautifully arranged standing on the freehold land purchased for the permanent structure by Father O'Halloran.'[48] His future building programme, moreover, called for the construction of a school. A printed leaflet told the inhabitants of Ealing that 'the mission has made considerable progress,' and 'over £5,000 has already been expended upon it'.[49] Some debts still existed, but this plea recognized that 'the time has come when school accommodation must be provided for the children'. O'Halloran asked his mission to contribute £1,000 for the construction of this new school building. Within a few years, therefore, it seemed that Father O'Halloran had effectively built up the mission and provided for the spiritual needs of the area's faithful. According to him, 'in less than two years I purchased Mattock Lodge, with the grounds attached; erected a church; [and] opened schools for all grades and conditions of children'.[50] Ealing represented the first real accomplishment of his priestly career; 'my congregation swelled and swelled, and my weekly receipts are better, in proportion, than any church of any denomination in Ealing.' But the peaceful situation began to disappear. O'Halloran's fiery personality and his past stormy relations with Cardinal Vaughan almost invited trouble.

In 1895, for example, the parish priest from nearby Hanwell wrote to Archbishop's House and complained that 'O'Halloran was drawing away the people from their allegiance to the good reverend father of Hanwell'.[51] The Vicar-General, Father Michael Barry, heard the complaint, but passed no judgement. Also, the construction of the new church in Mattock Lane caught the attention of the diocesan officials. O'Halloran did not, as required, petition for the necessary ecclesiastical permission. Another element, however, hurried the eventual explosion. During the summer of 1897, the arrival of the Benedictine monks from Downside pushed the affairs at Ealing to the brink of crisis. After the Benedictines had accepted Cardinal Vaughan's invitation to settle in the suburb, the Cardinal simply informed Father O'Halloran that he no longer required his services, 'and that we . . . arranged, with the approval of the Apostolic See, to place the mission of Ealing under the charge of the Benedictine Fathers'.[52] Father O'Halloran, however, defiantly and publicly announced that he would not surrender his claim to Ealing peacefully.

After he received the shocking news from Archbishop's House that he must give up the title of Ealing to the monks, whom he considered to be mere interlopers, Father O'Halloran wrote to Prior Ford at Downside. This letter contained hints of the emotion and vituperation which would emerge and burst forth during the next several decades. The Ealing priest told Ford that he had just received the notification from the Vicar-General that he must leave Ealing, and told the Prior that he 'had worked up this new mission in a manner spiritually and financially in every way satisfactory'.[53] 'My work has succeeded and is going on well, and there is no fault whatever to find in it,' he informed Ford, and 'I have today informed the Vicar-General to acquaint the Archbishop that I have not the slightest intention of resigning the rectorship of Ealing.' If he must, O'Halloran claimed that he would take his case to Rome. Moreover, Father O'Halloran beseeched Ford and asked him not to send the monks into his parish: 'I now appeal to you, as an Order of religious men, not to be the cause of bringing on this quarrel between my Archbishop and myself . . . and that perhaps you would not come.' He recounted the numerous ways how he had laboured, and related that he had spent a considerable amount of money on the mission. And if Ford refused to listen to this logic, O'Halloran told him that the English Benedictines along with Cardinal Vaughan would shoulder the responsibility for a gross injustice. 'Imagine, then, my astonishment that because you want Ealing I MUST GO – after all my labour and the money I spent,' O'Halloran wrote. 'Why not ask for a new mission – virgin soil – and let me and my work alone.' Ford did not respond. The Benedictines were keen about Ealing and Cardinal Vaughan wanted Father O'Halloran out of the Westminster Archdiocese.

Not only had he expended time and money on the Ealing mission, but Ealing represented the one example of stability and achievement in O'Halloran's life. Although he had admitted that he was not a priest of Westminster and had agreed to take the Ealing mission only on a temporary basis, the sudden and abrupt action of Cardinal Vaughan seemed to him both unfair and unchristian. He resented handing over his success to a group of monks from Somerset. Not only did the past troubles between himself and Vaughan contribute to the intensity of O'Halloran's reaction to the arrival of the Benedictines, but he admitted later that he had already cultivated a violent dislike of religious orders. Father O'Halloran maintained that his hatred of the regular clergy began as soon as he arrived at Mill Hill to begin his studies for the priesthood. 'Before I came to London, and entered Mill Hill, I knew little about the conflict between the diocesan clergy and the religious orders,' he wrote, and it was 'in Mill Hill that I heard of the bitterness between 'seculars and religious'.[54] According to O'Halloran, it was Cardinal Vaughan himself who had encouraged this anti-religious-order atmosphere. 'The writings of both Manning and the present Cardinal were severely hostile to the claims of monks, and from these writings I imbibed a distrust for all monks.' 'It was Dr Vaughan . . . and no other,' O'Halloran continued, 'that led me to look upon monks as the greatest curse on earth to the Church and State.' He maintained that Cardinal Vaughan, who had recently invited the Benedictines to take over his mission, represented the arch-enemy of religious communities. 'While I was a student in Mill Hill,' Vaughan '. . . led me to regard the religious orders with anything but a friendly eye.' O'Halloran was a priest about to be dispossessed of his mission, but his contention that Vaughan had fostered a hatred of religious orders as intense as O'Halloran claimed had no foundation.

During the summer of 1896, Father O'Halloran tried to negotiate with Archbishop's House; he pleaded for his right to remain in Ealing. He approached the Vicar-General of the Archdiocese of Westminster, who replied that 'it is the Cardinal's desire that you should look out for another diocese'.[55] Regardless of the signed document which acknowledged that he belonged to the Diocese of Middlesbrough, he protested his right to remain in London. But Father Barry responded that 'a rule [exists] in this diocese that priests who leave Mill Hill are not to be accepted for this diocese. . .'[56] The Vicar-General, however, told O'Halloran that his pastoral work in Ealing was praiseworthy, and no fault could be found with the administration of the mission. And he also emphasized that past history or personal differences had not influenced Vaughan's decision to give the mission to the Benedictine monks. 'It is simply for the sake of the principle involved,' Barry informed O'Halloran, and 'having in view the order and good government of the diocese.'[57]

Nonetheless, Cardinal Vaughan tried to soften the blow to O'Halloran's pride and integrity. He repeated the words of the Vicar-General: 'there is a rule in this diocese that priests who leave Mill Hill are not to be accepted for this diocese . . . [and] other English bishops act on the spirit of this rule'.[58] The Cardinal also suggested an alternative. 'You can allege this rule as a reason for applying to [a] Scottish or colonial Bishop,' he counselled. Moreover, according to Vaughan, he worked 'to avoid the painful necessity of having recourse to an extreme measure . . . [and] obtained from his own Bishop a kind promise to offer him a Mission, if he would apply for it.'[59] The Cardinal also assured O'Halloran that he could 'submit his case to the arbitration of any Bishop in England, and that we would abide by the decision'. Finally, Cardinal Vaughan 'offered him the benefit of the Diocesan Commission of investigation, if he would appear before it'. The Ealing priest snubbed the Cardinal's gestures at peace and compromise. For the time being, O'Halloran refrained from making any public statements, yet he persisted in his determination to remain in control at Ealing.

An uneasy calm characterized the autumn of 1896, but the omens did not augur well for a peaceful settlement of the Ealing problem. The Downside community had already purchased Castle Hill House, and the monks were anxious to settle in Ealing. Archbishop's House had already warned the Benedictines in December 1896 that Father O'Halloran might make trouble for them. In January, an official of Westminster informed Prior Ford that O'Halloran 'shows no sign of surrender'.[60] Moreover, the monks should exercise diplomacy and be sensitive, not belligerent, towards their clerical neighbour. By February 1897, Vaughan confidently informed Prior Ford that he believed that O'Halloran would not present a serious difficulty. Yet the

Cardinal understood that the transfer of jurisdiction in Ealing would inevitably cause problems. He informed Ford that he had 'given O'Halloran notice that on 28th March the Benedictines will take over the Ealing Mission', but the monks were also told that they could not expect to take possession of O'Halloran's church or the mission property.[61]

According to Cardinal Vaughan, Father O'Halloran 'persistently refused in offensive language to leave the mission',[62] and, when threatened with ecclesiastical punishment, O'Halloran's response sounded more like a declaration of war. 'Death alone removes me from the Rectorship here,' he informed Archbishop's House.[63] Even at this early date, Prior Ford tried to reason with O'Halloran. Ford wrote and told him that 'it is impossible to go round the Church . . . without a feeling of deep sadness at the thought that a priest of your zeal might be destroyed'.[64] English Roman Catholics were soon treated to the spectacle of a rebellious cleric flouting the expressed commands of the Archbishop of Westminster.

Cardinal Vaughan could not tolerate this disobedient priest. Moreover, the scandal of prelate, cleric, and monks feuding threatened to besmirch the picture of a unified English Roman Catholicism which Vaughan and his predecessors had struggled to create. On 8 April, therefore, Father Michael Barry, the Vicar-General, informed Father O'Halloran that 'the Archbishop was grieved to hear that you have paid no attention to his direction that you should give up the Mission of Ealing into the hands of the Benedictine Fathers'.[65] Barry also drew attention to O'Halloran's boast that he would 'not retire and . . . [would] continue to serve the Mission'. The Vicar-General enumerated the following facts to Father O'Halloran: he promised in writing 'to leave Ealing whenever he [Cardinal Vaughan] should call upon you to do so'; the Ealing Mission 'has been canonically made over to the Benedictine Fathers with the full consent of the Holy See'; and Cardinal Vaughan promised not to force him to retire from Ealing until 'he had arranged with your own Bishop to give you a Mission in his Diocese to which you canonically belong'. Father Barry reminded O'Halloran that he had been given an opportunity to argue his case that he belonged to Westminster, and had a right to remain in the diocese, before any bishop in England, but had declined the offer. Barry contended that Cardinal Vaughan had presented O'Halloran's 'claims before the Diocesan Commission of Investigation', and reminded him that he had been given the opportunity to attend the meeting. The Commission, according to the Vicar-General, 'decided against you upon the evidence, which consisted of documents in your own hand, and the facts of the case'. Because of this disobedience and obstinacy, Archbishop's House communicated the following judgement to Father O'Halloran:

> The Cardinal is under the painful obligation of giving you formal notice by this letter that he has withdrawn the Diocesan faculties which you have hitherto held, and that he forbids you to say a public Mass at Ealing on Sunday, unless you

publicly announced that you will obey the decision which has been given, and at once hand over the Mission to the Benedictine Fathers.

On the following day, Cardinal Vaughan canonically entrusted Ealing to the care of the Benedictine monks living at Castle Hill House. Vaughan directed Dom Bernard Bulbeck 'to announce to the Catholics within the Mission of Ealing that the pastoral care of this Mission of Ealing has been confided to the Benedictine Fathers exclusively'.[66] The faithful of the area were also to be instructed that 'no other Priest within the Mission holds faculties of jurisdiction from me'. After an expression of encouragement, Vaughan instructed Dom Bernard to urge Ealing's Roman Catholics 'to follow and obey their lawful spiritual Superiors'. These actions on the part of Archbishop's House, however, did not hinder Father O'Halloran, who refused to recognize the claims of the Benedictines to the Ealing mission. In spite of the suspension of his priestly faculties, he continued to say mass and to adminster the sacraments to his Mattock Land flock. One week after O'Halloran had been informed of his suspension, Cardinal Vaughan announced to the Roman Catholics of Ealing that officials from the Archdiocese of Westminster would meet with members of the congregation on the afternoon of 17 April at Castle Hill House to explain the changes which had taken place in respect to the Ealing clergy. O'Halloran still remained intransigent; stronger medicine was needed to bring peace to Ealing. On 21 April 1897, therefore, Archbishop's House issued a formal Decree of Suspension which banned the priest 'from the use of all ecclesiastical faculties,' and branded Father O'Halloran a 'refractory cleric'.[67]

Paradoxically, in light of his past behaviour, O'Halloran remained quiet, and the Cardinal vowed to keep him silent. Cardinal Vaughan took the case to the Propaganda in Rome. The judgement, as expected, supported the position of the Cardinal. The Cardinal Prefect of the Congregation declared that O'Halloran belonged to the Diocese of Middlesbrough, that he 'held office of Rector in the Mission of Ealing . . . in a temporary way', and that although his faculties were suspended, 'continues to the grave scandal of the faithful, to celebrate Mass and to administer the Sacraments'.[68] The Cardinal Prefect directed Vaughan to act in the following manner:

> I therefore request your Eminence to make known to the said priest that this Sacred Congregation gravely blames his conduct, and wishes him to retire from Ealing as soon as possible; and in the meantime your Eminence, in the name of the Sacred Congregation, will give notice to the faithful not to go near this rebellious priest.

In May, the Vicar-General again visited O'Halloran, and read him the strongly worded letter from Propaganda. Soon after this, Father O'Halloran received a personal letter from the Cardinal Prefect in Rome which severely rebuked and scolded him. This document told O'Halloran that he remained a priest of the Diocese of Middlesbrough and described his refusal to relinquish

Ealing to the Benedictines as an act of 'contumacious obstinacy'.[69] Moreover, 'you have gone as far as to despise the suspension from the exercise of all sacred functions ... and most wickedly, and to the great scandal of the faithful, you have continued to say Mass and sacrilegiously to administer the Sacraments'. The Prefect warned Father O'Halloran that his actions might lead him 'headlong into the way of perdition' and pleaded with him to 'do your duty, asking pardon for what you have done and betaking yourself, for obedience sake, to the Bishop of Middlesbrough'.

Father O'Halloran chose to disobey this direct command from Propaganda, and declared that he would not 'resign in favour of the Benedictine monks'.[70] 'If there be a scandal in Ealing, it is produced by the violent and illegal conduct of Cardinal Vaughan and the monks,' he replied to Propaganda. Roman Catholics still attended the services at his church, and O'Halloran continued to describe himself as the legitimate priest of the Ealing area. One Roman Catholic paper, the *Universe*, expressed shock to learn 'that the Rev. O'Halloran obtains sympathy and support from Catholics in Ealing'.[71] The newspaper attacked the 'atrocious guilt of taking part in sacrilegious actions', and implored 'the misguided Catholics who support this unworthy priest to examine their conscience in the sight of God'. The *Daily Chronicle* also reported that the Sunday masses were well attended.[72] The *Westminster Gazette*, however, predicted that O'Halloran would suffer because of 'the Cardinal's suspensory order upon the weaker members of the flock'.[73] 'So long as the faithful are not driven away by the archiepiscopal thunders from Westminster,' the article concluded, 'he is prepared to stand his ground.'

Vaughan, therefore, was forced to take even stronger measures. Ealing Roman Catholics must be alerted to the presence of a wolf among the flock. The Vicar-General informed Dom Bernard that the Cardinal Prefect of Propaganda had given permission for all correspondence dealing with Vaughan and O'Halloran to 'be translated and circulated among the people'.[74] Rome's case against Father O'Halloran must be explained to the Roman Catholics of the area: 'The Benedictines should read these letters to their people and distribute copies of them among the people frequenting O'H's chapel'. Vaughan also issued a public condemnation and denunciation of the priest, and told his clergy to read it from the pulpits of the area's Roman Catholic churches. 'We have no choice,' the announcement stated, but 'to call upon those concerned not to allow themselves to be misled, but to listen to the voice of their Bishop.'[75] This circular, 'Notification to the Catholics in Ealing and the Neighbourhood,' chronicled the background of the dispute between Cardinal Vaughan and Father O'Halloran and printed the priest's signed statement that he did not belong to the Westminster Archdiocese. Vaughan addressed the people of Ealing in the following manner:

> With deep pain and regret we find ourselves at last compelled, in obedience to an instruction from the Apostolic See, to issue a public and official notice, to the effect

that the Rev. Richard O'Halloran has been canonically suspended from the use of all ecclesiastical faculties, including that of saying Mass; that his place of worship is not recognized as a Catholic Church or Chapel, and that no Catholic can frequent it, or receive Sacraments from him, without sin.

During the summer of 1897, Father O'Halloran slowly began to respond to Cardinal Vaughan's public chastisements. Initially, he tried to sow seeds of distrust between the recently arrived Benedictine monks and the Cardinal. O'Halloran wrote to Vaughan in July and accused the Ealing monks of saying 'the blackest things about you'.[76] According to one of his informants, the monks alleged that 'no lady will allow her maid to come near you – either Catholic or Protestant', and he told the Cardinal that 'they hinted as much as they dare about me'. 'These untrustworthy Benedictines' constantly alluded to 'something very black against your past,' O'Halloran claimed. The ethos of this letter remained restrained as he tried to darken and damage the character of the Ealing monks: 'It seems to be incredible that the monks (no matter how bitter you and they are against me) could be guilty of such wicked malice and falsehood towards me'. But this tactic did not work. Vaughan forwarded O'Halloran's letter to Dom Bernard with the comment that the women who made the allegations must have 'been deceived'.[77] Even if charges of libel could be brought against Father O'Halloran, it 'would be most fatal' to pursue them. To taunt him unnecessarily would be disastrous, Archbishop's House advised the Benedictines.

From the beginning of this clerical battle, the Benedictines had adopted a cautious approach to the problems they encountered in Ealing; reserve and diplomacy characterized their response to the O'Halloran problem. Abbot Snow, capturing the spirit of this policy, wrote to Prior Ford during the turbulent month of April and confessed that he did 'not see what we can do about O'Halloran except keep quiet and await events . . . and do our best not to get mixed up in the quarrel'.[78] 'It will be a scandal and he will probably say and do things that will shock even-minded people,' Snow maintained, and 'I think our cue should be to say as little as possible and at present do merely the bare requisites of the mission work.' The monks, however, did try to inform the area's Roman Catholics of Father O'Halloran's shaky ecclesiastical status. In April, O'Halloran complained to Ford that 'your monks have been round the houses of my flock' and have made several damaging accusations:

that I hold no diocesan faculties; that I am outside the pale of my church; that it would be sinful to be present at the services in my church, that my church was no more than any Baptist or Methodist chapel; that the Cardinal did not know that I was building the church in Mattock-Lane; [and] that I am in defiance of the Pope.[79]

'These statements are all – each and everyone of them absolutely untrue,' he tried to convince Ford.

Although the Benedictines had hoped that Father O'Halloran would strike camp and leave Ealing if ignored, it soon became apparent that he was preparing for a long siege. After the public condemnation of the priest by Vaughan, Abbot Snow informed Downside that several concerned people had approached him and warned him that O'Halloran was prepared to 'hold out to the bitter end'.[80] Although Roman Catholics slowly began to desert the Mattock Lane church for the orthodoxy of the Ealing Benedictines,[81] Dom Bernard soon dashed any hope for a quick victory and peace. Writing to Ford in October, he stated that 'O'Halloran is flourishing and [he] told his people his church would be crammed full by another year'.[82]

Attacked by prelate and monks, Father Richard O'Halloran finally responded in June 1897, and the secular press became the major platform for his bellicose rhetoric. On 19 June, the *Middlesex County Times* reported that the Benedictines had arrived in Ealing and occupied Castle Hill House. The same issue also printed a letter addressed to Vaughan written by Father O'Halloran. He informed the Cardinal that he would appeal to Rome against 'the unjust and uncanonical intrusion of the Benedictine monks into Ealing'.[83] Moreover, he argued, this drastic action would emphasize 'the conduct both of your eminence and of those monks towards me and my flock before and since their arrival in my mission'. On 10 July, the paper printed the letter sent by the Cardinal Prefect of Propaganda Fide to O'Halloran. His terse response and explanation followed. 'We believe in the primacy of the Bishop of Rome as the supreme shepherd of the whole Catholic Church,' he wrote to a member of his mission, but 'we do not allow that supreme or absolute power as attached to the See of Westminster.'[84] Emotion then dislodged logic: 'It is not an act of schism to refuse obedience to a law or precept of the Supreme Pontiff, or other ecclesiastical superiors, provided this refusal does not amount to a disclaimer of all subjection to him; nor even then if there be any doubt of his authority.' A few sentences later, however, O'Halloran proclaimed his loyalty to church superiors. 'We accept the Bishop of Rome's authority,' he pleaded, 'and in all things lawful and canonical and reasonable we faithfully carry out the will and wishes of Cardinal Vaughan, who is our Archbishop in union with the Apostolic See.' The spectre of an ecclesiastical insurrection, however, soon caught the attention of the local inhabitants. One anonymous letter-writer, a non-Catholic, argued that the facts of the case and the weight of the evidence proved O'Halloran wrong, and he suggested that the Ealing priest should 'give in at once'. 'Against Rome he is powerless.'[85]

The *Middlesex County Times* realized that it had stumbled on to a sensational story involving religion: a Roman Catholic priest confronting and disobeying a Roman Catholic Cardinal. The paper printed Cardinal Vaughan's 'Notification', and then dispatched a journalist to meet this new ecclesiastical celebrity of Mattock Lane. The interview with Father O'Halloran was published under the title, 'He Fears That He Is In Physical Danger'.[86] Commenting on his signed statement disclaiming that he belonged to the

Archdiocese of Westminster, O'Halloran argued that the Vicar-General had promised that the document would never be used against him. Moreover, 'on the advice of eminent canonists', he had signed the document believing that his 'canonical position would be unaffected'. O'Halloran also argued that 'the undertaking . . . [he] signed had no reference to the Ealing idea', and that his assignment to Ealing was never intended to be temporary. The earlier pronouncements and decisions from Rome concerning his case, he told the interviewer, lacked objectivity and knowledge of the facts of the case. As for the suspension imposed by Cardinal Vaughan, O'Halloran remarked: 'I regard these censures as invalid, and I am therefore, entitled to disregard them'. 'Whatever the issue,' he boasted, 'I shall remain in Ealing.' When asked if he felt threatened with physical harm, he replied: 'Yes, quite serious'. In the same edition of the paper, Father O'Halloran also received some support and encouragement. A letter referred to Cardinal Vaughan as a prelate 'backed up by innumerable priestly friends and relations and a rich monastery of monks thrown in . . .'[87] 'To ruin the work of such a man at the caprice of a Cardinal,' O'Halloran's nameless champion wrote, 'is wicked in the extreme and merits the censure of every honest, right-thinking man'.

As the O'Halloran drama escalated, it caught the attention of the larger London papers. The *Daily Chronicle*, for example, introduced its subscribers to the Ealing fracas in July with an article entitled 'Arbitrary episcopal action', which explained to its readers that the 'resistance of the secular priests to the encroachments of the religious orders is the story of a universal conflict that has to be measured by centuries'.[88] Soon, several letters dealing with the subject of 'Roman Catholic Discipline' appeared in the columns of the *Daily Chronicle*. One of Father O'Halloran's parishioners wrote that 'until the Courts of the Church have heard Father O'Halloran I cannot see why we should leave him'.[89] A London priest also shared some of O'Halloran's misgivings about the misuse and abuse of episcopal power, and argued that 'for a long time [there has been] an uneasy feeling that the parochial clergy are so many chessmen in the hands of their Bishops'. If the Ealing priest could prove that Cardinal Vaughan had wronged him, the writer claimed that the priests of London would 'back him up'. Another cleric sympathetic to Father O'Halloran drew attention to the 'anomalous position of the English priesthood', and expressed a hope that this 'would soon be a matter of ancient history'. In its next several issues, the London daily continued to stoke the fires of religious emotionalism. One story, headlined 'The Ealing Scandal: A Strange Story,' declared that 'the question raised would affect the liberty and happiness of every Roman Catholic in England'.[90] And the paper emphasized a traditional rivalry and suspicion within England's ecclesiastical history: the jealousy between the secular priesthood and the religious orders. 'In another way [the questions involved] affect the vitality of the Church itself for it is evident that we are in the presence of an organized attempt on the part of religious orders to seize the well-established mission of the secular clergy.' The *Daily Chronicle* also expressed surprise that Cardinal Vaughan has 'lent himself to methods which, however familiar they are to the monkish fraternity, seem strangely out of sympathy with his own known geniality of disposition'.

The press, therefore, quickly turned the Ealing crisis into an issue which revolved around an alleged attack on the rights and privileges of the secular priesthood. In a letter to the editor of the *Daily Chronicle*, O'Halloran flatly denied all the accusations and charges made by the Cardinal against him. He also questioned the validity and legality of Vaughan's authority to suspend him: 'I am not suspended, but the Cardinal's power to suspend is suspended'.[91] Proclaiming that he was a priest of the Archdioceses of Westminster, he declared that 'the Benedictines have no "legal title" to Ealing . . . Neither the Cardinal nor the Propaganda can set aside the Ten Commandments or the natural law of justice.' The rights of a secular priest, he proclaimed, have been violated for the sake of Benedictine monks. In a hostile article, the *Daily Chronicle* supported Father O'Halloran and asked 'whether or not the great religious ordes should replace the humbler secular mission priests and rectors whose work has been so faithfully rewarded'.[92] In an attempt to embarrass Vaughan, the paper also declared that 'the issue is simply whether or not Cardinal Vaughan, or any other prelate of the Roman Church, is empowered by canonical authority to remove from his care of souls a popular mission priest in order to make room for two or three Benedictine monks, who desire to enter into the fruit of his successful labours'.

But the Cardinal also found support for his Ealing policy. A Franciscan from Crawley responded to the *Daily Chronicle* and attacked the paper for its unfounded and biased support of 'the rebel' O'Halloran.[93] Another correspondent professed that 'it is ridiculous to talk of the secular priests being ousted by the religious orders, and to hear the Benedictines spoken of as an aggressive Order is exceedingly funny to anyone who knows anything of them'.[94] Nonetheless, the *Daily Chronicle* saw the Ealing affair as an excuse to poke fun at the Roman Catholic Church in England, and it used O'Halloran to illuminate the internecine conflicts of this foreign religion. Lead stories, such as, 'Regulars v. Seculars' and 'Aggressiveness of the Monks', exposed the infighting in Vaughan's church. A letter from one of O'Halloran's faithful parishioners captured the policy of the paper: 'Was it honest or honourable for the monks of Downside to enter the parish of Ealing when they knew that the resident priest had protested against the Cardinal's power to remove him, and the trial had not taken place?'[95]

If the *Daily Chronicle* emphasized ecclesiastical civil war, the *Daily Mail* chuckled at the sight of a disobedient cleric defying the proud Archbishop of Westminster. In an article, 'A "Rebellious" Priest: Fighting Against Ecclesiastical Superiors', the *Mail* told its readers about the suspension of the local priest by Cardinal Vaughan and noted that 'the usually peaceful parish of Ealing is now convulsed to the very core by the bitterness of this ecclesiastical dispute, which is almost without precedent in the annals of the church'.[96] A reporter from the paper also visited Father O'Halloran, and later retold the story of the unjust and illegal treatment the priest suffered at the hands of the Cardinal. On 20 July, it printed the text of the 'Notification', and gleefully emphasized the division within the Ealing faithful: 'the support that the Roman Catholics of Ealing still extend to the "silenced" priest' is recognized by the authorities at Archbishop's House.[97] As the conflict flowed over the boundaries of Ealing, the Roman Catholic press rushed to defend the honour and integrity of their Archbishop and to condemn the behaviour of Father O'Halloran.

The Roman Catholic papers did respond to the happenings in Ealing, but they did not waste as much ink as their secular counterparts. After calling attention to the publicity O'Halloran was receiving in the columns of London press, the *Catholic Herald* simply announced that 'by a Papal decree, the ecclesiastical privileges of the Rev. Richard O'Halloran have been withdrawn owing to the refusal on his part to comply with an order of his Eminence Cardinal Vaughan'.[98] In its next edition, the paper pointed out that 'O'Halloran appears ... to be doing all he can to foment trouble in the Archdiocese of Westminster'.[99] Moreover, 'Cardinal Vaughan has done nothing which he needs to conceal or blush for, but on the contrary he has shown to this man the utmost Christian charity ...' As for the Benedictines, they 'are persevering with their mission at Castle Hill, which is intended to replace the closed one at Ealing'. The *Universe* drew attention to O'Halloran's nationality and wrote that 'the notoriety created by the Irish priest at Ealing ... ought to have convinced that foolish ecclesiastic that there is no use in falling out with his superiors in the hierarchy'.[100] One article came close to emulating the vituperation and venom of O'Halloran's rhetoric. 'We are of the opinion,' the *Universe* smugly declared, that 'O'Halloran's conduct is most reprehensible and unjustifiable, and is such that no true-hearted priest would be guilty of'. It urged Ealing's Roman Catholics to boycott the Mattock Lane chapel. But the *Universe* also printed a letter sympathetic to O'Halloran which told the editor that 'if you knew him by his good works you would add to your article a few of his good points as well as his one fault'.[101]

The *Catholic Times* published several of Father O'Halloran's letters without comment during August 1897, but in the autumn it abandoned any pretence of neutrality. It denied O'Halloran's accusation that Cardinal Vaughan had ordered the Catholic press not to report on the happenings at Ealing, and termed O'Halloran's letters 'incoherent'.[102] Moreover, it continued, 'his rhetoric is running away with his logic'. A week later, subscribers to the *Catholic Times* were told that 'if every priest were to act on Father O'Halloran's principles, diocesan government would be impossible'.[103] A priest of Westminster pointed out that 'the attempt to represent this as a dispute between the seculars and regulars is hardly honest ... The regulars have nothing to do with the dispute,' the writer claimed, 'which lies entirely between a secular priest and the diocesan and chapter of a secular diocese whose right to rule the diocese and to be obeyed is challenged.' The paper soon decided to terminate the discussion of the Ealing scandal. After acknowledging the fact that the editor had received numerous letters on the subject, an announcement signalled the end of the O'Halloran debate: 'the pages of a popular newspaper such as the *Catholic Times* are not the proper medium for investigating and deciding complicated questions of canonical procedure'.[104]

By the summer of 1897, therefore, Father O'Halloran's plight and his battle with the Benedictine monks had been popularized by the local and metropolitan press. And the problems at Ealing refused to die a quiet death. O'Halloran remained adamant: he would not leave Ealing peacefully. He declared his intention 'to remain here . . . in opposition to the authority of the Cardinal Archbishop'.[105] 'The Cardinal knows me and he knows that I am fighting for the truth . . . [and] nothing but the truth will reduce me to submission'. Appealing to the emotionalism of the secular-religious argument. O'Halloran proudly declared that he was 'only doing what other priests should have done when driven from pillar to post'. The Benedictines became intruders, 'who were doing their utmost to attract my people away from this church'. 'So far they have attracted a good many of their bodies,' he told the press, 'but I know that I shall have their souls . . . [and] in time they will all come back.' He also disavowed the authority of Cardinal Vaughan to discipline him or deprive him of his priestly faculties. 'In reality it is his own power over me which is suspended, and consequently all censures . . . are not only unjust, but invalid.' O'Halloran also enjoyed some support from the residents of Ealing. The *Middlesex County Times* reported that 'a committee has been formed to raise the necessary funds to assist Father O'Halloran in his fight for justice'.[106] 'As the fight will be to secure a better status for the Catholic clergy in England,' the secretary and treasurer of this organization announced, 'it is hoped this appeal will be responded to by the clergy and laity of the Catholic Church and the friends of justice'.

The press continued to report on the Ealing crisis, and the columns of the local paper became a pulpit for O'Halloran to distribute his views. In September, for example, O'Halloran publicly thanked the readers of the *Middlesex County Times* 'for the many letters of sympathy which . . . [he] received in consequence of the later difficulty which caused such grief to the loyal and faithful worshippers of SS. Joseph and Peter'.[107] He urged his friends to attend the services at his church and to send their children to his school, which he planned to enlarge. Although he had proclaimed his determination to remain in Ealing, a faint offer of compromise and peace suddenly appeared: 'We interfere with no man . . . there is room enough in this world for all Christian men to labour for souls'. But this did not constitute surrender. Two weeks later, the same paper reported that 'the Rev. Father O'Halloran meditates a permanent stay in Ealing, judging by the fact that recently he had all the mortar rubbish, which looked so unsightly in front of his church, removed'.[108]

The last month of 1897 saw only two stories dealing with Father O'Halloran appear in the press. The local Ealing paper printed his response to an article in the *Catholic Times*[109] and at the end of October he launched his last attack of the year. 'The Cardinal,' O'Halloran declared, 'has no more right to send the monks into my mission and attack me, as he has done, than a highwayman has a right by violence to knock down and plunder a respectable citizen, and then abuse him.'[110] O'Halloran accused Cardinal Vaughan of 'an abuse of his jurisdiction and of gross injustice in bringing monks into Ealing'. Finally, he blamed the Cardinal and the monks for having caused the scandal at Ealing. The year ended with a strange report in which O'Halloran announced that 'the Pope removes all sentences of censures of excommunication in whatever case impaired'.[111] Moreover, 'Father O'Halloran . . . urged his flock to cling close to the Apostolic See of Rome and to avoid all those who in Ealing were causing division and bringing scandal on the Roman Church.'

As the Benedictines of Castle Hill House began to extend their ministry to the Roman Catholics of Ealing, and as Cardinal Vaughan progressed in his negotiations with the monks about their liturgical responsibilities at Westminster Cathedral, the tense situation in Ealing remained relatively calm. The new year, 1898, opened with a press story detailing the life and activities of O'Halloran's church,[112] and another which reported that Father O'Halloran had been 'confined to his room through a severe attack of rheumatic fever',[113] an illness which would last for nearly two months. The Mattock Lane Church continued to survive. The *Middlesex County Times* reported the baptisms and marriages conducted by Father O'Halloran and announced the schedule of services to be conducted at 'Saints Joseph and Peter's Roman Church' along with those of its nearby rival, St Benedict's of Castlebar Road.[114] But O'Halloran could not avoid publicity. In October 1898 he became involved in a bitter exchange of letters in which he defended the Ealing Anglican priest, Rev. W. Ranger of St Saviour's, who was associated with illegal and Romish ritual actions. 'Now no man in Ealing can accuse the clergyman of St Saviour's of dishonesty or of seeking worldly ends,' he wrote, and 'it is a fact known to all that the cream of the Church of England priests is among the Ritualistic party.'[115]

During the last days of 1898, Father O'Halloran again seemed to extend the olive branch to the Benedictines. He wrote to Prior Ford at Downside and made the following proposal: '. . . you monks have and carry on a separate mission on the Castle Bar Road . . . there is room enough and to spare for both missions'.[116] 'If you do this the cause is ended.' O'Halloran warned Ford that if no compromise was reached he would publish a book and expose the duplicity of the Cardinal and the Benedictines, and the 'responsibility for its publication will *rest* entirely *on the monks*'. This publication would vindicate his position and restore respect to his character. 'Rome will no doubt read the book,' he threatened, 'and all England and the Catholic world will look on to see *if you monks* succeed in your aggression.' The option became clear. 'Once more I offer you the choice of a separate mission here and let me undisturbed . . . or my public vindication of my position.' Ford chose not to respond to this offer.

At the same time as he was trying to woo the monks into a compromise, Father O'Halloran became involved in a scheme to undermine their integrity. When Dom Bernard Bulbeck was preparing to retire as the first parish priest of St Benedict's, the Benedictines faced a threat potentially and traditionally more dangerous than the invectives of O'Halloran: the possibility of a anti-Roman Catholic outburst fanned by a visit to Ealing by an ex-Franciscan. The Rev. F. G. Widdows, pastor of the Church of Martin Luther, Hackney, lectured at Shaftesbury Hall during November 1898. The gathering did not proceed without incident: 'A little knot of young rowdies also in attendance resolved that, if they could not prevent it, the audience should hear nothing of the sort'.[117] A connection between the appearance of his anti-monastic speaker and Father O'Halloran surfaced. Widdows admitted that he sympathized with the plight of O'Halloran and claimed that 'it was fortunate for Father O'Halloran and his flock, for if they were in a Roman Catholic country the congregation would speedily be persecuted out of existence'. After addressing the evils of religious life, the speaker claimed to have had tea with the Benedictines of Castle Hill House. When he was asked to prove this contention, a fracas broke out in the hall and the police rushed in to restore order. Widdows then explained the manner in which he had suffered at the hands of Roman Catholics. Consequently, 'he wished to warn his countrymen' of this danger.[118] He then touched on his life as a friar. 'He had never up to that time seen things to scandalize him,' the speaker claimed, and he then 'gave a description of things he had seen while in the monastery and . . . these things began to make him think.' Tantalizing his audience with stories and rumours of immorality within monastic cloisters, he gave an example 'of one order being so corrupt that the Pope ordered them to wear beards so that they would be unable to disguise themselves in the nunnery.' But Widdows' opponents in the crowd refused to remain quiet, and according to one report 'outside the little crowd of ejected rowdies used language that was painful and free . . .'[119] On the following Wednesday, he presented a talk on 'Monkish Imposters: Ancient and Modern,' but unlike his first lecture, protesters did not interrupt this presentation. If the intention of the speaker was to unite his listeners against the Ealing Benedictines or to enlist support for O'Halloran's campaign against the new arrivals, the plan failed. No anti-Benedictine or anti-Catholic demonstrations materialized.

One incident independent of O'Halloran and Widdows did occur, however, which might have mushroomed into a Maria Monk campaign against the Ealing Benedictines. In October 1899, Dom Gilbert Dolan reported that he had recently anointed a nun at a local convent. She suffered a breakdown soon afterwards. 'She was "clean gone" and had to be watched all night,' he lamented.[120] Dom Gilbert explained what happened next to the authorities at Downside.

Left alone for a few minutes while the sister in charge went to report her condition to Fr. Bernard, she got out of the window, and half dressed as she was, made for the garden, through the hedge across the field and into one of the new roads close by.

Fortunately, a man who worked for the convent and whom Dom Gilbert labelled 'a Prot', saw 'here and induced her to go to his home where his wife made here comfortable'. But this strange incident did not escape unnoticed by the Ealing locals. According to Dom Gilbert, 'the brutes who saw the poor thing jeered and behaved badly', and 'now in addition to the O'Halloran business, we are likely to have the "escaped nun" cry for a time'. Dom Gilbert's final comment on the subject revealed a touch of English stoicism. 'I began to think,' he ended the report of the incident, 'that Ealing is a lively place.'

By 1898, therefore, the new Benedictine foundation in West London had survived the hostile words of Father Richard O'Halloran and the adverse publicity of the press. Even an ex-friar who lectured on the alleged lurid details of conventual life failed to dampen the spirit or halt the progress of the Benedictines. Property had been purchased for expansion, the construction of a new church undertaken, and the energy of a new priest, Dom Gilbert Dolan, began to generate a vibrant spirit. The policy of not publicly engaging O'Halloran also helped to ensure the stability of this new monastic foundation. Ford had successfully orchestrated this approach. 'The only wise policy in regard to Fr O'Halloran is (I am convinced) to leave him alone,' he wrote to one of the Ealing monks in December 1898, and 'the great thing is to go on with work of our own and leave him alone.'[121] Ford warned this Ealing monk to guard his words and actions concerning Father O'Halloran. 'Dont [sic] go to see the Cardinal and dont [sic] talk to others about the necessity of "doing something" about Fr. O'Halloran,' he continued, since 'there are plenty of those who would like to see us fail at Ealing.'[122] Ford's order was succinct: 'Your text is to let Fr. O'Halloran alone, and discourage anyone who fusses and talks about his doings'.

But this approach did not muzzle the Mattock Lane cleric. In one of his last letters before he left Ealing, Dom Bernard Bulbeck commented on the activities of his rival. He informed Downside on 10 March 1899 that 'Fr O'Halloran ended his sermon on Sunday with a flourish of Defiance'. [123]

CHAPTER III

Consolidation and Expansion: The Ealing Benedictines at the Turn of the Century

W hen Dom Gilbert Dolan, OSB, arrived in Ealing on 5 January 1899 to take charge of the new Benedictine foundation, he brought with him a varied background and a tenacity of will which influenced his tenure as superior. A native of Kentish Town, he was born on 2 February 1853 and was sent to Downside where he received his early education.[1] He entered the novitiate in 1870, and was ordained a priest at Downside in 1878. While at St Gregory's, he showed a keen interest in architecture and religious history and, as the community's librarian and archivist, 'he collected and bound up a large number of pamphlets . . . relating to English Catholicism since the Reformation'. In 1884 he was sent to work on the missions, and served successively at Liverpool, Warrington, Woolton, and Dulwich. In London, he became one of the monks associated with the so-called House of Historical Studies under the tutelage of Dom Aidan Gasquet. Afterwards, he was appointed as a chaplain to the Benedictine nuns at Stanbrook, a post he retained until he was assigned to take charge of the new mission in Ealing.

Dom Gilbert always exhibited a keen interest in the history of the Benedictine missions throughout England and their presence in the capital city; consequently he believed it was his vocation to work to strengthen the Benedictine tradition at his new post. A gifted preacher, he enjoyed the reputation of 'originality of mind [which] gave to his sermons an interest peculiarly his own'. A confrère later noted that the secret of his influence lay deeper than his obvious rhetorical skills: 'Behind and beneath the gentle, cheery temper was a depth of spirituality and a love of prayer which, overlooked by many in the days of his activity, came out in the last years of his life so plainly that none could fail to see'. Loved by the parish he helped to mould at Ealing, it was recorded that, when his superior finally decided to re-assign him in 1907, 'the whole congregation . . . begged [the Abbot of Downside] to reconsider his decision'.

Numerous difficulties and problems confronted Dom Gilbert at Ealing: the O'Halloran affair, the relation of the Benedictine monks to Cardinal Vaughan's new cathedral, and those usual problems associated with any new foundation, such as manpower and finance. But Prior Ford had the highest confidence in Gilbert Dolan's ability. 'No one perhaps besides myself realizes the heavy work you have in front of you at Ealing,' Ford informed him.[2] 'It is comparatively an easy thing to start a mission, but at Ealing you are beginning a monastery,' he continued, 'and within a few years we want to see a monastic church there and a Community attached to it.' Ford told Dom Gilbert that he would face difficult financial obstacles, especially in respect to the future purchase of real estate and construction costs, but these must be overcome. Prior Ford's commission to his fellow Benedictine seemed Herculean. 'If we are to be a monastery at Ealing we must have room enough for a school, sufficient ground to enable the community to be out-of-doors without being obliged to go out into the streets, [and] land for monastic buildings.' And this represented only the beginning. 'As we shall be serving the mission,' Ford continued, 'we shall want room for public buildings for the use of the people, reading rooms, boys' recreation rooms, guild rooms, besides the Church and its special buildings.' Dom Gilbert was also told that he already faced a debt of £15,000 to £16,000. But in addition to this bleak but challenging forecast, Prior Ford guaranteed Gilbert Dolan his support and backing.

In respect to this large debt, Prior Ford assured Dom Gilbert that 'you will have the last penny I can afford to send you, but the burden left to you will be very heavy'. Ford suggested that he utilize the obvious goodwill and support of the parishioners to tackle the money problem: 'when they are contending with these early difficulties [they will] remain as a tradition of faith and piety in the Congregation'. Wealthy benefactors, therefore, must be found. Again, Ford tried to minimize the difficulties by saying 'it is the wish of the Holy See that we should found this monastery at Ealing and have a Community there'. Ford reminded Dom Gilbert that for 'many years I and others have looked forward to a time when we might have a house in which there would be community life, and from which we should be serving a parish'. Ealing, moreover, only represented the beginning of a grand design which could secure for the English Benedictines a permanent foundation in the capital. In concluding his commission to Gilbert Dolan, Prior Ford emphasized this vision: 'If we succeed at Ealing, who knows that we may live long enough to see our idea of a monastery in the thick of the East of London realised'.

The problems associated with Father O'Halloran and his Mattock Lane chapel had also influenced Ford's decision to send Dom Gilbert to Ealing. The Downside Prior told Dom Vincent Corney, a monk already stationed at Ealing, that he was 'quite as alive as the Cardinal or yourself to the need of Fr Dolan being there . . . [because] he is wanted not so much to do something as to ignore Fr O'Halloran, and those who fuss about him, . . . [and] to keep things quiet.'[3]

Dom Gilbert did accept his new post with reservation and caution; but he quickly set about to build up his parish by his encouraging words, actions, and example. He told his congregation on his arrival that he had come 'to relieve the venerable priest – Father Bernard Bulbeck – who for the past eighteen months had conducted the mission under very difficult circumstances'.[4] Everyone must work together, the faithful of Ealing were told, and all should remember that 'a Catholic congregation was always a unique body, because it was a divine instead of a human institution'. Dom Gilbert quickly alluded to the construction of a proper church, and stated 'that it was a very great privilege for anyone to help build a sanctuary for the Most High'. He reminded his parishioners that it was the presence of the Blessed Sacrament 'which prompted the erection of handsome churches and the carrying out of a beautiful ritual'.

Dom Gilbert's energy and dedication immediately bcame apparent to the Catholic inhabitants of Ealing. St Benedict's Day 1899, for example, was celebrated with pomp and ceremony. With the obvious exception of Father O'Halloran, the neighbouring clergy were invited and heard Abbot Snow canonize 'the work of the Benedictine monks from the time of St Benedict to the present day, showing the prominent part they played in the history of Europe'.[5] The local paper also recorded in great detail the Holy Week services held at St Benedict's and reported that Dom Gilbert publicly acknowledged various gifts from his parishioners which included 'a handsome chalice of Parisian workmanship . . . a silver thurible, a missal, six altar candlesticks, and a tall paschal candlestick of mahogany gilt'.[6] In more sober language, the same column acknowledged that Holy Week was also celebrated by Father O'Halloran in his chapel. During the summer, 'the annual dedication of England to St Peter, ordered by the Catholic Bishops, was made' at the Benedictine mission.[7] In his sermon, Dom Gilbert told the congregation that 'the deep devotion of the English people to the person and See of Peter was one of the facts of history'. 'To be in communion with the See of Peter was the true test of Catholicity and Apostolicity,' he concluded, and 'those outside the Catholic Church were fully aware of this distinctive mark of Catholicism, for they have coined those terms of reproach and words of abuse – Romanism and Popery'. Under Dom Gilbert Dolan's leadership, therefore, the Ealing mission began to develop into a lively urban parish, and he immediately turned his attention to the construction of a parish church.

If the construction of a proper church represented the mark of stability and vitality of a Roman Catholic community, then the self-assurance and confidence of the Ealing Benedictines surfaced long before the arrival of Dom Gilbert. Originally, in accordance with Cardinal Vaughan's directive, services were conducted in Castle Hill House, but Prior Ford soon entertained dreams of a grand abbey church. In August 1897, Ford directed the monks at Ealing to tell their parishioners that they could expect a suitable church in the near future, and the priests were directed to 'begin at once to get subscriptions' and to 'tell the Congregation at once that plans are being prepared for a stone church'.[8] Ford personally chose Frederick Walters, who designed Buckfast Abbey in Devon, and the architect submitted a design similar to a fifteenth-century East Anglican church, complete with two flying towers. The proposed church would face south on Marchwood Crescent.

In the spring of 1898 the Council at Downside discussed the question of the future Ealing church, and asked to see the plans for the building and to know 'the estimation for the *whole* church'.[10] Dom Osmund Knight informed Ford that the council thought the plan to borrow £6,600 was 'reasonable and desirable', but without more information it was 'almost like a leap in the dark *for them*'. Some members of the Council continued to express serious reservations. One member believed that 'we have no power to allow the prior to borrow £6,600 from the Missionary Fund [since] it is a matter that must go before the whole familia'.[11] Moreover, there was some concern voiced that the President 'has already spent about £3,000 on Ealing'. Ford replied to these queries and remarked that he understood that the Council was far from unanimous about his plan 'to build a really fine Church at Ealing'.[12] Financial considerations, therefore, forced him to trim his sails. Consequently, Ford suggested to the Council that if '£6,600 seemed to be too great a venture', he would ask for only £4,400 and build only two bays.

Two weeks later the Downside Council met again to consider the future of Ealing's church; and after its deliberations, Dom Osmund relayed the results to Prior Ford. 'They approve generally to having a good church at Ealing,' Ford was told, 'but they are far from enthusiastic about the present plan because it conveys so little information.'[13] In respect to the loan, one member strongly objected that the Council might not have the power to authorize an amount this size. He argued that Prior Ford 'must go to the whole familia, and backed this up by a letter from the President whom he had consulted'. This monk, Dom Alphonsus Morrall, a member of the Regimen, pointed out that 'all were equally of [the] opinion that as we had neither plans, nor specifications, nor estimates, we should be acting in a most unbusiness and imprudent manner to commit ourselves to anything'.[14] In spite of these rather serious reservations, the Downside Council 'gave its consent to the loan as far as they legally can, i.e., on the understanding that you can justify your petition with the President General'.[15]

The Council unanimously believed that 'the consent of the familia should be asked even if not of obligation'. This report stated that it was 'evident the council did not want you to come into direct conflict with the President General'. 'We feel quite sure that neither the President nor familia will voice any objection to the loan,' the letter concluded, 'and the council thinks it is only prudent and reasonable to get the consent of the Conventus.'

Ford wrote to his Benedictine friends and asked for suggestions. Abbot

Snow offered some practical objections to Prior Ford's plans. The church appeared to be too long, the east end would be 'inconvenient and unnecessarily expensive,' and the body was too wide.[16] Ford also asked him if he would agree to a plan to petition the Abbot President and the members of the Regimen for an advance of £4,400 from the Missionary Fund to begin work on the new church. Snow replied and told him to push on with the plans for the building and confided 'that we must commence . . . as soon as we can'.[17] The Abbot also abandoned his characteristic caution and told Ford that 'the circumstances are such at Ealing that we cannot delay the building until we have sufficient [funds] in hand'. Dom Aidan Gasquet also supported Prior Ford's plans to build a proper church. 'I do not think there can be two opinions as to the need of doing something at Ealing,' Gasquet wrote the Prior, 'everyone who has seen the place I think must be satisfied that ultimately it will be one of the best missions near London'.[18] Gasquet raised some questions about the estimated cost and design, but essentially agreed with Ford's vision for the Ealing church.

By the end of June, therefore, Ford was ready to move. He would again approach the Downside Council for its approval and then take his case to the Abbot President of the Congregation. He scheduled a meeting of the Council for the end of the month. He sent the members a draft of his petition to President O'Gorman and stated that he would seek the approval of the Downside Council for the scheme. Moreover, he wanted his Council to approve a motion that the money for the church 'should be a loan from the missionary funds'.[19]

Within a week, the Council met at Downside to discuss Ford's letter and petition to Abbot President O'Gorman. It briefly recounted the history of the Ealing foundation and emphasized that 'the congregation is already increasing and it is the universal opinion that as soon as a Church is built, the mission will develop rapidly and be capable of supporting a large church'.[20] He reminded the Fathers that services were currently conducted in Castle Hill House, which had already proved too small and inadequate. Commenting on the plans for the church, Ford noted that the plans for the nave had been prepared, and the estimated cost for this ranged between £14,000 and £15,000. But at the present time, he pointed out, it was only feasible to build two bays, which would cost approximately £4,460. The petition asked the Abbot President to approve the funding. Again, Dom Alphonsus Morrall raised some objections to Prior Ford's plans; he continued to question the authority of the Downside Council or the Abbot President and the Regimen to allocate the requested funds. All members of the Downside community should be consulted. He also questioned the wisdom and prudence of borrowing the money from the Missionary Fund. But Dom Alphonsus' objections failed to impress the Council, which approved Prior Ford's petition to the President and his suggestion that the money should come from the

Missionary Fund. On 4 July, the Regimen approved Prior Ford's request to begin construction of a church at Ealing and to spend the amount agreed upon by the Downside Council. The Mission Fund would provide the financial support.

Within a month after his arrival in Ealing, Dom Gilbert Dolan founded an altar society in the parish 'with the object of arranging for the reverent care and adornment of the sanctuary, with special regard to the requirements of the new church in course of construction'.[21] Dom Gilbert's avocation as an architect also immediately surfaced. He told Prior Ford that four bays, not two, should be the immediate goal.[22] And he also offered suggestions dealing with the design of the chancel, the nave and the clerestory. For the time being, he believed, the roof should be temporary because 'when the church comes to be completed the permanent and elaborate (and expensive) wooden roof could be added to the clerestory [sic].' He also sent to the Downside Council a series of sketches for the proposed interior and exterior of the church. Dom Gilbert emphasized that 'from the quiet and stately increase in the congregation I think we should be fully warranted in providing . . . additional accommodation'.[23] Moreover, Dolan pleaded with Prior Ford that a larger church was 'so necessary . . . for the more dignified rendering of the Church's services'.

In February 1899, the local press announced that a new Roman Catholic church had 'been commenced on land at the northern end of Charlbury Avenue'.[24] The article reported the dimensions of the future place of worship and claimed that 'the building will rank among the finest ecclesiastical structures of the neighbourhood'. With a touch of nostalgia, the *Middlesex County Times* favourably compared the width of the proposed monastic church to one of 'the best known of the old Benedictine churches of London – the abbey church of Westminster'.

During the summer the pages of *The Tablet* informed English Roman Catholics about the construction of the new church in Ealing. A letter from the Benedictine community there explained that 'every effort has been made to provide for the needs of the Catholic population by the erection of part of a new church'.[25] But more money was needed to turn this dream into a reality. Dom Gilbert begged the 'Catholic public to assist us in our work' and argued that 'as our local resources are but small we must make our appeal to friends at a distance on behalf of our new church'.

The perseverance and courage of Prior Ford triumphed; by the end of 1899 a section of the church had been completed. For months, Prior Ford and Dom Gilbert agonized over the opening ceremony. Should 'our opening be a modest one, as beseems our condition, or an ambitious affair to suit our expectations,' Dom Gilbert queried Ford.[36] The two monks addressed a series of possible problems dealing with the celebration: would Cardinal Vaughan attend; who would preach; and who would take charge of the music? Dom Gilbert hoped that the Downside choir would come and present an 'object lesson in

Eccles[iastical] music'. 'I don't want a "monastic" opening to be marked by any display of smart musical talent,' he told Prior Ford, and 'that for public purposes and for real effect a choir of monks . . . singing a plain Chant Mass would be more acceptable to the bulk of people, and more appropriate, than the best amateur performance, which might be quite in keeping elsewhere.'

The spirit of the ceremony corresponded to Dom Gilbert's wishes. The *Downside Review* proudly announced that on 25 November 1899 'the choir twenty-five strong, started on the longest journey the Downside choir, as a body, has ever made'.[27] The article explained that 'a portion of the new Church at Ealing was to be opened, and as it was the first Church that the English Benedictines have opened in the Diocese of Westminster, it was thought appropriate to make the opening service a throughly Benedictine function'. Prior Ford sung the mass; Cardinal Vaughan preached.

Dom Gilbert Dolan's vision for a grand church continued to expand; additional construction must proceed. Consequently, he approached his superior at Downside during the summer of 1901 and mapped out his plan for the future of Ealing's church. After noting the progress at the mission, he asked Ford the following question: 'isn't it worthwhile considering whether it is time to enlarge the church by building say the ground floor of the nave, 3 or 4 bays?'[28] 'We could do with the accommodation and use a good deal of the present as Sanctuary,' he argued. 'At present anything like a function is impossible.' Dom Gilbert also enclosed numerous sketches of the proposed floor plans and his conception of the exterior. His dreams, however, failed to materialize, and the church was not enlarged.

But bricks and mortar were not the only concern of Dom Gilbert Dolan. Parish life continued to flourish. At first, he expressed some apprehension about the future of a vibrant congregation at Ealing: 'Slowly Catholics are coming to settle, but there is a lack of houses at reasonably low rent, say £40 [per annum]'.[29] Several months later, he told Downside that 'some more people have been around lately looking for houses'.[30] The trend continued, and the membership grew. 'The congregation is increasing,' Dolan boasted to Ford in September 1899.[31] 'We have about 100 at Mass (11.00) on Sundays now; and sometimes well over that.' He reported that several families planned to move into the parish, and told Ford that 'it will probably be necessary soon to have a third Mass on Sunday'. After the opening of the new church, the influx of Roman Catholics into the Benedictine parish increased. Ford was told that 'since the opening about five new house holders have come or taken houses – and on Sundays the church is quite full'.[32] This growth in attendance, according to Dolan, also represented 'a valuable addition to the income [and] Sunday offertories are also nicely on the rise'.

After the Christmas holidays, Dom Gilbert again optimistically reported that 'almost every week brings new people to the parish and we seem suddenly to have sprung into existence as a large congregation'.[33] In the Missionary Statistics for 1899 which he went back to Downside, Gilbert Dolan estimated the number of parishioners at 360, the population of Ealing being 37,000.[34] Dom Gilbert noted that the figure represented the number of Roman Catholics 'in the district near St Benedict's, and extending halfway to Hanwell . . . No episcopal boundary line has yet been designated, and this has led to some slight unpleasantness with the Hanwell neighbours'. This annual census also recorded the following: nine baptisms, one marriage, one death, two converts, and twenty apostates. He ended his first-year report with this insight: 'The bulk of the congregation belong to the upper middle class, and their children with 3 exceptions attend Catholic Colleges or convents.'

Throughout the next year, the number of Roman Catholics continued to swell. Dom Gilbert informed Downside that 'the quarter seems likely to bring us four new households . . . [and] one or two other people are thinking of coming here'.[35] Easter Sunday that year represented a high-water mark. 'We had [a] very large congregation at Easter,' Dom Gilbert proudly wrote,' 243 at first Mass and over 200 communions; and 120 at [the] 2nd Mass.'[36] He did not fail to point out that 'this compares well with our 83 and 72 respectively on Easter Sunday last year – as did the offertory £10.10s. this year against £6.10s. later year'. The 1900 parish census, taken after the boundary with Hanwell had been drawn, recorded 332 Roman Catholics, thirteen apostates, six converts, and sixteen marriages. Two members of the parish had died during the year.

Well-publicized activities testified to the vitality of the Benedictine parish. The Auxiliary Bishop of Westminster, Dr Brindle, who according to the press had led a distinguished military career as a chaplain 'under Lord Kitchener to Khartoum . . . and [who] received the Distinguished Service Order,' administered Confirmation in February 1901.[37] The *Ealing Gazette* printed extracts from the Bishop's instructions to the candidates, which also congratulated the Ealing Benedictines for their quick and visible successes in the suburb.[38] The monks were also anxious to prove their patriotism through their devotion to the memory of the late Queen Victoria. From the pulpit, Dom Gilbert read the Cardinal's letter which stated that 'it would not be fitting to give even the appearance of wishing to claim the Queen as a member of the Catholic Church, [and] these offices (Mass for the Dead, Solemn Absolution, the Funeral Office) could not be performed for her'.[39] However, Ealing Catholics could 'take their part in the civic mourning of the nation, and where there were church bells, they would be tolled and the flags hoisted at half-mast'. In his sermon, moreover, Dom Gilbert eulogized 'the life of the Queen, emphasizing the noble example she had set both in her family and public life'.

The surprising growth of the parish perplexed Dom Gilbert. In August 1901, for example, he told Abbot Ford, who was elected Downside's first Abbot on

26 September 1900, 'that various new families are coming here . . . so we are going ahead'.[40] Holidays did not even diminish church attendance. 'In spite of half the Congregation being at [the] seashore,' he noted, 'the Sunday attendance is full, i.e., about 300 at the two Masses.' It was also the character of the parish that also puzzled him. 'There are signs of that moving restlessness which is a growing feature in suburban life,' he wrote in 1902. 'I have an appalling list of some 15 or 16 Catholic families or detachments which have come and gone in my three years here; and some others are soon to be on the way.'[41] 'It is true we have some new people,' he mused, 'but the new arrivals scarcely fill the places of the old, and of course it takes time to get to know them.' Dom Gilbert maintained that because of the railway, many new families journeyed to Hanwell, and because of the new church at Acton, he feared 'a still further diminution on Sundays'. 'One hopes for the best, but somehow there is not quite the feeling of buoyancy and progress that we had a year ago.'

Dom Gilbert's cloud of despair about numbers, however, quickly disappeared. He recognized the need to increase the number of masses on Sunday to accommodate another group of English Roman Catholics. 'I sh[ould] have a third Mass at St Ben's (9.30),' he told Ford, 'as that would catch several who otherwise go to Acton or Hanwell for 9.00 Mass . . . and would prove highly convenient for a number of golfers who come out to the numerous links on this side of London.'[42] And the trend continued. In the following year he told Ford that 'every week almost brings us news of newcomers, several with families . . . so the church accommodation question becomes more acute'.[43] The parish records also dispelled Dom Gilbert's gloomy prediction. In 1902, for example, he estimated the number of parishioners at four hundred and he recorded ten baptisms. In the following year, the membership increased to five hundred and sixteen were baptized. Marriages totalled six for 1903 as compared with three for the previous year. The figures for 1904 confirmed this growth within the Benedictine parish: number of parishioners 550, baptisms 19 and marriages 4.[44]

Dom Gilbert's horizon also began to expand beyond the frontiers of Blakesley Avenue and Charlbury Grove. In 1899, he alerted Ford that he had seen news reports that 'a working men's town [is] soon to be begun at South Ealing'.[45] According to this press story, five hundred houses were to be constructed immediately, and an additional five hundred were scheduled to follow. In the eyes of Dom Gilbert, this expansion presented a golden opportunity. Since this proposed settlement bordered on St Benedict's, he informed Downside that 'our parish will before long need a chapel of ease, or school chapel . . . and unless we supply the priest and energy someone else will be called in'. Dolan urged Ford to act. 'It won't do to leave the ground open to O'Halloran,' he argued, 'nor to see our parish cut into its most populous part if we can supply its spiritual needs.' Downside did not respond. But again in 1901, Dom Gilbert urged Abbot Ford to take action in regard to South

Ealing. 'It should be our endeavour . . . to secure a site – or in some way to open a chapel of ease in South Ealing,' Dom Gilbert recommended, 'well within our own district so as not to trespass on the Brentford mission, not too far from St Ben's to prevent its being easily served as a *Chapel of Ease* from here.'[46] Three reasons forced Dolan to make this suggestion: a Benedictine presence in the area would 'be a capital check to the schism' of O'Halloran; 'a chapel there abouts would be more really useful to the poorer part of the congregation than St Benedict's'; and finally, he regarded this district as the special or exclusive territory or property of the Ealing Benedictines. 'I don't want outsiders to come in and do it in a way detrimental to our interests,' he forcefully informed Abbot Ford, and 'if we do it ourselves we can guard against the drawbacks possible or probable of the Card[inal] or someone else stepping in.' Downside, however, would not be swayed by Dom Gilbert's arguments, and the dreams for a chapel in South Ealing vanished.

But Dom Gilbert Dolan's urge to expand and branch out was not limited to the immediate local area. Soon after his arrival in Ealing, he approached Ford and asked him for permission to become the confessor to the convent at Kensington Square. This job, he believed, would not jeopardize the work in Ealing, and 'the £10 or £12 a year – or whatever it is will be very welcome'.[47] Another reason also explained his enthusiasm: 'it might be useful in itself as making oneself agreeable to an influential community strongly disposed to favour Benedictines'. Ford gave his approval. Dom Gilbert also sought other areas for Benedictine expansion, and his master plan became grandiose. Discussions about staffing Lulworth, on the Dorset coast,[48] and later Dom Gilbert's wish to branch out within London into Kentish Town and Ditcham, near Petersfield in Hampshire, failed to materialize.[49] Moreover, he also told Ford that a local secular priest said 'he hoped to see all these West London missions in Benedictine hands – Ealing, Hanwell, West Drayton as well as Brentford and Acton, which the respective pastors would gladly relinquish'.[50] 'A big programme,' Dom Gilbert informed the authorities at Downside, 'but not likely – just yet – to be seriously suggested.'

Dom Gilbert Dolan's primary duty, however, concerned the foundation at Ealing; stability, financial solvency, and a community life based on Benedictine principles took precedence over monastic empire-building. Castle Hill House had served as the original residence for the monks, but the old rambling Georgian mansion was badly in need of repairs. In response to a question on the Mission Statement on when the house was last painted, Dom Gilbert caustically responded, 'Goodness knows'.[51] He also wrote to Ford and told him that the dwelling urgently needed a cooking stove. 'Just at present we manage with great difficulty to get the cooking done with an oil stove, [but] that can't go on with a full house as we have now.'[52] Dom Gilbert pointed out the lack of furniture and the need to refurbish the servants' rooms. In fact, the entire place needed vast and expensive work. Internal and external repairs were estimated to cost approximately £448 to make Castle Hill House habitable.[53] In spite of these inconveniences, Dom Gilbert was able to report back to Downside that the small community was 'comfortable and happy'.[53] 'The domestic questions and the financial are those most urgent now,' he reported. He noted that the housekeeper, Mrs Simpson, and Lizzie, the cook, 'do all the housework between them'. A young lad would be desirable to help the women, but Dom Gilbert admitted that he hesitated to hire any additional help 'because just now *real money* is wanting'. He also maintained that the community could survive on '£3 a week with economy'. But the question of improvements to the house and financial problems were not Gilbert Dolan's only concerns.

In September 1899 Dom Benedict Weld-Blundell had received a new assignment from the officials at Downside, and he left Ealing. With no replacement in sight and Dom Bernard Bulbeck still in failing health, Dom Gilbert approached Downside for assistance. 'The Sunday work comes rather heavy,' he informed Ford, 'and as Fr Bernard is scarcely able to get through Mass sometimes . . . I am puzzled to know how much longer he will be useful in that way.'[54] According to Dolan, Dom Bernard had spoken of 'his growing weakness, and extreme sense of fatigue . . . [and] he thinks his heart is failing, or that he eats too much'. To replace Dom Benedict, Ford proposed to send Dom Vincent Corney to Ealing. When reports reached Gilbert Dolan that Dom Vincent would be assigned to the Ealing mission, Dom Gilbert asked about his knowledge of French. A local convent, with several French-speaking sisters, had requested a chaplain, and the additional income would help. 'The person should be of an early rising and punctual habit and possessed of enough French for his work there,' Dom Gilbert told his superior.[55] When Dom Vincent Corney arrived shortly afterwards, Dom Bernard was seriously ill again. 'The old man has caught a chill and his heart is weak,' Dolan reported, 'and he has to stay in bed till the doctor comes tomorrow.'[56] He was forced to cancel some masses and also to seek the services of another priest. A fortnight later, Dom Gilbert reported back to Downside that the doctor had suggested that Dom Bernard must 'have a warm wintering place'.[57] Alton had been suggested as a possible venue for Dom Bernard's recovery, and Dom Gilbert seized the opportunity to suggest that the Benedictines purchase a seaside grange for the community and send the ailing Dom Bernard there. 'Every place is secured by seculars or Regulars except Seaford,' Dolan pleaded in vain, 'don't let *that* be lost!'[58] During the next week, Dom Bernard Bulbeck finally left Ealing and retired to Acton, but illness still continued to plague the Ealing Benedictines.

After the Christmas holidays of 1899, the monks moved from Castle Hill House to a nearby residence, 2 Marchwood Crescent. But Dom Vincent's health cast a pall on this monumental move. Dom Gilbert again reported that one of his monks was sick: 'He has been three of four days in bed and seemed to be getting over the bronchitis and influenza, and his temperature was going down, but last night . . . he took a turn for the worse'.[59] Dolan also told Ford that Dom Vincent became hysterical and began to dry for no apparent reason. He also reminded his superior that the Holy Child of Jesus Sisters, with whom the Benedictines had been negotiating, would soon inhabit Castle Hill House. Consequently, 'there should then (or very soon) be means for a third active, or fairly active priest.' Dom Gilbert ended his tales of woe on an optimistic and positive note: 'we can jog along for a while'. Economically, moreover, there was some hint for a bright future; the year ended with a surplus of £34.6s.[60]

Moreover, additional revenues could be generated if tenants could be found to occupy Castle Hill House. Both Ford and Dolan began a search to find a community of nuns to rent the house when it became apparent that the monks would vacate the dwelling. The Nazareth nuns of South Ealing had been asked to consider opening a school at Castle Hill House, but they refused to commit themselves immediately. In February 1899 Dom Gilbert visited the convent, although he sensed that they were in no position to make a decision. But, he told Ford,' the M[other] General's veto on a branch Day School unless 12 pupils be assured has been withdrawn'.[61] Moreover, the Servite Sisters had also expressed a desire to transfer one of their communities to Ealing and they had already started to price property in the area, but they would not consider Castle Hill House. In early summer, Dom Gilbert informed his superior that he had 'been nun-hunting: Notre Dame is no go – but the Mayfield people [The Society of the Holy Child Jesus] are more promising'.[52] This group had already expressed a keen interest in Ealing. 'They seem inclined to settle here,' Dom Gilbert recorded, 'and if they will take the house, good.'[63] Moreover, this group enjoyed solid social contacts, and consequently, he wrote, 'just the people for Ealing'.

Within a week, the Mother-General at Mayfield asked two of her sisters from their London convent, Cavendish Square, to travel to Ealing and explore the possibilities for a new foundation there. Dolan's reaction was hopeful: 'she and her companion seemed very well satisfied with the looks of Ealing as a promising field for their work and development, and expressed themselves as hopeful of the M. General's consent'.[64] Moreover, this community of sisters also fitted into the Benedictine educational prospects. According to Dom Gilbert, the sisters were 'not . . . adverse to having a department for small boys'. After these two visitors remarked on its suitability for a school, Dolan quoted a yearly rent of £150 for Castle Hill House. His enthusiasm grew as the sisters told him that they want 'a *suburban* opening, easily reached from Cavendish Square' and he assured them that Ealing was 'just the place'. Dom Gilbert ended this optimistic letter to Downside with a prediction that the Mayfield Sisters would be comfortably settled in Castle Hill House by the autumn.

In July, it appeared that these sisters would indeed become the monks' new neighbours. The nearby Nazareth Sisters, whom he had contacted earlier, informed Dom Gilbert that they did not think they could commit themselves to a foundation in Ealing. More importantly, they told Dom Gilbert that they would welcome the Mayfield Sisters into the area, and they had already told this to Cardinal Vaughan.[65] And the Mayfield Sisters were interested. 'I presume we shall soon see the *H. Child* sisters make definite arrangements,' he told Downside, because 'the Rev. Mother and another called yesterday [and] they were very keen on the place.' A letter from the Mother-General confirmed this sense of buoyancy. After her visit to Ealing, the superior told the Ealing Benedictines that she 'was most favourably impressed with the neighbourhood'.[66] She also told Dom Gilbert that the General Council planned to meet during the middle of July to discuss the possibility of an Ealing foundation.

Consequently Dolan had reasons to be enthusiastic about the success of this project, and the additional income from the rent was not the sole reason. A Benedictine school now seemed within reach. He told Ford that the Mayfield Sisters 'are as good a lot for educational purposes as can be had – and I don't know if we can do better than have them'.[67] Dom Gilbert next approached Cardinal Vaughan and sought his permission for the nuns to move into Ealing, and he reported back to Downside that the Cardinal 'would place no difficulty in the way provided that [the] Nazareth at South Ealing were not injured, as they were first in the field'.[68] Dolan also informed the South Ealing convent of the Nazareth community about the possibility of the Mayfield Sisters living in Ealing, and demanded a definite answer about their future plans in Ealing. 'I am writing a sort of ultimatum to the Rev. Mother there,' he informed his superior at Downside, 'asking for a definite reply as to their opening a school at Castle Hill House or close by.' Dom Gilbert's abruptness surfaced. He told Ford that the Nazareth Sisters were ill-equipped to staff a school: 'Their French exclusiveness and preponderating Frenchness make them unsuitable for our purposes'. Unlike the Mayfield Sisters, the Nazareth community never seemed enthusiastic about teaching young boys, 'one of our greatest needs here.' At the end of the month, the sisters of South Ealing finally told Dom Gilbert that they had no desire to expand into his mission. He believed, consequently, that the Society of the Holy Child Jesus of Mayfield would answer his prayers.

In August, Dolan visited the Mother-General at Mayfield, who 'was bent on opening at Ealing'.[69] But she informed him that no move could be made until the end of the year. Details had to be worked out, and moreover, the Mother-General wanted 'definite and formal permission in writing from the Card[inal].' Dom Gilbert informed her that the Nazareth Sisters had no intention of moving into Castle Hill House, but 'the brief assent . . . [was] not enough' for her. And disquieting news reached him from Mayfield. In October, the superior there told him that 'His Em[inence] the Card[inal] has explained himself and has made conditions that make it impossible' for a move to Ealing. She did not reveal the nature of the Cardinal's stipulations. Consequently, Dom Gilbert visited Vaughan in the middle of October. During this meeting, according to Dolan, the Cardinal 'practically withdrew his opposition to the Holy Child nuns coming.'[70] Dom Gilbert told Ford that Cardinal Vaughan planned to visit South Ealing soon, and 'if they find they [Nazareth Sisters] really mean not to come, [will] at once authorize the H. Child nuns settling here'. After the visit, Archbishop's House failed to notify the Benedictines of any decision. The Mayfield Sisters continued to voice their desire to come into Ealing, so Dom Gilbert decided to bring pressure on the Cardinal. A week before Christmas, therefore, he informed Vaughan that several families in his mission continued to ask about the possibility of a local Catholic school. Dolan's motive was simple: 'I hope his conscience will not allow him to delay'.

The new year brought exciting news; Cardinal Vaughan had finally arrived at a decision concerning the future of Ealing. Dom Gilbert joyfully informed Ford: 'last night the Card[inal] sent his permission for the H. Child Nuns to establish themselves here'.[71] 'I have sent the permit onto the M. General at Mayfield and hope there will be no delay in that quarter.' Shortly afterwards, the Mother-General notified Dom Gilbert that she intended to submit the Ealing proposal to her Council before the end of the month. Although other communities of women, for example the Ursulines of Jesus, had recently enquired about Castle Hill House, both Dolan and Ford favoured the Mayfield Sisters, and both Benedictines were confident that they would be their neighbours in Ealing. But in February, it appeared that this bubble might burst. The Superior-General, Mother Angelica Croft, regretfully notified Abbot Ford that her Council had decided '*not* to make any foundation at Ealing'.[72] She apologized and explained that 'sickness and death have been very busy amongst us of late'. Ford's response expressed stoicism and disappointment. The Abbot replied that he 'was very sorry to hear . . . about Ealing,' and he informed her that he would advertise in the Catholic press to find a tenant.[73]

Because of the Cardinal's blessing and the earlier positive signs from Mayfield, this sudden change of events jolted the Benedictines. Eventually they discovered the real reason behind the nuns' change of heart from one of the Holy Child Sisters who was stationed at Blackpool. She revealed what happened to a friend, and this eventually found its way into the hands of the Benedictines. This person explained that 'on consideration we found the Cardinal's permission for our work there so very uncertain in spite of Father Dolan's protestations that we could undertake anything.'[74] Consequently, a sister was sent to London to talk with the Cardinal. An official of Archbishop's House met the sister, and in the course of their meeting, he contradicted an earlier statement made to Dom Gilbert: he explained that if the sisters took 'day scholars for a higher school [this] would injure them a little'; and moreover boarders 'would be a serious injury to them'. The secretary related that the Cardinal 'was emphatic in saying we [the sisters] were only to take the poor of the parish.' Because of this interview, the Mayfield Sisters decided not to expand into Ealing.

For some unknown reason, however, the Mother-General surprised Abbot Ford in April and informed him that her Council had voted to reconsider the Ealing proposal. She simply pointed out that 'some changes have taken place in our affairs which alters some of our circumstances'.[75] Prior to this meeting, a delegation of the Mayfield Sisters had visited Dom Gilbert and inspected Castle Hill House. Business considerations now took centre stage; monks and nuns discussed the need for repairs to the house and the question of rent. The sisters 'did not think the rent £200 too high'.[76] Dom Gilbert also promised his support in trying to secure pupils and boarders, but he maintained that 'our hands are tied till they had made up their minds to come'. He told the nuns that if they decided to come to Ealing, 'we could at once let it be known in various ways and quarters, and thus induce new residents and families in the neighbourhood'. Dolan then informed Abbot Ford of the meeting with the nuns and argued that the possibility of these people at Ealing took precedence over the cold facts of economics: 'the ultimate benefit to the mission by having a first-rate establishment such as they would soon possess would far outweigh any immediate gain by letting the place, e.g., to lay tenants or to any second-rate sort of nuns'.

The past anxieties and disappointments of the Benedictines quickly turned to joy. The Council of the Mayfield Sisters gave their consent. 'They have decided to come to Ealing,' Dom Gilbert wrote to Downside.[77] 'The M. General will send some pioneers to take up their abode early in August and . . . to be ready to open school in September.' But the necessary negotiations with the nuns contained some difficulties. At the end of May, their solicitor, Charles Russell, contacted Ford and began talks. His first letter also suggested that the arrival of the Mayfield Sisters in August might be a bit too premature. Before any arrangement could be finalized, he suggested to Abbot Ford 'that there should be a clear understanding in an ordinary business-like form as to the terms upon which the house and grounds . . . should be held by them and they have asked us to advise them and to communicate with you'.[78] Ford soon realized that the Mayfield Sisters had hired a tough and seasoned solicitor, who immediately insisted on two important points: the nuns 'should have the right at any time during the currency of their Lease to purchase from you the freehold of the premises at a price to be agreed upon now'; and the lease should contain stipulations which would allow the nuns 'to put an end to it at certain intervals . . . and we suggest that they should have this right at the end of every five years'. But this was not all. Russell objected to the proposed rent of £200, and he also insisted that extensive repairs be carried out at Castle Hill House.

Dom Gilbert wanted a compromise. He wrote to Abbot Ford and suggested that Downside could sell Castle Hill House and some of the grounds to the nuns. Dolan knew that Ford opposed this, but he listed the advantages of such a move: the money realized could help pay off the debt; and a sale would mean getting 'rid of a large and expensive house and grounds, save ourselves the rates and taxes, and the imminent cost of making up the road in Charlbury Grove'.[79] Moreover, Dom Gilbert argued that the money needed to repair the house represented a staggering amount, and he advised Ford to 'let the nuns ... do their own repairs, in their own way and at their own time.' Finally, Dolan addressed the sensitive issue of rent. Here again, his desires to secure the nuns became clear. He suggested that the Benedictines accept Russell's offer of £150 instead of the original £200, and in the future the monks 'might insist on £50 or £60, or after three years £100 a year for the chaplain's salary.' Gilbert Dolan sensed disaster and informed Abbot Ford that he had contacted the Sisters of the Assumption, Kensington, and asked if they were interest in coming to Ealing. Ford, however, viewed the situation in a different light. Somewhat shocked by the new demands of the Mayfield Sisters, he replied to their solicitor and informed him to make it perfectly clear to the nuns that the property was not for sale. Moreover, both parties had already agreed to a yearly rent of £200.[80]

Russell continued to press the Abbot to reconsider the sale of the property, and noted that 'we were only consulted by our clients last week and we were of course unable to previously advise them'.[81] After an exchange of letters, Russell informed Abbot Ford that the Mother Superior had agreed not to press for the sale of the estate, but did insist on a twenty-one year lease 'determinable ... at her option at the end of three, seven or fourteen years at a rent of £150 per annum'. [82] Moreover, the monks must refurbish Castle Hill House prior to any legal agreement. Ford replied and stated that he would consider an option, but only at the end of the fifth, tenth, and fourteenth year, but he would not agree to undertake repairs to the house until estimates were drawn up, and he would not budge from the rent of £200.[83] Throughout the summer, the nuns continued to demand that the Benedictines repair Castle Hill House. Appealing to Dolan's sympathetic nature, the Mother Superior justified the hire of Mr Russell and told the Benedictine that 'we poor nuns need a lawyer to look after our affairs'.[84] The nuns also complained that the monks 'have not met them in a proper spirit over the details of the arrangement and that you [Abbot Ford] are trying to strike a bargain greatly to their disadvantage'.[85] But Ford remained steadfast and told the solicitor that if he was 'compelled to put the house into "habitable repair" there is no reason why ... [he] should agree beforehand to reduce the rent'. Moreover, he threatened 'to accept the best rent ... in an open market'.

Dom Gilbert Dolan languished in the middle of these negotiations; from his point of view it was imperative that the Mayfield Sisters come to Ealing. He believed that the nuns were 'shilly-shallying over Castle Hill Ho[use]', and he told Abbot Ford that 'the important thing was their making a foundation in Ealing'.[86] And if they were interested in buying property in the Ealing area, he had already informed them that some real estate in nearby Amherst Road had recently come on the market. Dom Gilbert also forced Abbot Ford to modify some of his intransigent views. Since it was apparent that the nuns wanted to come to Ealing, he argued that 'repairs of some kind must be done before anybody can live in the place, and the sooner they are done the better'. Again, Dolan addressed the question of rent. 'If they only pay £150', he pleaded, 'they must be prepared to pay something for chaplain's services – at least after a bit.' Moreover, 'the educational and other interests of the parish will suffer if they don't come'.

After another encouraging visit by a delegation of the nuns in August, Dom Gilbert again wrote to Abbot Ford and emphasized their importance for the success of the Benedictine foundation. 'Unless we get a good teaching community – *a first-class* concern,' he told Ford, 'we cannot hope to entice good families to Ealing.'[87] A proper Roman Catholic education in Ealing was important: people 'won't come unless there is a good school for girls – and not any sort of a school – not a French school – but an up-to-date place, such as Mayfield, St Leonards and Cavendish Sq – the very best convent school in England'. Moreover, the future of a Benedictine school for boys would be jeopardized by the absence of the nuns. He argued that the existence 'of a first-class girls school will naturally facilitate our hope for a Grammar School – for the boys must next be catered for educationally'. 'The presence of a growing Catholic good-class congregation will be our best plea for our boys' school.' Not only would the nuns be useful for the future educational plans of the monks, but they would upgrade the parish: '. . . the congregation will practically continue to be one of "odds and ends" unless we have schools'. He closed his remarks by pleading with Abbot Ford to reconsider and to lower the rent; the lost funds could be made up by a chaplain's fee.

The Society of the Holy Child Jesus of Mayfield also wanted a speedy end to these negotiations, and the Mother-General informed Dom Gilbert that she wanted the matter settled. But letters still continued to be exchanged between Russell, the Benedictines, and the nuns. At every opportunity, the Mayfield Sisters sought concessions in respect to repairs and rents, and the monks did try to accommodate their wishes. In September, for example, Dom Gilbert informed Downside that 'the house is being put into repairs . . . [and] eight or ten men are busy about it, and already it looks a good deal smarter outside.'[88] During November, both groups of religious finally struck a bargain. Abbot Ford agreed to continue the repairs to Castle Hill House, and the nuns, to a compromise in rent. A wearied Ford informed Abbot Snow that the Mayfield

Sisters planned to arrive early in December. Concerning the final arrangements, he told Snow that 'we are putting the house into repairs and they will pay rent of £175 instead of £150'.[89] Dom Gilbert and the Ealing parish, and not the Downside community or the English Benedictine Congregation, had to raise the money for the necessary improvements at Castle Hill House.

The nuns moved into their new residence in January 1901, and on 14 January the five nuns began a school for girls. The original class numbered one boarder and five day-students. In spite of their success in securing occupants for Castle Hill House and the fact that a school had been opened, the Benedictines harboured some resentment against their new neighbours and their solicitor. 'While I do not wish to burden their coming to Ealing,' Ford told Mr Russell, 'I am not at liberty to put an unreasonable burden on the mission.'[90] Abbot Ford directed his feeling against the solicitor's unwavering demands. 'I wish they [the nuns] would find someone who is not a solicitor to arrange terms and confine the solicitor's business to drawing up deeds,' he complained to Dom Gilbert.[91] 'I have had nuns here for three or four years and have arranged all our agreements without solicitor or deed, binding ourselves by a written agreement and we had no trouble.'

It was not until 1902, however, that the formal and legal contract between the monks and nuns was concluded. Regardless of the wranglings and escalating demands of the nuns, the Ealing Benedictines had leased the property, and therefore enjoyed the added revenue from the rent. Moreover, a school for young Roman Catholic girls had been established in Ealing. And Dom Gilbert's initial reports to Downside were positive. In spite of the sudden change in the leadership of the convent, the school had grown in numbers and reputation. Dolan told Abbot Ford that the nuns 'seemed very hopeful of succeeding, as a good many ladies have been to see the school and seem to like it'.[92] When a new assistant superior arrived at the convent, Dom Gilbert interpreted the assignment optimistically. He told Abbot Ford that he was 'given to understand that this means a good deal, that the nuns think Ealing is growing into a first-class school à la Saint Leonard's'.[93] The new assistant's 'aristocratic connection . . . must be brought to bear on Ealing, to make the place a success'. With the promise of more students, Dom Gilbert Dolan reported that the nuns were 'sanguine of the place's future'. The arrival of the Mayfield Sisters and the opening of a school, however, did not solve all the problems which faced Dom Gilbert.

Domestic problems continued to plague Dom Gilbert and the Ealing community. In March 1900 he reported that Dom Vincent Corney had suffered 'another attack of nerves and an hysterical outbreak'.[94] Dom Gilbert told Abbot Ford that the doctor recommended a month of peace, quiet and rest. Part of the problem, Dolan believed, could be traced to Dom Vincent's assignment of hearing confessions in French at the convent of the Nazareth

Sisters. Well before this outbreak, Dom Vincent had already informed Ford of the 'difficulties of serving the Convent from such a distance'.[95] He reminded his superior at Downside that, when asked if he 'was prepared to hear confessions in French ... [the] answer was decidedly in the negative'. He admitted that 'it was a serious matter' and he was 'quite unequal to it'. Two days before this recent illness, Dom Vincent again complained to Abbot Ford that he had not received any response or answer to his last letter, namely, that he be relieved of his duties at the local convent. 'It is a matter which will not admit of any further delay,' he pleaded, 'for it is wrong of me to continue that work, and naturally enough the nuns themselves are anxious about it.'[96] Dom Wilfrid Corney, Dom Vincent's brother, wrote to Ford the same day and argued that Dom Vincent was unfit for convent work: 'when he does get unwell he gets nervous and anxious and that makes him worse; moreover he seems v[ery] much worried over the French confessions'.[97] He also related that the sisters became very disturbed over the 'irregularity of their chaplain'. With regard to Dom Vincent Corney's health, his brother suggested the following plan to his superior at Downside: 'My opinion ... is that it w[ould] be much better to give up the chaplaincy'.

Dom Gilbert also acknowledged that Dom Vincent was guilty of 'unpunctuality and irregularity' in his charge to the nuns.[95] Dolan had visited the sisters and asked the Mother Superior 'whether they could not rearrange the time of Mass'. She responded in the negative. Dom Gilbert also suggested that 'some modification of their hours might be made' because 'in England priests are few and ... they are at a greater distance from a resident priest than any convent in the country.' He also questioned the financial advantages of the stipend, £100, since little remained after the cab fare was deducted. But the nuns would not compromise. Consequently, Dom Gilbert told the Downside authorities that a healthier and stronger man should be appointed to attend to the spiritual needs of these women. 'In view of the near future when I suppose we are to have six here,' Dom Gilbert reasoned, 'you will not care to give up a place which will occupy one man's time.' After noting the good qualities and popularity of Dom Vincent, Dolan ended his report on a note of frustration: 'Don't any of the younger generation talk French?' Ford responded that he would try to find a replacement, and even hinted that Dom Vincent should be removed from Ealing because of his frail health.

But Dom Gilbert strongly resisted this suggestion. 'From the point of view of the *Mission* interests,' he argued that it 'would be undesirable to make a change just now'.[100] Dom Vincent was a well-liked priest who took a keen interest in parish affairs. Moreover, 'changing the staff so soon may prejudice St. Gregory's in the Cardinal's eyes, [which] is not worth consideration'. But Abbot Ford reminded Dom Gilbert of the 'serious obligations to attend regularly and properly to the Convent, and it will not do for us to neglect it'.[98] Other considerations also confused the situation. 'It would not be right, and we should begin by losing our good name,' he continued, and 'we have not even the excuse of too much work.' In a letter to Abbot Snow, Ford admitted again that Dom Vincent seemed 'unable to do the work at [the] Ealing convent,' and he confessed that he might have to replace Dom Vincent with another monk.[102]

A compromise eventually emerged; duties at the local convent were to be shared. Dom Gilbert agreed to go to the convent on Thursdays and hear the confessions of those who could speak English, and Dom Vincent would continue to say mass, hear French confessions, and preach. By the end of the year, however, even Dom Gilbert began to question Dom Vincent's usefulness to the Ealing mission. 'Fr. Vincent Corney has been poorly once or twice lately,' he notified Downside.[103] 'Fr. Vincent always gets an attack if I press him to do any extra thing, like preaching here, etc; so it doesn't pay to ask him.' 'If Southall is added to our hinterland,' he concluded, 'he might (*perhaps*) be energetic there.'

The economic horizon appeared brighter. Although the surplus for 1900 amounted to only £17.17s.5d,[104] as compared with over £36 for 1899, the year could not be considered a financial failure. The yearly report noted, for example, that the offertory collection and bench rates had increased since the previous year. Moreover, over £425 had been expended on the new house at Marchwood Crescent and on the church. And Dom Gilbert emphasized this point in a letter to Downside: 'As all the heavy bills for furnishing [the] house and Church, benches, organ, etc., next year should show a better balance'.[105] Dolan, therefore, remained cautiously positive and remarked that 'at present our heads are just above water'.

But the health of Dom Vincent continued to cloud this optimistic state of affairs. In early February 1901, Dom Gilbert informed Downside that 'Fr Vincent is still in the hands of Dr Caley, and will not be fit for any work on Sunday or for some time yet'.[106] He urgently requested that Abbot Ford send someone to help out with the increasing parochial duties. Consequently, several short-term priests were assigned to St Benedict's during this period, but Dom Gilbert was not satisfied; he believed that their hearts were not in the work of the Ealing mission. His words and actions probably perplexed his superiors at Downside. On the one hand, he had campaigned for a chapel of ease, expansion into Southall, and the foundation of a network of Benedictine houses from Ealing to serve the London area. But on the other hand, he had a difficult time staffing the home base at Ealing and was not satisfied with the help which Downside sent him. Manpower became an urgent priority. In a subtle but demanding manner, he reminded Abbot Ford of the original agreement between the Benedictines and Cardinal Vaughan: 'It helps me to realize how quickly the time is passing and that by 1902 we are to have six fathers here'.[104] After he jogged the memory of his superior, Dom Gilbert simply asked if Abbot Ford 'could . . . not spare one now'. He pointed out that 'the Sunday work comes hard when practically both F Vincent and I have double duty; and the strain of the two Masses and two sermons is becoming serious'. Dolan maintained that, with the opening of the electric tramway into Ealing, the congregation would increase, and 'it would be desirable to have another to relieve one of us of the Sunday work'.

Again, Dom Gilbert did not succeed in obtaining the addition of a healthy permanent priest for Ealing. Ford had not lost interest, but the negotiations with the nuns over the lease of Castle Hill House, his vision and dream for a Benedictine school in the suburb, and the unresolved problems concerning a Benedictine presence at Westminster Catherdral monopolized his time and energy. Dom Gilbert, therefore, tried to shame Ford into sending an additional priest to work at Ealing, and he emphasized the bright future of the mission. In October, for example, he proudly announced that 'two postulants' had already sought admission to the Ealing community.[108] The first wanted to live at Ealing as an oblate while continuing to work in the city. The second expressed a wish to become a Benedictine lay brother. 'This begins to look hopeful,' he boasted, and informed Abbot Ford that 'we shall want one or two quiet steady men of the good lay brother type for our priory here.' Moreover, new members 'would help financially and besides be of use in the church and choir'.

As a result of this unexpected interest in the Ealing Benedictines, Dom Gilbert's mind again began to wander and he dreamed of a grandiose monastery rising on the summit of Blakesley Avenue. He told Abbot Ford that it was 'desirable to get as much accommodation . . . into our projected building as possible'. 'To restrict ourselves to the rooms absolutely necessary for the six resident fathers (required by our compact with the Card[inal]) would not do.' If a shortage of money would not permit the immediate construction of a proper monastery, Dolan suggested another solution to the possible overflow of candidates: 'three or four smaller cells for "adventitious" people' like the two recent applicants 'would be a wise provision – even if something of the fine appearance and large scale . . . of apartments has to be sacrificed'.

But the internal problems which Dom Gilbert faced at 2 Marchwood Crescent dampened this enthusiasm. Dom Richard O'Hare, who had been sent to help out at the undermanned Ealing mission, broke his leg, and Dolan estimated that it would 'be five or six weeks at least before he can use his leg'.[109] 'It is a great disappointment,' he lamented, 'as he promised to be so active after his long period of retirement.' In addition to his 'irregularity and unpunctuality' in respect of his convent duties, Dom Vincent's sickness also flared up again and continued to plague the smooth operation of Ealing. This time the complaints were not limited to hostile letters from the convent. The Mother Superior, according to Dom Gilbert, had brought the issue of the chaplain's lacklustre performance to the attention of Archbishop's House, and consequently 'had more than once exposed us to remarks of an uncomplimentary nature – no less trying because they happen to be true – from the Bishop Auxiliary and the Vicar-General to whom the complaints are forever being made'. For the future of the mission, its smooth operation, and the reputation of the Benedictines within ecclesiastical circles, by the autumn of 1901 Dom Gilbert Dolan painfully reached a decision which he had put off for a year. Dom Vincent Corney must go. Dom Gilbert emphasized his confrère's chequered medical history and recommended the following to Abbot Ford: 'I see no other course open to me than to beg you to consider the desirability of placing some one here who can do his work sufficiently'. The services of another monk became imperative, and Dom Gilbert's request again revealed a sense of frustration coloured with sarcasm: 'How the Masses here . . . and S. Ealing are to be said I don't know . . . if you [have] anybody to spare at least for a time it would be a kindness to send him'. He concluded with a sense of urgency. 'At present I am practically single-handed.'

Regardless of his failure to secure stable and healthy assistants, the financial diagnosis of 1901 revealed that the Ealing mission represented a solid and worthwhile investment. The revenues for the year climbed to £691.2s.10d, and the expenses were estimated at £600.18s.4d[110] An increase in the number of churchgoers meant a corresponding jump in the Sunday collections and the Bench Rent. Abbot Ford's assessment and report to the Downside Chapter on the condition of the London mission also confirmed Ealing's solvency. He drew the attention of the Chapter to the yearly statement and pointed out that in addition to the rent accrued from the Orchard Dene estate, Castle Hill House, now occupied by the nuns, produced an annual rent of £175.[111] Moreover 'a legacy of £20 has been used to pay off the Church debt'. The 'Mission in Ealing is now self supporting', he declared, and he also acknowledged the kind gifts of money from the Ealing parishioners which were used to purchase the following: the altar, rich fittings, vestments, a large American organ valued at £70, and the benching. In the future, a school would also greatly contribute to the income. As for immediate plans, Abbot Ford told the Council that funds must be found quickly to finance the building of a priory. In addition to economic progress, another obstacle in the growth and direction of the Ealing mission was finally dismantled: a peaceful solution to the debates over what group should chant the Divine Office at Westminster Cathedral was finally reached.

As late as February 1901, the public still believed that the English Benedictines would staff Westminster Cathedral and conduct its liturgy. The monks also thought they would be called upon to participate in some manner in the cathedral's worship. The *Ealing Gazette* reported that 'Cardinal Vaughan has allowed it to become known that he intends the grand metropolitan cathedral now approaching completion to mark the restoration of full and open honours to the singings of the offices from Matins to

Compline and it is to the ancient Benedictine order . . . that he has committed the restoring task. . .'[112] The paper drew attention to the local Ealing monks and stated that 'if one may judge by comparison, then what has already been done in Ealing the suburb is a notable augury of what will be achieved in mighty London'. This forecast proved to be wrong.

Other considerations forced Cardinal Vaughan to alter his original dream concerning the Benedictine monks and Westminster Cathedral. The cardinal's biographer wrote that 'it may be doubted whether, under any circumstance, Cardinal Vaughan would have consented so far to bind the hands of his successors in the See as to hand over to a Religious Order the possession of a chapel in the Cathedral in perpetuity'.[113] Moreover, a recrudescence of the old rivalry between the secular and religious clergy might erupt if both had duties connected with the new Westminster. In order to escape this impasse, Vaughan even proposed that an outside party, the French Benedictines of Solesmes, be invited to London. Not surprisingly, this scheme was resisted by all parties: the English Benedictines, the secular priests, and interested members of the laity who voiced their horror in the pages of the Roman Catholic press. Consequently, Vaughan put aside his chief reason for inviting the Benedictines into Ealing and opted for the obvious solution: the secular clergy would render the liturgy at his cathedral. In *The Tablet*, he announced that 'the best arrangements sometimes leave room for regrets, and we confess that we should have been glad if it had been possible to see the cowls of the Benedictines back in Westminster, and to know that there were opportunities for joining their religious chant'.[114] With much sorrow, Vaughan concluded: 'and yet, apart from the old associations which cluster around the site of Westminster, is it not after all better, and more in accordance with the fitness of things, that the Secular clergy themselves render the Liturgy in the new Cathedral?'

Although the Westminster Cathedral question had finally been settled, Dom Gilbert Dolan still had to wrestle with the internal problems of the Ealing mission. Sent to Ealing in the autumn of 1901, Dom Richard O'Hare soon edged out Dom Vincent as the chief source of concern and worry for Dom Gilbert. The conflict arose out of the strained relations between the cleric and the parish housekeeper, and it appeared that Dolan was even prepared to sacrifice his fellow monk for the success and stability of the foundation. After suggesting to Abbot Ford that he make arrangements for Dom Richard's return to Downside, Dom Gilbert informed Ford that 'the housekeeper protests that she will not stay on unless he leaves; his ways and temper are so trying'.[112] Apparently something in the priest's past history forced Dolan to take this drastic action. He told Abbot Ford that even 'Fr President today spoke strongly about the risk we run in keeping him here after recent events'. This mysterious letter brought a visit from Ford to the Ealing mission, but no action resulted.

Probably despairing of any resolute action being taken by Downside, Dom Gilbert wrote again and informed the Abbot that 'since your visit on Saturday last things have not been pleasant and the housekeeper positively refuses to stay in the house ... unless Fr Richard goes'.[116] This 'very inconvenient revolution', as Dom Gilbert referred to the situation, arose from stories and rumours which the Ealing housekeeper had heard from a former employee of Dom Richard. 'In any case it is extremely painful to have such things said about a priest,' Dolan candidly admitted, and '... I confidently ask you to apply the obvious remedy.' He begged Ford for a replacement, and concluded that 'the continual presence of a source of constant domestic friction and of daily anxiety is enough to paralyse anybody'. Still, no decision or action came from Downside.

Dom Gilbert would not budge from his insistence that Dom Richard must depart. Within two days after his last letter, Dom Gilbert again wrote to Downside and informed Abbot Ford that within the past days the situation had 'assumed rather a painful shape from the silly gossip which is almost inevitable under such circumstances'.[117] 'The matter I find is pretty well known and I should not wonder if there is a nice kettle of fish before long.' He also announced that he had fired the troublesome housekeeper and concluded that 'the crisis is ... painful and I hope a scandal may be averted'. Dom Richard was finally re-assigned. But the replacement who joined the already incapacitated Dom Vincent, Dom Odo Langdale, also proved to be disruptive to the harmony of the Ealing foundation. Again, it was the South Ealing convent which provided the spark.

Despite the list of complaints from the Mother Superior, the acknowledgement of his many faults by Dom Gilbert, and the recognition that the job of chaplain at the Convent of the Nazareth required a responsible priest, Dom Vincent Corney was allowed to remain and function, although on a reduced schedule. But even this arrangement proved disquieting to the nuns in South Ealing. Realizing that Dom Gilbert had not responded to her wishes or requests in the past, the Mother Superior wrote directly to Downside in the spring of 1902. She apologized to Abbot Ford and remarked that she found it unpleasant to complain, but the chaplaincy demanded immediate attention. 'It is no news for you that Father Vincent Corney is of very delicate health and that the duties of Chaplain to our convent are very hard upon him,' she explained, and '... the order and regularity of the convent suffer too much from his being unable to come punctually in the morning.'[118] 'I am sure, dear Reverend Father, that you would not tolerate it in any of your colleges,' she scolded the Abbot. The sermons, religious instructions, and catechism lesson had also suffered and deteriorated. Not knowing that Dom Richard would soon leave Ealing, she suggested that he replace Dom Vincent. The Mother Superior ended her letter with an appeal to Abbot Ford's conscience and a mild threat: 'If you cannot arrange matters for us, we shall be very sorry to part with the Benedictine Fathers, but I know that His Eminence would not refuse to give us a chaplain.' Ford responded quickly and told the nuns that they would 'be attended to more regularly'.[119] He apologized to the Mother Superior and told her that other business and a spate of sickness at his monastery had prevented him from making changes or appointments earlier.

Within a month, Abbot Ford assigned Dom Odo Langdale to take Dom Richard's place at Ealing. He would also become the chaplain to the South Ealing sisters, but unfortunately this change in personnel did not heal the breach between the monks and the nuns. Shortly after this appointment, the Mother Superior again approached Ford and informed him that 'we are painfully disappointed'.[120] She complained that Dom Odo was worse than Dom Vincent in regard to punctuality, and that 'he always seems discontented and makes himself as unpleasant as he can'. 'His ways seem so strange to the nuns and the children!' His sermons and instructions also fell well below the standards expected by the nuns. According to the Mother Superior, Dom Odo had also complained of the high cost he had to pay to hire a cab to take him to South Ealing. Consequently, she again placed the entire blame for the troubles on the Benedictine Fathers: 'it is not our fault if St. Benedict's is so far from the convent.' 'You knew from the beginning what work your Fathers were undertaking,' she reminded Ford, and moreover, 'we are made to feel that we are a burden.'

The Mother Superior then issued an ultimatum to Downside. If supply at the convent did present a burden, 'we can have our own chaplain, and get a regular religious service, and . . . live on friendly and kindly terms with our priest, as we always try to do for our part'. Ford answered this now familiar letter and told the Mother Superior that he was 'sorry to hear . . . about the chaplain'.[121] He promised to speak to Dom Odo and admitted that he could not understand why 'the chaplain should not be punctual'. But Abbot Ford also seriously challenged some of the Mother Superior's statements. In the first place, the cost of transportation to the convent did represent a significant amount of money and, he maintained, 'when the charge for the cab is deducted from the stipend, there is not much for the maintenance of the priest'. Secondly, Dom Gilbert gently but firmly reminded her that the chaplain had other duties at St Benedict's. He could not be considered the exclusive and sole property of the sisters.

Neither the corrections of his religious superiors nor the complaints of the Mother Superior reformed the lax habits of Dom Odo. In May, the Mother Superior again took her case to Abbot Ford and told him that she was 'extremely sorry to be obliged to tell you that we cannot possibly continue with Father [Odo] Langdale'.[122] She then reeled off the usual list of complaints: tardiness, 'uncivil manners', unprepared sermons, and inadequate religious instructions. 'I earnestly beg of you,' she implored, 'to remove Fr Langdale as soon as possible, and if you cannot give us a suitable chaplain because you consider the trouble too great and the stipend insufficient, I will see the Vicar-General to make other arrangements.' Ford's response to this letter was terse: 'I am sorry to hear that there is still cause of complaint about the service of your convent'.[123] He told the Mother Superior that he would come to Ealing and meet with her during the following week to make the necessary arrangements for a change. Dom Gilbert also confirmed the lack of professionalism and the slipshod manner in which Dom Odo performed his job at the convent. Dolan confessed to Abbot Ford that the 'situation at South Ealing is more strained than ever'.[124] He informed the Abbot that he had already seen Cardinal Vaughan and had 'obtained faculties to hear such English confessions there need be'. Moreover, he continued, 'several refused flatly to go to D. Odo again'. But Abbot Ford somehow managed to diminish the anxieties of the Mother Superior since Dom Odo was still functioning as the convent's chaplain in July 1902. The atmosphere at South Ealing, however, remained cool. Dom Gilbert reported to Downside that 'things seem no pleasanter down there though here there has been less friction'.[125]

Yet domestic problems continued to haunt Dom Gilbert Dolan and the Ealing Benedictines. Dom Vincent's health remained unpredictable, and he had even insulted some of the parishioners.[126] Moreover, he begun to show his discomfort at being assigned to Ealing and to find faults and shortcomings with the mission. For example, he had developed negative views about the Ealing parish and their support of the monks. Commenting on the possibility of collecting funds to finance the church and to help liquidate the debt, he told Abbot Ford that 'our Ealing people are too "grand" for collecting small funds'.[127] And Dom Odo still represented a source of possible trouble. Dom Gilbert, therefore, continued to assume more and more of the parish and monastic responsibilities until Dom Sebastian Cave arrived in Ealing on 29 September 1902 to replace Dom Odo. Dolan also had another problem: Father Richard O'Halloran refused to remain quiet.

Censure by the ecclesiastical authorities had hurt O'Halloran's credibility and status as a Roman Catholic cleric, but it did not silence him nor dampen his enthusiasm. In order to compete with the construction and the expansion undertaken by the Benedictines, Father O'Halloran also had to build. According to one of Dom Gilbert's reports to Downside, 'He has – so he says – received some money and talks of beginning to build [a] church and presbytery almost immediately'.[128] 'I wish the cardinal w[ould] issue another *plain* notification against the man,' Dolan told Abbot Ford. 'The "Schism" talks of building,' Dom Gilbert informed Downside several days later, and he related a story that Father O'Halloran had 'received a legacy from a Catholic lady who had lived in Windsor Rd, toward the erection of a Catholic Church at Ealing'.[129] If this rumour were true, Dolan suggested that Cardinal Vaughan should question the will: 'Mr O'H has certainly no claim to the money, and I should think a case would be made should the Cardinal care to contest the will.'

Other stories and reports, such as, O'Halloran saying mass at a convent in

Bath and financial assistance being given to his cause by the Prior of Ampleforth, demonstrated that O'Halloran would not be satisfied with irenic retirement. Moreover, sarcasm and ridicule became his weapons in a renewed attack against his enemies, the monastic intruders. In early March 1899, Father O'Halloran wrote to the President of the English Benedictine Congregation, Dom Anselm O'Gorman, and related an alleged incident when he overheard Dom Gilbert Dolan, who was *'in the next room – and in utter ignorance that we heard every word he . . . [was] saying'.*[130] According to O'Halloran, his Benedictine rival tried to steal some members of his congregation, and he sneered at this attempt: 'But it is amusing how your monks work with such prudence . . . when your monks will have captured their hare it will be *time enough to skin him'*. Father O'Halloran prodded President O'Gorman to send this letter to Dom Gilbert 'and let him see that we hear and know all he says when he comes *under the same roof with myself'*. He ended on a caustic note: 'I hope you keep the record of my letters . . . they will amuse if not interest posterity showing how you found the Ealing monastery'.

O'Gorman complied with Father O'Halloran's wishes and sent Dom Gilbert a copy of the accusatory letter. In reply, Dolan admitted that he did visit the home of one of O'Halloran's parishioners, but he maintained that it was impossible for Father O'Halloran to hear any conversation 'unless one shouted'.[131] Dom Gilbert told the President that Father O'Halloran 'has misrepresented the business – or rather invented most of it . . . Obviously embarrassed, Dom Gilbert went to great lengths to deny O'Halloran's story; he emphasized that he stayed only a few minutes, and even drew a sketch of the house for the Abbot President to demonstrate the impossibility of O'Halloran overhearing his conversation. 'The whole thing is a piece of bluff,' he declared, and he maintained that O'Halloran was merely angry at the thought of losing members of his flock to the Benedictines and other nearby parishes such as Acton. Unsuccessful in his attempt to blacken the Ealing Benedictines and failing to receive any satisfaction from President O'Gorman, Father O'Halloran again took his battle against the monks to the columns of the press.

The target of this attack was again Cardinal Vaughan, and the issue dealt with the status and future of the breakaway parish in Mattock Lane. The *Middlesex County Times* printed an open letter from Father O'Halloran to Cardinal Vaughan. It represented another direct challenge to the authority of the Cardinal, who had suspended him from his priestly duties. O'Halloran smugly informed Vaughan that 'the District Council have sanctioned the plans for our proposed new buildings, and the contractors will begin work soon'.[133] Moreover, Father O'Halloran continued, a certain Father Murphy from the Newport Diocese had 'resigned his rectorship in that diocese . . . [and] has kindly come to assist me in my efforts to teach the true Roman Catholic religion . . . to the inhabitants of this flourishing suburb'.

And he could not resist an assault on the Benedictine monks. O'Halloran contended that the education of the children in their faith remained his primary goal, but 'a gang of schismatical monks . . . have dared to enter this peaceful secular mission, have broken up all the schools, and have coerced the children to attend Protestant schools'. His accusations became more preposterous and ludicrous: 'at this present moment there are three of these monks living in Castlebar Road, whose sole mission in life is to scandalize the Protestants, make the unity of the Roman Church a mockery, and cause all the Catholic children to be educated under Protestant teachers'. Vaughan has condoned this. O'Halloran accused the Cardinal of fooling the Pope into believing 'that the return of England to Roman unity is but a matter of years, whilst all the time you [Cardinal Vaughan] and the monks are doing your utmost to bring our Holy Father into contempt'. Father O'Halloran ended this emotional diatribe by announcing his intention to expand and to commission his parishioners to collect funds for this purpose.

Some Roman Catholics reacted to Father O'Halloran's provocative rhetoric. *The Universe* printed a letter warning Catholics against 'certain unauthorized people who of late have been engaged in collecting funds for a so-called Roman Catholic school in Ealing'.[134] Dom Gilbert informed Downside of O'Halloran's latest invectives and posed an interesting question: 'Is it worthwhile, or desirable, to test his letters as libel?'[135] The cost involved in a legal settlement might outweigh the advantages of a successful outcome, Dolan mused, 'but if the man were brought to book he might and would be more careful in the future'. Moreover, 'to pay damages he might not unlikely have to sell up his chapel and so legal action would tend to break the schism'. Vaughan also replied to Father O'Halloran's latest outburst, but did not suggest any possible action or discipline against this cleric. He simply clarified Father O'Halloran's status as a Roman Catholic priest. Writing to the *Middlesex County Times*, the Cardinal informed their readers that 'this priest has been for a considerable time suspended from the use of all ecclesiastical faculties'.[136] 'The Rev. O'Halloran is free according to the civil law, like anyone else in England to establish a sect of his own and to invite adherents,' Vaughan went on but, he stressed, O'Halloran's mission was not recognized by the Catholic Church; neither he nor his establishment was in communion with the Roman Church.

Predictably, the battle heated up after Cardinal Vaughan's statement appeared in the press. One of the Mattock Lane parishioners rushed to support Father O'Halloran's wish to launch a campaign to build a school.[134] But it was O'Halloran who orchestrated the campaign against Cardinal Vaughan and his Benedictine allies. His lengthy reply to Vaughan's letter rehashed the previous arguments against the Cardinal's actions, that is, he again explained his 'justification in refusing to hand this secular mission over to the Benedictine monks'.[138] He proclaimed his loyalty and re-affirmed 'faith to the doctrinal authority and discipline of the Bishop of Rome,' but denied 'that the Archbishop of Westminster is the head of the church'. Vaughan, according to this logic, had no power or authority to dismiss any cleric and the Cardinal had acted towards him in a dishonest manner. O'Halloran also challenged Cardinal Vaughan to publish those documents which the Cardinal claimed he had received from Rome which gave the Ealing mission to the monks. Commenting on the document which he had signed promising to leave Westminster, Father O'Halloran still maintained that Vaughan had 'procured it by the most dishonourable methods that ever disgraced any transaction between a bishop and a priest'.

O'Halloran dismissed the ecclesiastical suspension from Archbishop's House as a 'farce', and labelled Cardinal Vaughan's 'conduct in this dispute as unworthy of an archiepiscopal administrator of the Holy See to the English Nation'. He also accused the Cardinal of scandalizing both Roman Catholics and Protestants.

> You, a Cardinal, create division, schism, scandal, and all manner of uncharitable-ness; those who loved are now coerced by you to hate each other; simple women are frightened through fear of hell to side with the monks, and give money to their support; and all this because a faithful secular priest refuses to violate his vows by surrendering a secular parish to the rapacity of monks.

Father O'Halloran concluded his defence by claiming to be the rightful and canonical rector of Ealing, and laughed at the accusation of heresy and schism. The Benedictines were interlopers who must leave Ealing: 'the monks are intruders, who should go back to their monasteries to which they are vowed'.

Sides were drawn, and the friends of Father O'Halloran and the monks supported and championed their respective party in the local press. One critic of O'Halloran accused him of 'dirt-throwing . . . scurrility' and 'venomous attacks'.[139] 'If the monks never came to Ealing alienation would have ensued as a matter of course.' This correspondent also suggested that Father O'Halloran's past was tainted with stories of impropriety while he ministered in the North and in the Bow, London. Another argued that O'Halloran 'allowed himself to be cut off from union with the Catholic Church . . . and started a new sect'. The writer warned loyal Roman Catholics not to support or contribute to his school-building scheme. A week later, another compared O'Halloran to Martin Luther and proclaimed that he belonged to 'the Ritualistic sect of Protestants, who . . . are known . . . as absolutely defiant of all authority'.[140] This individual, a 'Resident Catholic', urged the faithful of Ealing to reject Father O'Halloran and to 'show their view of the question by attending either the Benedictine or . . . Hanwell Church'. One letter, however,

captured the spirit and consensus of those who supported the claims of the
Benedictine monks: the entire affair at Ealing was sad. 'I am sure there is a
very genuine feeling of regret that so estimable a priest ... as Father
O'Halloran should have become separated from the Church ... and it can
only be hoped that he will eventually recognize his error, and thus avoid in
time the terrible consequence of leading others astray.'[138]

But others pictured the monks as the culprits. One individual rose in defence
of Father O'Halloran, who fought 'for the rights of the secular priests, [and]
who has not lost the courage of manliness to own to it'.[142] Moreover, this
supporter of the Mattock Lane priest argued that 'the Cardinal's suspension
is a deception and farce'. Another Ealing resident pointed out that the monks
'attempted to seize a mission before that mission was vacant, thereby doing a
great injustice' to Father O'Halloran.[143] The Benedictines had become 'tools
to oust a hard-working and deserving priest from the fruits of his labour'.
'Why are they not in the monastery now,' this writer asked, 'and not
wanderers on the face of the earth causing strife and bitterness where they
settle and undoing the work that God's priest has so successfully commenced?'
Another letter characterized Vaughan as 'wicked', the monks as 'schismatic',
and encouraged O'Halloran 'to stick to his little church till his body is carried
out'. An Anglican onlooker also urged Father O'Halloran 'to agitate the whole
world till justice is granted to him.'[144]

This duel raged throughout the autumn of 1899, and it appeared that
Roman Catholics continued to desert Father O'Halloran for the orthodoxy of
the Benedictine monks. In September, for example, Dom Gilbert Dolan
informed officials at Downside about 'that latest thing in scurrility from
Mattock Lane,' and boasted that more and more families were abandoning
O'Halloran's parish.[145] Father O'Halloran, however, fought to preserve his
respectability. In another letter to the *Middlesex County Times*, he pleaded
that 'in publicly attacking the Cardinal and the monks' he was 'not only
discharging a sacred duty, but following the example set me and taught me by
the saints'.[146] Yet his rhetoric remained savagely brutal. He described the
Cardinal as 'a slanderer ... worse than Lucifer, more unjust than Pilate, and
the greatest living foe to Papal supremacy and the reunion of England with
the Apostolic See'. O'Halloran argued that 'the schismatical' monks enjoyed
'no more right to plunder and feed [themselves] than King Humbert* has to
rob the Apostolic See'. In spite of these harsh invectives, Father O'Halloran
portrayed himself as an injured priest, and he continued boldly to proclaim
his loyalty to Rome. And attempts to besmirch the character and motives of
the Benedictine monks remained powerful weapons in his arsenal. When
O'Halloran found out that a Dominican from Haverstock Hill had been
scheduled to preach at St Benedict's , he wrote to the superior and informed

*The reference is to King Umberto I of Italy (1878–1900).

him that 'these monks are schismatical intruders.'[144] 'Rome is fully aware of this quarrel,' he stated, 'and pending a decision from Rome no monk or priest should join *and take sides* publicly in this dispute.' Consequently, O'Halloran told the Dominican Prior to 'consider this letter as a protest against any Dominican Father preaching in the Benedictine conventicle here'. Nonetheless, a member of the order did occupy the pulpit of St Benedict's in November.

Early in 1900, Father O'Halloran again tried his luck with the President of the English Benedictine Congregation, Dom Anselm O'Gorman. In March, he attempted to blacken the character of Dom Gilbert Dolan. 'I wish to bring the following serious matter before your official notice,' Father O'Halloran began, and he painted the following picture:[148] 'An Irish maid servant in the employment of . . . [the] sister of the Anglican Vicar of St John's Ealing . . . has complained of the greatest annoyance and threats of a spiritual and physical nature caused by your monk the Rev. G. Dolan.' O'Halloran then listed a litany of accusations against the Benedictine monk: he 'calls continually at her place of employment interrupting her at her work'; Dom Gilbert had claimed that the Pope hated O'Halloran and had excommunicated him; and he cautioned the maid to stay away from the Mattock Lane church. Dom Gilbert allegedly told this woman to contact other 'Irish girls who heard mass [there] and to tell them of the eternal damnation in hell' awaiting them. Moreover, Christ 'was not in the Holy Communion . . . ' at Father O'Halloran's parish. O'Halloran also alleged that 'if she did not do what he [Dolan] told her, he threatened to get Fr Powell to flog her'. O'Halloran then tried to describe his motives or concerns as those of a Christian, and he urged the Abbot President to investigate the matter. 'Such conduct is most grave,' he continued, and 'it disgraces the Gospel of Christ and violates the laws of England by terrorizing over a free born subject of the Queen . . .' Finally, 'it is such conduct that makes the name of monk hateful in England and gives a bad name to all genuine and God-fearing Roman Catholics.' O'Halloran concluded by threatening to tell the girl to bring the incident to the attention of the magistrate. He also sent a copy of this letter to Dom Gilbert.

On the same day, Father O'Halloran sent a similar letter to Cardinal Vaughan. He complained that 'such gross conduct is causing enormous scandal to souls and making the name of Roman Catholics a disgrace'.[149] O'Halloran repeated the charges that one of the monks had annoyed a servant girl at her place of employment, and he mentioned that this might result in action being taken by the local magistrate. Vaughan, like Abbot President O'Gorman, informed Dom Gilbert of O'Halloran's actions. The Ealing Benedictine immediately informed the President of the English Benedictine Congregation that he did not know the Irish girl and, consequently, never called on her. Again, Dom Gilbert wanted to use the law to muzzle O'Halloran: 'legal threats would sober the poor man'.[150] Dom Gilbert also claimed that he had 'a constitutional horror of house maids and . . . [was] not in the habit of talking hell fire and damnation to anyone'. 'So is it to be be an action for libel?' he queried the Abbot President.

But the Benedictines did not use the power of the law, and O'Halloran's campaign to damage Gilbert Dolan's priestly character continued during the summer. O'Halloran believed that Archbishop's House would lend a sympathetic ear. In June, he informed the Benedictine priest that he was forwarding a complaint against the monks to Cardinal Vaughan and that he had also 'formally applied *for trial* in Rome'.[151] This letter, which Dom Gilbert also received, revealed the hatred and anxiety of a man fighting to maintain the integrity of his parish against a group of monks who, he believed, had violated his rights. Although he had previously branded Cardinal Vaughan as a fraud and a cheat, O'Halloran humbly appealed to his sense of justice. He informed the Cardinal that the Benedictines had been spreading a lie that the Protestant monk, Ignatius of Llanthony, had preached at Mattock Lane. 'I need not tell your Eminence that this is a base falsehood invented by the monks,' O'Halloran thundered, 'and circulated to serve their own selfish and unholy designs.'[152] He then lectured Vaughan on his responsibilities: 'when your Eminence gives the charge of souls and entrusts the cause of religion in England to such barefaced liars – can you wonder that great scandal prevails in England – that thousands of your people are ceasing to believe in the priesthood or the need of the sacraments and that Protestants are getting to lose that respect for the church which they had in the time of Manning?'

Both Cardinal Vaughan and Dom Gilbert Dolan chose not to respond to this shocking attack. Consequently, Father O'Halloran became more outrageous and vindictive. In July, he again wrote to Archbishop's House and accused the Ealing monks, who 'by nature and habit [are] both liars and cowards', of sending him threatening anonymous letters and of publishing letters in the local press attacking him under the cover of a pseudonym.[153] In an attempt to flatter the Cardinal, O'Halloran praised the character and dedication of the Mill Hill priests as 'simple, grand, noble, generous, fearless, and God loving . . .' But, on the other hand, 'these monks and regulars with their vows made and *never kept* sicken me'. 'They love the *bottle*,' he continued. 'It is branded clearly on their faces.' Father O'Halloran's accusation of monastic alcohol abuse continued. He related a story about a Benedictine who 'would never preach before he swallowed a full bottle of port . . . [because] it was necessary to "gargle" his throat.' Again, he appealed to the loyalty and sobriety of the secular clergy and begged the Cardinal to remove the monks from Ealing. Any friend or supporter of the Ealing Benedictines must be warned of their wickedness. When O'Halloran learned that a community of nuns planned to settle in Ealing and to open 'a convent . . . in conjunction with the Benedictine monks', he warned the Mother Superior that the monks were 'schismatical' and did not hold a canonical title even to be in Ealing.[154]

During the summer of 1901, Father O'Halloran consolidated his attacks, and published a small pamphlet, *Cardinal Vaughan and Father O'Halloran: The Rights of the Secular Priests Vindicated*. This publication chronicled the history of the stormy relationship between the priest and Cardinal, contained all the important documents, complete with O'Halloran's interpretations, and portrayed the Benedictines as crafty and vindictive people. Hatred of the Cardinal coloured every page. O'Halloran described Vaughan as a crafty, deceitful fiend, a prelate who sought illegally to deprive a poor cleric of his rightful benefice. The attacks against the monks reached new heights of arrogance. 'Rome should confine all monks forthwith to their cells,' O'Halloran sneered, and 'the monks had no right to invade or to come to Ealing.'[155] The greed of these capricious monks caused the troubles in Ealing; 'the strain of this Ealing scandal and schism shall ever stick to the Order of St Benedict'.[156] The concluding sentence announced that this publication did not represent the last hurrah of a disgruntled secular priest:

> I could not surrender Ealing; I cannot do so now. It is mine by canonical right; I am the lawful pastor; the flock here is mine; and the Benedictine Monks are schismatical intruders – 'wolves in sheeps clothing'.[157]

The year 1901 also saw Father O'Halloran journey to his homeland in an attempt to get funds and support for his mission. Ireland, he believed, would surely help one of its native clergy to spread the Gospel throughout Protestant England. Consequently, he made two trips to Ireland, but his presence was not greeted with enthusiasm. In 1901, he visited Dublin twice, and had also commissioned some friends to solicit funds for his work in Ealing. The *Irish Catholic*, however, warned the faithful against O'Halloran and his begging campaign. The paper pointed out that the Archbishop of Dublin disapproved of Father O'Halloran's tactics in Ireland, and it repeated the archiepiscopal warning that Roman Catholics should 'subscribe to no work – no religious work – without his written authority'.[158] During the following year, O'Halloran again travelled throughout Ireland, but the faithful were again told to avoid him unless he possessed the official approval from the local bishop or from Cardinal Vaughan. The *Freedman's Journal* printed a story about a man collecting money on behalf of Father O'Halloran and told its readers not to donate any money unless the individual could produce a letter of introduction from the proper ecclesiastical authorities.[159] Still, the lacklustre reception did not discourage him; nothing would drive him from Ealing.

CHAPTER IV

Consolidation and Growth: The Early Twentieth Century

T he Benedictines had always wanted to establish a school at their Ealing foundation. But because of his past problems with the Jesuits in Salford and because of his support of St Charles in Bayswater, Cardinal Vaughan's invitation to Downside explicitly forbade the foundation of a school other than a public elementary school. Nonetheless, the monks continued to dream. During the summer of 1899, Dom Gilbert Dolan wrote to Ford and told him that the Dominicans planned to open a boy's grammar school at Haverstock Hill, and remarked that 'our time will come some day, I hope'.[1] Dom Gilbert also worked to soften the Cardinal's resistance with reports of pressure from the Ealing parishioners. 'I have told the Cardinal of some new families (with children) who have come to live here,' he told Downside, 'and of others writing about educational possibilities.'[2] In 1901, Dolan continued to try to convert Vaughan, but the Benedictine admitted it had been difficult to arrange a meeting with the prelate.[3]

Therefore, the growing population of the mission, the want of proper educational facilities, and reports of the unstable condition of St Charles soon turned wishful thinking into reality. In the spring of 1902, Abbot Ford seriously begun to search for space. He told Dom Gilbert that the scheme must proceed quietly and prudently. 'All we can do is to provide private tuition for such boys as are in the neighbourhood,' he explained to Dom Gilbert.[4] 'Even this would be difficult, but it is the only way to begin,' Ford continued, and 'the first step is to get an exact list of the boys with their ages and to ascertain what they require teaching.' Ford sensed that a school might cause a financial loss, and he told Dom Gilbert that as soon as an estimation of the enrolment could be calculated and the amount to be charged for tuition estimated, 'we should know how much exactly we stand to lose'. Ford also had definite ideas on the nature of Benedictine education to be offered at Ealing on lines similar to Downside:

> ... the education and training of Catholic youth was an apostolate and monastic work. If boys of the upper class were to be prevented from attending the great public schools of England, with all the dangers to their Faith and practice which such an attendance might entail, then Downside must be made ... efficient in every branch of education.[5]

83

But the main responsibilities for the new educational apostolate fell not on the shoulders of Dom Gilbert, whose energies were absorbed by parochial work and the elimination of the debt. Abbot Ford surprisingly entrusted the planning of the new school to Dom Vincent Corney, whose health was still questionable and whose work with the nuns in South Ealing had been lacklustre. Dom Vincent, however, embraced this challenging commission with pronounced enthusiasm. At first, he did not know the extent of Ford's plans except that the Abbot wanted a school at Ealing and that he would play an instrumental part in its foundation. Dom Vincent sensed his Abbot's cautious approach, but he pledged his time and support. 'With your sanction,' he wrote Ford, 'I would work away at it and do what I could to make it a success.'[6] 'But from our conversation I quite gathered that the scheme had not yet got your sanction.' It seemed, therefore, that Abbot Ford realized the benefits that a Benedictine school would reap, but his actions remained far from decisive. The very question of Ealing had also raised the issues of financial considerations, manpower, the future commitment from Downside, and these tended to blur the future.

Dom Gilbert and Dom Vincent estimated that Ealing had eighteen Roman Catholic youths who might be attracted to a Roman Catholic school run by the monks. Of this number, two had already applied for admission to any future Benedictine school. If these figures seemed unconvincing, the self-confidence and optimism of the Ealing monks swept away doubts as to the wisdom of starting a school within their parish. Their basic argument served as an introduction to a report which the community sent to Abbot Ford: 'In the following statement an attempt has been made to arrange in a connected and methodical manner some of the reasons why it appears to us to be for the advancement of Religion and for the welfare of the mission that a Catholic High School be established in Ealing'[7] Dom Gilbert and Dom Vincent presented eight points which argued for immediate and decisive action from Downside. The first demonstrated that an increasing number of Roman Catholics had moved into Ealing, and their educational needs must be met. Although Gilbert Dolan had repeatedly stressed the close relationship which he hoped to establish between the monks and the respectable element of the area, he also emphasized the needs of 'Catholic families of limited income'. These people could not afford to send their children away to boarding schools, and therefore 'day schools are becoming more and more popular with parents'. This report told Abbot Ford that parents 'like their sons to combine the refining influences of home life with the advantages of a school education'. But the proposed school at Ealing would not limit itself exclusively to the needs of the poor. The second point noted that 'there is no provision [in the area] for the well-to-do class'. The Benedictine school, therefore, would open its doors to both the rich and the poor of Ealing.

As much as they stressed the needs of the underprivileged, the contemporary

Downside Abbey, Somerset, in the early years of the twentieth century. It was Downside which founded and staffed Ealing Priory until 1947

Dom Bernard Bulbeck, OSB   *Dom Gilbert Dolan, OSB*

The young Ealing community around 1909. Standing: Dom Cyril Rylance, Dom Denis Goolden. Seated: Dom Leo Almond, Abbot Hugh Edmond Ford, Dom Sebastian Cave

Abbot Cuthbert Butler, OSB. As Abbot of Downside he continued to dream of a strong and independent monastic community at Ealing

Dom Wulstan Pearson, OSB, first Bishop of Lancaster

Ealing Priory church, 1922

class prejudices of the Benedictines emerged in the next argument. The report maintained that the only schools which catered to the wealthy were located at Wimbledon and Bayswater, and neither could meet the demands of that class. Wimbledon was unsuitable because it was 'quite inaccessible to this side of the Thames'. St Charles, Bayswater, could easily become a powerful rival to a Benedictine school, but this was unlikely to happen for two reasons. The area's families disliked the thought of a daily train trip into London, and 'another objection raised by some of the parents against St Charles is the class of boy which largely frequents it . . . [because] the class is not as good as it was'. According to the authors of the report, 'the better class of people have moved further out of town and there is only the rougher and less independent class left in the neighbourhood . . . [and] the tone and manners of the school have deteriorated'. Without offering an explanation, Abbot Ford was told that the wealthy have also objected to 'the foreign element which of late years has been on the increase'. The Ealing Benedictines stressed that their objections and reservations about St Charles should not be interpreted as arrogance. The future Benedictine 'school is not intended to compete against St Charles, but rather to provide for those who object to St Charles and for the well-to-do class which can afford to live further out of the smoke and smog of London'. But would the new Ealing school hurt the already weak Bayswater school? The Ealing report answered in the negative: 'the consequent loss to St Charles by the opening of a school in Ealing will be proportionally slight'.

The fourth point re-echoed a constant and important theme for Edwardian Roman Catholics: Protestant England must be converted. 'It is part of our duty,' the report contended, 'to provide not only for the spiritual needs and training of Catholics, but also to lead souls outside the church into the fold of Christ.' Weakly argued, this point told Downside 'that a school would be probably a powerful engine for the diffusion of Catholic influence among the non-Catholic portion of the population'. Father O'Halloran held centre stage in the fifth reason for the establishment of a school. The Ealing monks noted that the informed element of the population, Roman Catholic and non-Roman Catholic, recognized O'Halloran as a sham, but 'the great majority view the matter very differently'. The reputation and honesty of the Roman Catholicism had been sullied by this renegade priest, and 'among the best means to recover our position surely is the establishment of a well-conducted High School'. O'Halloran also figured in the sixth point; his public boasts about building a school near his Mattock Lane church frightened his Benedictine neighbours. Although it appeared that O'Halloran's scheme would probably fail, the Ealing report argued that 'it does not do to let him take the lead . . . in providing for an acknowledged want'. 'If it is of importance to "snuff out" Fr O'Halloran,' this reasoning continued, 'it may be said generally that the more St Benedict's becomes a centre of importance and influence the more superfluous and undignified will the position of Fr O'Halloran appear.'

Another strong argument in favour of a school run by the Benedictines stressed that non-Catholic schools certainly attracted members of the parish. Fearing the loss of souls, the report told Abbot Ford that 'the exact number thus attending Protestant schools in the four adjoining parishes . . . cannot be inconsiderable'. Moreover, a number of people, which the Benedictines estimated to be approximately thirty, had already moved out of the parish in search of a Roman Catholic School, and consequently this adversely affected the growth of the parish. Roman Catholics who might have settled within the boundaries of St Benedict's have already elected to live near a school, the two monks told Ford. Comparing the number of Roman Catholics in Ealing to that of Wimbledon, the report pointed out that 'the growth of the Ealing mission is stunted by the want of a school'.

This rambling and redundant statement ended by stressing that a Roman Catholic high school for boys would not only serve Ealing, but would also accommodate the needs of the surrounding areas of Acton, Chiswick, and Brentford. It appealed to Abbot Ford's conscience and maintained that 'the absence of one is detrimental to souls and a great hindrance to the growth of the mission'. Ealing, therefore, could easily become the educational centre for Roman Catholics in the west of London. Religious communities, moreover, conducted schools in a more professional fashion that those run by 'an isolated secular priest'. The above reasons, some valid, some pompous, and some irrelevant, were summed up in an urgent plea to Abbot Ford and the Downside community: 'All these considerations seem to point to the advisability of committing to the Benedictines . . . the institution and conduct of a high school in Ealing'. In addition to this statement from the members of the Ealing mission, suggestions from a Cambridge confrère also graced Abbot Ford's desk.

Writing from Cambridge in May 1902, Dom Cuthbert Butler urged Abbot Ford that far-sighted and forceful actions were required if Ealing was to succeed. 'Ealing is at present in an impasse,' Butler argued, and 'I have been thinking over it a good deal and I feel moved to give you the outcome of my cogitations.'[8] He did not emphasize the school. According to Dom Cuthbert, the problems and difficulties of Ealing revolved around questions of personnel and finances. Dom Cuthbert, a rising star at Downside, urged that Dom Gilbert Dolan be re-assigned immediately. 'It is clear Gilbert will not be able to carry the thing through,' Butler reasoned, and he suggested either Dom Bede Cox or Dom Meinrad Fulton as the replacement. Of the two, however, Dom Bede emerged as Butler's first choice for the job. Dom Cuthbert, moreover, wanted Ealing to be run as a proper Benedictine priory: 'if Bede goes to run Ealing as a Priory, my word! it will be a priory'. Butler claimed that Dom Bede would 'beg and energize his level best'. For Ealing to survive and flourish, Downside had to place full confidence in the new superior, and the monks stationed there must also be of a superior quality. 'You must give him from the first at least one man that he wants,' Dom Cuthbert urged his Abbot, and you 'must not plaster him with crooks and cranks'. Butler suggested the name of one monk, but then mused that 'the only hesitation is on how he would take on the "Priory" part of the business – choir, etc.'.

According to Dom Cuthbert, a new and daring superior supported by a few courageous monks would mould Ealing into a first-class religious foundation. But manpower alone was not enough; Downside must also open its coffers and generously support its London foundation. 'Here you must be reasonable and equitable and not a Shylock,' Dom Cuthbert argued. He also pointed out that to ask a superior to 'pay off a debt of £12,500, with accumulating interest, and keep six men, and add to the church when needed – is to expect something absolutely impossible.' 'No sane man will undertake such a thing,' Butler reasoned. If Downside continued to follow a half-hearted approach, Dom Cuthbert maintained that the Benedictine motherhouse 'better give it up at once' and try to sell the property to the Cardinal or another religious order. Pusillanimous policies must be abandoned immediately. Realizing that only a mere fraction of money invested would be recovered, Cuthbert Butler pointed out that 'Ealing is a foundation, and we make it because we believe it is for the good of Downside, and we must be prepared to spend money on it'. Moreover, the current practice of keeping the mission and priory accounts separate seemed to him 'useless and impossible': 'it is an institution to be worked as a single unity'.

Dom Cuthbert Butler believed that Ealing should not be saddled with a huge and burdensome debt. Ealing 'should pay Downside what interest it can'. He also questioned Abbot Ford's policy of quick and instant repayment and claimed that this would make it impossible for the foundation 'to farm any funds of its own for the next fifty years or more'. Butler's lengthy letter ended with a prophetic argument which will later be associated with his name: 'some definite arrangements must be made which the man who runs the place recognizes as possible and reasonable and compatible with putting Ealing on a permanent footing'.

Dom Cuthbert Butler's sense of urgency fell on deaf ears; Downside could not comprehend his plea for swift and resolute action. Abbot Ford's response to his confrère's programme epitomized this approach. 'Your letter makes me despair,' he finally wrote to Cambridge.[9] Ford admitted that the financial questions were confusing and also that the Downside Council had failed to formulate any new plans for the Ealing foundation. Abbot Ford realized that changes were imperative, but he lacked the initiative or determination to bring about any far-reaching programmes. In the minds of some, therefore, the status quo became the acceptable policy. 'It looks as if things will remain as they are until some external force moves us on,' Ford sadly told Dom Cuthbert, 'and then we shall probably have to pay more than if we had taken things in the right time.'

But pressures from the Ealing community and the gentle but firm urgings of Dom Cuthbert Butler shook Abbot Ford out of his monastic lethargy, and he slowly began to take steps to direct the establishment of the future Benedictine school at Ealing. He ignored Dom Cuthbert's advice that Ealing needed new leadership, and both Dom Gilbert and Dom Vincent remained. But he accepted Butler's suggestion that a strong and well-qualified captain was needed to pilot the school during its infancy. Ford, therefore, approached Dom Sebastian Cave, First Prefect (equivalent of Headmaster) at Downside's school, and appointed him the headmaster of Ealing's future school. Ford had definite ideas about Dom Sebastian's duties. Writing to the Abbot President of the English Benedictine Congregation, the Abbot announced that Dom Sebastian was going to Ealing, and stated that he would not ask Archbishop's House for faculties for the new headmaster. He told Gasquet that he did 'not want Ealing to be looked upon as a mission only – nor do I want him to be regarded as a missioner but as a "conventual"'.[10] Dom Sebastian Cave was a perfect candidate. The *Downside Review* expressed a sense of loss, but also rejoiced that Ealing would benefit from Dom Sebastian's professionalism and experience: 'the work he is undertaking is one of serious importance and demands both energy and experience . . . [and] we cannot think a better choice could be made, but we are very sorry to miss Father Sebastian from the school'.[11]

Louis Sebastian Cave was born at Desboro, Northampton, on 26 April 1866.[12] He came to Downside in 1875, was clothed in the habit in 1885, and pronounced simple vows in 1886. Archbishop Scarisbrook ordained him priest on 17 September 1893, and this was followed by his nine-year career at Downside School. Dom Sebastian, an avid cricketer, looked the part of a schoolmaster: six foot three inches tall, and to many, the 'type of an athletic Briton'. Austere by nature, he maintained a reserve and restraint in his dealings with people. Consequently, he enjoyed the company of few intimate friends. If his appearance suited his task as pioneer headmaster at Ealing, he nonetheless felt uneasy in the world of academics and scholarship. A contemporary remarked that 'he had no fund of conversation or literary background, no interest in books or study'.

Dom Sebastian Cave arrived at his new assignment on 29 September 1902, and within a week the long-awaited Benedictine school was opened at 39 Blakesley Avenue. The *Middlesex County Times* reported that the presbytery of St Benedict's Church 'has been removed from Marchwood Crescent to 39 Blakesley Avenue . . . where it is the wish of his Eminence Cardinal Vaughan, a Catholic Grammar School has been opened'.[13] Monks and students shared this building. The first prospectus for the Ealing Catholic Day School, written by Dom Sebastian, emphasized that 'the school is under the management of the Benedictines from Downside Abbey assisted by qualified lay teachers'.[14] A short description of the course of instruction, English, Mathematics,

Sciences, French, Latin, Elementary Drawing, Typewriting, and Shorthand, testified to the addition of practical business skills into the traditional curriculum. Moreover, the prospectus pointed out, 'in addition to the head-work every boy should learn some handicraft in connection with his drawing, such as carpentry, wood-carving, book-binding, basket-making, etc., for which special arrangements can be made'. For boys over the age of ten, the fee was £6.6s.0d a term; for those under ten, £5.5s.0d. Parents were also told that special accommodation would 'be made for boys who are preparing for the Public Examinations'. Cave's philosophy or approach to education departed from the traditional Roman Catholic view: he wanted to introduce some aspects of the English public school system into Ealing's new school. Dom Sebastian wanted to emphasize discipline and to instil a sense of responsibility into the older students by encouraging co-operation between them and the staff.

The inauspicious beginning and the handful of students did not discourage Dom Sebastian Cave; the expansion and growth of the Benedictine school became his primary goal in life. Two months after the school opened, he wrote to Abbot Ford and outlined his plans. He told Ford that he had printed 150 prospectuses and that there was even a good chance of two Protestant youths enrolling. Cave's main point, however, did not concern the trickle of students entering, but his burning desire to turn Ealing into a boarding school: 'I do wish we could get get the question of *boarders* settled,' he told Abbot Ford, and 'I could then . . . lodge them out in the congregation'.[15] The Cardinal, who had placed strong restrictions on the establishment of a school at Ealing, appeared to be the chief obstacle, and the Benedictines wanted to avoid any rash action which might alienate Cardinal Vaughan. But the headmaster proposed a solution which might circumvent the Cardinal's prohibitions. Dom Sebastian emphasized that the idea originated with a layman and did not come from any of the Ealing monks. According to this plan, Abbot Ford should educate his 'church students *here*, and let them finish by two years at Downside.' Cave argued that many of the monks pursuing Orders had experienced difficulties and trials during their years of preparation, and he believed that this happened because of 'too much familiarity with things' at Downside. This scheme, he believed, might convince the Cardinal to modify his condition. 'The idea of their being destined for the priesthood could be more in evidence here than is possible at Downside,' he continued. Moreover, 'most of them get "spoilt" at Downside by having a good time of it'.

Abbot Ford's reaction, however, lacked the dynamism and excitement of Dom Sebastian's letter. He told Dom Sebastian to accept the two non-Catholic youth and also informed him that 'we do not require the Cardinal's consent for you to have boys whom you lodge out with a member of the congregation'.[16] As for the possibility of educating 'church students', Ford's remarks revealed his cautious but diplomatic nature: 'Just at present I am not a good person to approach the Cardinal [but] I shall remember what you say about the church boys'. Abbot Ford dashed Dom Sebastian's dreams by ending his letter with a query about the progress of shrub planting in front of the church.

But Dom Sebastian Cave refused to settle for anything short of a proper boarding school. Musing on the possibility that Cardinal Vaughan might object to any Benedictine school in the archdiocese, Cave philosophically remarked that 'it will go on somewhere or other'.[17] Dom Sebastian continued to pressure Abbot Ford for approval of his boarding school. 'I am sure Dom G[ilbert] could get boarders sanctioned by the Cardinal,' he argued, and his competitive spirit began to surface: 'with boarders – well we'd beat Wimbledon tomorrow'. But this question did not monopolize Dom Sebastian's first months at Ealing. He had to attend to other school business such as budgets, enrolment, and problems of space. Requests for additional monks for the faculty also began to appear in his letters home to Downside. Moreover, publicity suddenly became a priority. Although the school roster showed only three students, some residents of the area began to visualize hoards of unruly children invading their peaceful enclave. Some of the locals had already complained about the noise, but Dom Sebastian dismissed the seriousness of this action. 'The boys can hardly be a nuisance,' he told Abbot Ford, since 'they have only a quarter-hour's recreation here and are confined to the back garden.'

Growth and expansion dominated Dom Sebastian's plans for his school as the second year opened in 1903. Again the question of boarders became important. In February he continued to exert pressure on Downside. Quoting a Jesuit friend, he tried to convince Abbot Ford that 'Grammar Schools . . . never pay expenses'.[18] Even six lodgers would defray costs. Ford's advice to Dom Sebastian was realistically brutal: 'keep the position which has to be solved – don't dream dreams'.[19] But Dom Sebastian would not give up. During the following month, he informed Abbot Ford that Cardinal Vaughan was seriously ill, and noted that 'a more sympathetic "figure head" might mean a small boarding school'.[20]

And the school had become popular. The enrolment had increased to seventeen students, and this provided the catalyst for Dom Sebastian to re-open the question of lodgers. Moreover St Charles, Bayswater, founded in 1864, closed its doors in July 1903. In the autumn of 1903, therefore, Dom Sebastian wrote to the Abbot President of the English Benedictine Congregation, Aidan Gasquet, and asked him for advice on how to pursue the question of a boarding school at Ealing. Gasquet replied and advised Dom Sebastian to ask Abbot Ford to approach Cardinal Vaughan, and the Ealing headmaster followed this suggestion. Dom Sebastian sensed that some tension existed between the Cardinal and Abbot Ford, but nonetheless, he asked Ford to 'catch him before he goes to Rome'.[21] A bit impatient with his superior, Cave urged Abbot Ford to 'do this at once, *before* you have any little misunderstanding with him'. 'I only want to get the principle settled,' he pleaded, and when 'this is once settled we can look around and shall know what to aim for'.

Abbot Ford continued to waffle on the question of boarders at Ealing. He was also more sensitive to the Cardinal's prejudices against a boarding school run by religious. In November 1903, Ford again tried to restrain Dom Sebastian and again tried to articulate the Downside policy. His tone was clear and abrupt. 'You have forgotten what I have told you about boarders,' he reminded Dom Sebastian.[22] Moreover, 'the Cardinal objected to our opening a boarding school, but said that he had no objection to our taking in a few boys to lodge with us.' For the time being, therefore, Ford ruled out any sudden drastic change at Ealing: 'this leaves us at liberty to have as many boarders as our present accommodation will permit'. Ford adroitly pointed out that 'it would not be wise to go to the present Archbishop'. A conservatism coloured Abbot Ford's approach to working with Archbishop's House, and he told his headmaster that he had little knowledge of Cardinal Vaughan's thinking on the future of Ealing's school apart from the original arrangements. To demand more might distress the Cardinal, who might then 'not allow even the limited permission which we now have'.

But Abbot Ford's restraints could not destroy Dom Sebastian's dream of a grand Benedictine school at Ealing. A proper building must house the future boarders, and consequently, the two subjects became synonymous. The question of the locality and the type of the building became important, and again Cave's independence of mind surfaced. The Ealing headmaster wanted to detach the school from the presbytery, and he appealed to Abbot Ford for authorisation to purchase some land. He had his sights set on 'Hermosa', situated on Ealing Common and therefore closer to the railway station. The construction of a new school a distance from the monastic foundation, Dom Sebastian believed, constituted a wise move. 'It would be insane to build *here* with a view to a school,' he told Abbot Ford, because 'as soon as it was built we might find ourselves allowed to take in boarders and then the building would not suit.'[23] Moreover 'a large school here [close to the presbytery or church] would decrease the value of the neighbouring property,' but 'Hermosa' offered many advantages: close to transport and 'a fairly respectable playground.' If the property had to be sold in the future, it might be an ideal site for a hospital or hotel. But, he believed, the mission fathers must remain at their present location, 39 Blakesley Avenue. There were serious disadvantages of moving both the clergy and the boys to this new location. Far from the church, the priests would 'grumble at the distance and they'd (as they do now but quietly) grumble at having boys and pianos about the place'.

Even a temporary building close to the church did not suit Dom Sebastian. Commenting on the possibility of an iron building, which he caricatured as 'tin tunnels', he told Ford that it would lack dignity and 'would not compare well with other schools here such as Durston House.'[24] Appearance weighed heavily in the competition for students; the so-called 'tin tunnels' amounted to a liability. Consequently, Dom Sebastian recommended 'buying outright for £1000 or better . . . and running it [the school] as a separate house'. A solid and attractive house could always be re-sold at a profit. Dom Sebastian, trying hard to convince his superior, pointed out that a school at 'Hermosa' would occupy little space, and consequently the rest of the estate could be leased. Realising that Downside planned to enlarge the Ealing church and construct a larger presbytery, Dom Sebastian did not want to get stuck with the old priests' house on Blakesley Avenue, which he believed was a bad location for a school. 'With a school up in "their parts" we might get two or three Protestant children, who would have to go a long way to get to school.'[25]

The administration of his small school also gave Dom Sebastian some headaches. The enrolment continued to climb, and the headmaster worked to improve his staff and curriculum. He recognized the importance of Science, Mathematics, and Modern Languages, and he also remained committed to the value of handicrafts and carpentry. The second prospectus reflected the growing sophistication of the Benedictine school. Neater in appearance than the rough premier issue, this 1904 prospectus emphasized three new aspects: the proximity of the school to the District Line and Great Western Railway stations, the nearby school operated by the nuns at Castle Hill House, and an attempt to meet the needs of the business world through the study of subjects such as English, Modern Languages, Mathematics and Science.[26] Suggested by Abbot Ford, this approach attempted to increase the appeal of Ealing to those interested in a career in business or commerce.

Trained teachers were required to teach these courses. In his letters to Abbot Ford, Dom Sebastian constantly emphasized the need for qualified teachers, especially monks from Downside. He explained that he taught five hours daily, and this detracted from the necessities of administration. Moreover, classroom responsibilities made it impossible for him to make important contacts in Ealing. Dom Sebastian also told his superior that games must not be minimized. At the end of 1903, he told Abbot Ford that the purchase of playing fields for cricket was imperative for the future of the school, and he had already visited a nearby site and made enquiries.

By the beginning of his second academic year at Ealing, therefore, Dom Sebastian Cave had formed definite and concrete plans about the future of the Benedictines' school.[27] As for housing, he believed that a temporary iron building would not entice either students or attract parents; financially it would also prove unprofitable. Moreover, it was impossible to obtain a freehold close to the mission because there existed 'a condition [of] *no Boys' School*' in the residential area. Downside, therefore, must purchase 'Hermosa'. A boarding school continued to remain the keystone of his master plan, and three reasons supported his argument: Jesuit friends advised him that day schools did not pay; seven genuine offers of good-class boarders' expressed an interest; and finally the Holy Child of Jesus Sisters at Castle Hill House claimed that a boarding school would help the fortunes of their school.

At times, Abbot Ford's caution defused Dom Sebastian's eagerness, but the headmaster continued to enjoy the confidence of the Abbot, who was committed to the existence of a reputable school at Ealing. In September 1903, Ford again extended his support and encouraged Dom Sebastian. 'I think with you that you ought to make the school as thorough as you can make it,' he wrote, 'for the name you get will stick for a long time, and if you get talked about as being efficient, the school will soon be supported . . .'[28] Ford urged Dom Sebastian to be conscious of Ealing's delicate financial health, but he also recognized that money had to be expended and invested. In the case of the cricket fields, for example, Abbot Ford realized that playing fields were essential, but he also urged Cave to 'get acquainted with all possibilities'.[29] When a lay teacher threatened to leave unless he received a rise in salary, Abbot Ford recommended that Dom Sebastian give him an increase. On the other hand, he supported the headmaster's plans to dismiss another teacher. Both monk and Abbot, therefore, laboured to establish the reputation and stability of their school during its infancy. Their styles, however, differed. Ford's caution and appreciation of diplomacy clashed with Dom Sebastian's enthusiasm. The latter articulated his philosophy in a letter to Abbot Ford: 'A half-hearted attempt at a school won't pay in any way'.[30]

Expansion and a flurry of activity were also evident in the life of St Benedict's parish. When the priests left Castle Hill House, they moved to 2 Marchwood Crescent, next to the church. And when the school began in 1902, the monks moved across the street and took up residence with the students at 39 Blakesley Avenue, which they had leased. As the school began to grow, it soon became apparent that a new presbytery was needed. Initially, Downside hesitated to commit itself to a building programme, and consequently Ford directed Dom Gilbert to enquire if 39 Blakesley Avenue could be purchased. 'This is the only remaining alternative to our building,' the Abbot told him.[31] By the summer, however, Abbot Ford realized that he might have to build. This required not only an expenditure of funds, but also the skills of a diplomat. In order to prevent any criticism from the Ealing populace, Ford told Dom Gilbert that the proposed building must 'be spoken of as the school' and not described as a clergy house.[32] Even in the deliberations with the Downside Council, Ford referred to the construction as the 'Catholic Day School and Clergy House'. However, the Abbot soon changed his mind concerning the policy on names. 'I find that to describe our new building as "school" would be dangerous,' he later informed the Ealing monks, 'as various authorities would insist on all manner of things, so it will be styled "clergy house".'[33]

Like Dom Sebastian, Dom Gilbert Dolan thought that the parochial and educational apostolates should be separate operations. He agreed with Dom

Sebastian and supported the headmaster's contention that the available property at Ealing Common, 'Hermosa', should be purchased for the school. In October 1903, after the construction of the new presbytery had started, Dom Gilbert told Abbot Ford that 'Hermosa' would be auctioned off soon and this was 'probably the last time it will be in the market.'[34] His arguments re-enforced Dom Sebastian's: 'the reasons which make it seem a desirable acquisition for [a] Grammar School and Chapel of ease purposes . . . appear as valid to me and those here who know Ealing . . .' In his attempt to dissociate parish from school, Dom Gilbert pointed out that the school would prosper at 'Hermosa' because of its proximity to trains and trams.

Moreover, the construction of a new presbytery might have a negative effect on the life of the Ealing mission. Dom Gilbert told Abbot Ford that the planned building might alienate some of the parishioners. The enlargement of the church, in their estimation, seemed more important and pressing. 'There is increasing difficulty in interesting people in what we are doing,' Dom Gilbert reported back to Downside, and a new house for the clergy might increase indifference. 'The public sees an ambitious and highly decorated fragment of [a] church, on which a great deal of money has been spent which might have been more advantageously expended in securing better accommodation.' Dolan believed that the lack of commitment and support from the laity stemmed from the apparent inability of the Benedictines to finish a project like the completion of the church. He noted that Cardinal Vaughan and other prelates, such as Bishops Brindle and Bellord, had already alluded to this. 'Our reputation . . . for common sense and prudence,' Dom Gilbert concluded, 'is evidently not on the increase.' It made no sense, he believed, to start a begging campaign for an 'ambitious looking priory' when the congregation had just responded to similar appeals to expand their church. Dom Gilbert then related the following incident: a wealthy parishioner had remarked to him that 'no sooner is a beginning made on one thing when a large five thousand pound job is undertaken . . . next door'. He told Abbot Ford that comments, such as 'those rich Benedictines', were becoming the response to their building campaign. Dom Sebastian also confirmed that some thought 'too much interest is not shown in the working of this mission'.[35]

Dom Gilbert sincerely believed that more than enough strain had been placed on the parishioners of Ealing. 'I wonder whether any other mission of 500 people is taxed in this way,' he asked Ford.[36] In addition to shouldering the resonsibility for finishing the church and being asked to fund a new residence for its priests, the congregation of St Benedict's 'is called upon to do a great deal more that, as a mission, it would ordinarily be called upon to do. . .' Dom Gilbert pointed out that the parish provided 'for the keep to a great extent of the Priest in charge of the Grammar School [Dom Sebastian] and the resident tutor'. In Dom Gilbert's opinion, Downside should commit its resources and money to the completion of the church. The needs of the parish must be addressed. Nonetheless, the construction went forward, and its symbolic importance was quickly noted. Commenting on the new building, the *Catholic Weekly* reported that 'solid proof of their zealous labours is now at hand in the opening of a very handsomely appointed and commodious' building.[37]

Yet Dom Gilbert Dolan had ample reason to take his line of attack in trying to address priorities: the mission had flourished. In his 1903 report to Downside, he noted with pride that his parish numbered over five hundred people.[38] The same document recorded that approximately four hundred attended Sunday mass,[39] sixteen were baptized, and six marriages performed. The Benedictine grammar school had enrolled nineteen students, and the school staffed by the Mayfield Sisters at Castle Hill House, ten. Pre-school children numbered thirty-six. Armed with these statistics, therefore, Dom Gilbert had pleaded his case for the needed extension of St Benedict's church to Abbot Ford. His argument was simple: 'the need of accommodation is increasing with the steady growth in the congregation'.[40] And projected future growth became an additional trump card. 'I hear of other people likely to come to Ealing, and I know that we have not enough sittings to give to people who apply for them.' Not only seating, but the church also needed an additional altar, a proper sacristy, and an enlarged sanctuary. 'There is scarcely room in the sanctuary for anything like a ceremony,' he complained, 'and altogether we are too confined for the decorous . . . carrying-out of the church work.' He also pointed out that the parish had recently opened a chapel of ease in nearby Windsor Road to take the strain off St Benedict's. Dom Gilbert opposed any temporary remedy to the overcrowding and proposed that the nave be extended by five or six bays. By doing this, he believed that it 'would justify us in doing *something*, and something permanent would be better than a temporary makeshift'.

Abbot Ford, however, had favoured the construction of the new building, but he still had not made up his mind on whether it should house the school or the priests. At first, he believed that the new dwelling should 'be devoted to the needs of the parish'.[41] Ford asked Dom Sebastian if 'it would . . . do to keep no. 39 and use it for school purposes only', for example, two class rooms and a master's room. To soothe the feelings of the new headmaster, Abbot Ford suggested that he could 'have three classrooms in the new building . . . [and] all meals would be in the new house'. Downside finally decided that the school would occupy the new building across the street from 39 Blakesley Avenue, where the monks would continue to live. Abbot Ford tried to explain the reasons behind this policy to Dom Gilbert. Ford told him that because of 'the money difficulties of combining the school and priory in one building, I think the simplest and most workable method is to let each have its own house'.[42] Ford, it seemed, favoured the growth and immediate expansion of the school. He told Dom Gilbert: 'if you have 39 [Blakesley Avenue] as a priest's house without any rooms occupied by the school, you will have enough for all parish purposes for the next year without rooms in the school'. Dom Gilbert had hoped to gain at least a foothold in the new building by asking for several rooms for parish activities, but Abbot Ford's decision had eliminated even this possibility.

Abbot Ford, therefore, had finally started to formulate a definite policy for Ealing's educational apostolate. But his actions and decisions ran counter to the wishes of Dom Gilbert and Dom Sebastian, who had fought to move the school away from the original property which surrounded the church. The plan to purchase 'Hermosa' was scrapped. Ford's rationale sounded blunt: 'the school can only succeed by being treated as part of the mission'.[42] He told Dom Gilbert that it was too soon 'to judge whether the mission benefits by its schools or not'. But he pointed out that 'where there are good schools attached to the mission, the property of the parish is considered to be in large measure due to the existence of the school'. Financial considerations also played a central part in his programme. The Abbot told Dom Gilbert that Downside must not become the paymaster for Ealing's educational ventures. The school cannot be expected to 'pay for its ... [upkeep] as yet,' he continued, but if 'it becomes clear that the school is no benefit to the mission it can be closed'. Consequently, Abbot Ford believed it was ridiculous to house the school in a building distant from the Ealing complex: 'If the school cannot be made to pay at the new house, still less can it pay if it has to take premises of its own.'

Usually cool and reserved, the Downside Abbot also responded emotionally to Dom Gilbert's attempt to clothe the Ealing mission in the garb of a poor cousin or the mantle of a martyr. 'I think you forget what Downside has done for Ealing,' Ford scolded Dom Gilbert, and he reminded the monks that 'no other mission has been helped to the same extent.' The Abbot pointed out that 'it was because of Downside money' that Ealing was 'able to get the chaplaincy at the Holy Child Convent – and that the mission has the benefit of the girls school there'. In addition to emphasizing the importance of the Downside largesse, he also attacked the alleged lack of initiative on the part of the Ealing Benedictines: 'And I doubt if any mission in London has done so little for itself'.

Dom Gilbert's tenure as parish priest at Ealing would last three more years. Apart from the tension between himself and Abbot Ford, the *de facto* separation of the leadership of the mission and administration of the school created problems. As early as 1903, Dom Sebastian complained to Abbot Ford about Dom Gilbert's lack of zest and enthusiasm. 'We want a young active man of ... missionary experience,' the headmaster informed Abbot Ford, 'one who would make the building of the church the work of his life.'[43] The occasional personality clash, difference of opinion and policy, and problems of jurisdiction also added to the tension between the parish priest and the

Ealing headmaster. At one time, for example, Dom Sebastian complained to Abbot Ford that Dom Gilbert had accepted a boy of questionable ability for admission at the grammar school without consulting him.[44] While students and monks were both housed at 39 Blakesley Avenue, problems of noise and space contributed to frayed nerves within the Benedictine community. But greater problems consumed the attention and energy of the monks.

The financial demands of the Ealing mission monopolized Dom Gilbert's time. The annual accounts revealed that the mission was slowly becoming solvent. In 1902, for example, the Mission Account recorded a profit of approximately £140.[45] Dom Gilbert drew Downside's attention to the fact that the church expenses were 'unusually heavy' because of the need to purchase more benches. Moreover, the move to 39 Blakesley Avenue and the increase in rent also meant additional expenditure. Dolan's prognosis, however, beamed with optimism: 'the general financial condition seems sound, and our prospects are slowly improving.' Moreover, 'the Grammar School shall pay its expenses at the end of the current year 1903.' But the next year did not turn out as prosperous as Dom Gilbert hoped. The increase in revenues over the previous year amounted to only £15. The income from the school, £8, also failed to meet Dom Gilbert's prediction of a large profit. In fact, an itemized account, which contained among other things, expenses for the upkeep of a tutor, meals for the students, and the additional rent, revealed that the mission had expended £145 to launch the new school. Philosophically, however, Dom Gilbert continued to remark that the 'school should some day pay this back'.[46]

The following year brought no relief from the financial burden of the school, and the uneasiness between the mission and school appeared in Dom Gilbert's annual statement. 'The expenses connected with the Grammar School have been a great drain on the finances of the Mission during the year 1904,' he claimed.[47] Including the £100, which he calculated was spent on the school, the balance for the year had increased to approximately £267. When Downside eventually separated the accounts of the mission and school in 1906, the balance of the Ealing mission stood at £221.[48]

The daily running of the mission did tax Dom Gilbert, but pressure put on him by Downside to liquidate the large debt owed to the Mission Fund, which had financed the establishment of the London foundation, also put a considerable strain on the parish priest. By January 1903, Ealing owed the Mission Fund £6,653, and the mother house, not surprisingly, was eager to collect this debt.[49] The property at Ealing had cost approximately £1,000, and the construction of the initial sections of the church, £5,343. Legal expenses, architectural advice, and surveying fees made up the rest of the debt. In spite of Dom Cuthbert Butler's advice to Abbot Ford, Downside had decided that the Ealing mission should, as agreed upon earlier, take responsibility for the liquidation of this debt. But a concerted effort had never been organized to repay Downside. Until 1902, for example, only £98 had been collected towards the debt.

In November 1902, Dom Gilbert Dolan began to act on the debt problem, but the initiative did not come from him. According to Dom Sebastian, 'this [was] all called by Dom Vincent starting the show'.[50] Nonetheless, Dom Gilbert finally approached the parish for help. He announced the seriousness of the problem from the pulpit and 'invited the heads of families to meet him in conclave'. Writing with approval that something had finally been done to lessen the financial obligation to Downside, Dom Sebastian told Abbot Ford that Dom Vincent felt 'somewhat put-out' because Dom Gilbert was stealing his thunder. However twenty-eight parishioners did attend the meeting convened by the parish priest, and pledged £117 towards the debt. Various annual subscriptions were also promised, and some present suggested that quarterly collections should become the established policy. Dom Sebastian again offered Downside some advice. He suggested that the money should be used to pay off the capital; the temptation should be resisted to put the money towards the increasing interest on the capital. By the end of the first month, £98 was collected.

This new departure pleased Abbot Ford, and he reminded Dom Gilbert of the magnitude of the debt, and suggested how Ealing might tackle this problem. 'With regard to the repayment of the debt,' Abbot Ford wrote to Ealing, 'I think we might let it be understood that all the money the people contribute, less 10%, should go to the reduction of the Capital'.[51] 'As Downside is paying the interest on the £1000 for the land,' he continued, 'I think that this £1000 should be paid off first.' Ford also told Dom Gilbert that any money which Ealing could spare from their mission account should go towards the interest. Abbot Ford also put Dom Vincent Corney in charge of the project, the so-called 'begging'.

Dom Vincent immediately printed a circular to be distributed among the parishioners of St Benedict's. It explained that the Abbot of Downside had requested him to head this appeal 'for a small contribution towards this good object'.[52] The parish soon learned that the debt exceeded £5,000, and one of Dom Vincent's explanations for its magnitude touched on the rivalry with Father O'Halloran. 'The difficulties under which we took on the mission in 1897 . . . and which are still existing are . . . only too well known.' Referring to the Mattock Lane chapel, he stated that 'much that was given for, and belongs to this Mission, has never come into our possession'. During the spring, the Benedictines also issued a printed statement, which itemized the extent of the debt in order to demonstrate to the parishioners the seriousness of the financial situation. In addition for the usual appeal for generosity, this statement thanked the parish for the contribution of £131 realized during the recent Lenten collection.

Abbot Ford continued to correspond frequently with Dom Gilbert and Dom

Vincent on the debt issue. He told Dom Vincent that he wanted to see the list of past donors and their addresses and also the drafts of any future circulars. Ford demanded that 'on the 6th of every month, you must send me an account, with [a] cheque for balance'.[53] The Abbot's advice was succinct: 'make a start and keep at it day by day, and you will soon see results'. In spite of these admonitions, Ford complained to Dom Sebastian that Dom Vincent rarely wrote 'as to what he is doing towards his begging'.[54] Upset with this lackadaisical approach to a serious problem, Ford had to reprimand Dom Vincent: 'You must get your begging into order'.[55] Abbot Ford again demanded a list of the contributors and a copy of the current circular. 'This will at least be a beginning,' he told Dom Vincent.

Dom Gilbert, however, expressed certain reservations about the timing of this fund-raising drive and how the parish might view it. He told the Abbot that some parishioners had pointed out that it was imprudent to launch a programme to reduce the debt, and at the same time build a new priests' house.[56] A number of the laity also told Dom Gilbert that they would rather contribute money for the completion of the church. Commenting on this impasse, Dolan told Abbot Ford that a benefactor from the parish had recently told him that 'he can't feel any particular interest in the debt fund seeing how inconsiderately the money has been spent'.[57] 'If friends in their candour feel like this,' Dolan warned, there is 'no wonder others share the feeling.'

Moreover, it appears that Dom Gilbert began to direct the money-raising project in place of Dom Vincent. He started writing monthly letters seeking advice and sent cheques of varying amounts to the authorities at Downside. A 'debt collection box' and constant notices from the pulpit reminded the parish of its financial obligations. Dom Gilbert looked for every opportunity to chip away at the debt or to soothe any bad feelings in his parish. He told Abbot Ford, for example, that St Benedict's planned to give him a gift of money on the occasion of his priesthood jubilee. 'I would like to be able to say that the money will be spent on the church at Ealing,' he informed the Abbot. 'I suggest this believing it would be the wisest policy and more likely to create a good impression, and create too good a precedent, than if it were to go elsewhere.'[58]

The Benedictine 'begging' did realize some results. During the first year of the campaign, the monks collected over £269 toward the elimination of the debt. The total capital debt stood at £6,384, but, the parish was informed, 'there has arisen, from arrears of interest, a new debt of £177.[59] Moreover, any funds which could be spared from the Ealing's mission account would be devoted to the elimination of the interest. Consequently, in 1904, the Ealing Benedictines announced a four-point programme: an effort to increase the number of annual subscribers to the debt fund; where possible, an increase in the amount already pledged; 'towards the payment of the interest we depend very largely on more generous offertories'; and finally, the Benedictines urged 'better results from the quarterly collections'. In 1904, therefore, the debt was again reduced; £282 had been collected.[60] Appeals to the charity of the parish continued to be the official programme of the monks, and Dolan used every platform to beg for money. In April 1904, for example, *The Tablet* mistakenly reported that the current church at Ealing was sufficient for the needs of the mission. Dom Gilbert wrote a letter to correct this false impression. 'I am in one sense, happy to state that this is not the case,' he pointed out, 'as our numbers have already outgrown the very limited space at our disposal.'[61] He told the readers that the debt still loomed large and that the 'local means to enlarge the church are not forthcoming'. Consequently, he pricked the conscience of Roman Catholics throughout England: 'I make an appeal through your columns to the generosity of the Catholic public to help us build up St Benedict's Church at Ealing.'

Problems connected with expansion and building and the financial dark clouds, however, failed to dampen the pastoral enthusiasm of the Benedictine monks or to halt parish programmes or activities. St Benedict's continued to grow and to minister to the needs of the suburb. In 1902, for example, both Dom Gilbert and Dom Vincent participated in a lantern lecture series sponsored by the Ealing borough. Dom Gilbert spoke on 'Scenes from the Life of St Benedict', and Dom Vincent on 'A Tour in Switzerland'. During the following year, Cardinal Herbert Vaughan, instrumental in the arrival of the Benedictines in Ealing, died, and St Benedict's took the opportunity to recognize its special relationship with the deceased prelate. A requiem mass was sung, and Dom Gilbert preached the sermon. He sketched the priestly career of Vaughan, noted his achievements at Salford, and pointed out that, 'brief as had been his rule over his archdiocese, it had been marked by many notable achievements'.[62] Dom Gilbert turned to statistics to illustrate how much Westminster had grown both in the number of churches and membership during the Vaughan era. In conclusion, he reminded the congregation that 'as founder of St Benedict's Mission the late Cardinal was entitled to the grateful prayers of the congregation of the church and mission'.[63]

Eager to make the acquaintance of the new Archbishop of Westminster, Francis Bourne, Dom Gilbert invited him to visit the parish on St Benedict's Day, 1904. Dom Gilbert's report to Downside bubbled with pride. He told Abbot Ford that Bourne, a 'teetotaller', was gracious, 'though not so much of a conversationalist as his eminent predecessor'.[64] The parish crowded in to attend Bourne's pontifical mass, and the local papers, along with the national press, reported the occasion. The *Ealing Gazette* printed the sermon in its entirety. After tracing the accomplishments of the Benedictine Order through-out the centuries, Bourne drew special attention to Ealing. 'The work of founding a new mission is surrounded by difficulties,' he told the congregation, and 'as you can see the beginning of what will one day be a very beautiful church and monastery has already involved a large outlay of money'.[65] The main theme of the Archbishop's message, however, dealt with the O'Halloran schism.

According to Dom Gilbert, six newspaper reporters attended the event, and Archbishop Bourne 'told one or two he wanted *all* he said to be carefully and fully reported'.[66] Bourne noted that 'we cannot shut our eyes to the special difficulty that attaches to the building up of the Catholic Church in this district'. 'Unfortunately,' he continued, 'as you know only too well, there is a schismatical chapel within the limits of this district.' He told the parishioners that Father O'Halloran enjoyed 'no kind of ecclesiastical recognition' and emphasized that 'the existence of that chapel is an act of open schism'. If anyone entered the doors of that church, they 'are sinning against the unity of the Holy Catholic Church'. The reports from the *Daily Chronicle* and the *Universe* both stressed the Archbishop's statement that Father O'Halloran was in open revolt against lawful authority.[67] Archbishop Bourne ended his message by asking for God's blessing 'on the fathers here that they may accomplish in Ealing, that work which St Benedict and his sons have done so wonderfully all over the world'.[68] Because of the visit and the supportive words of the Archbishop, Dom Gilbert believed that Ealing would experience friendlier relations with Archbishop's House than in the past. 'Before leaving the Archbishop promised to come again,' Dolan told Abbot Ford, and 'he promised a letter of encouragement for the extension of the church'.[69]

Changes in the status of other churchmen also had a profound impact upon the Ealing Benedictines. On 10 April 1906, Abbot Edmund Ford resigned as Downside's first Abbot. The Constitutional Crisis, the proposed school in Ireland, Downside's own educational apostolate, and the construction of the abbey church had taxed Ford's energies. Moreover, concerns over the new mission in Ealing contributed to his worries and failing health. According to his biographer, 'the community . . . was becoming increasingly anxious, for his progressive weakness could not be disguised, despite that fact his good spirits and general cheerfulness were, if anything, greater than usual'.[70] A holiday in Italy did not improve his health, and in August he offered his letter of resignation to the President of the English Benedictine Congregation, Aidan Gasquet. In it, Ford pointed out that his term ended in two years, but explained that he was 'no longer strong enough to do the work attached to my office'.[71] Gasquet accepted the resignation and replied the following day. 'I am greatly distressed, but cannot say surprised,' the Abbot President wrote, and 'of course, I will not stand out against what appears to me to be justified'.[72]

Abbot Ford's successor had already expressed a keen interest in the Ealing foundation. Born on 6 May 1858, Dom Cuthbert Butler had been appointed Head of the Downside House of Studies, Cambridge, in 1896. From there, he had written to Abbot Ford and expressed his opinion on Ealing and its future direction.[73] Dom Cuthbert was recalled to Downside in 1904, and in November 1906, the community elected him the second Abbot of St Gregory's.

But Edmund Ford did not spend the rest of his life in quiet retirement. The new Downside Abbot believed that Ealing might be the proper and suitable assignment for Abbot Ford. According to Butler, Ealing represented an example of Ford's vision of 'forming centres of community life outside Downside'.[74] 'Ealing was his own child, his own foundation.' At the age of fifty-five, therefore, Abbot Ford journeyed to the London suburb. In early May, a change in the composition of the Ealing community took place, and it was more radical and far-reaching than the assignment of an ex-Abbot. The *Downside Review* announced the new appointments: 'the following changes on the Mission have been chronicled . . . Abbot Ford and Dom Leo Almond have taken over the Ealing mission, and Dom Gilbert Dolan has been moved to Redditch and Dom Vincent Corney to Walton'.[75] The Ealing community now numbered four: Abbot Ford, Leo Almond, Denis Goolden (arrived in 1905), and Sebastian Cave. Dom Leo appears to have been Ford's hand-picked partner for Ealing. Ordained in 1881, he held several posts at Downside before he went to Swansea, where he remained until 1900.[76] When Ford was elected the first Abbot of Downside after the Constitutional Crisis, Dom Leo became his first claustral prior.

No letter or papers survive which record Dom Gilbert's and Dom Vincent's reaction to their new assignments, which they no doubt accepted with pious resignation, or their feelings on leaving Ealing. It was, however, a different matter with some of the parishioners of St Benedict's, who tried to fight the departure of their founder-priest. They circulated a petition which demanded that Dom Gilbert remain in charge at Ealing, and sent it to Abbot Cuthbert Butler. Butler responded immediately. He told the spokesman that by a quick response he hoped to avoid the impression that 'by delaying to give rise to the hopes that will not be realized'.[77] The Abbot began his reply cautiously: 'It does not surprise me that the congregation of St Benedict's . . . should be sorry at the prospect of losing Fr Gilbert Dolan'. He explained that he had sought counsel and 'gave the matter my careful consideration'. Consequently, he told the petitioners that he could not reconsider his decision. 'It naturally costs me a good deal to have to refuse such a Petition as the one that has come to me from so many of the congregation,' he explained, and 'I ask them to bear with me.' He ended his letter by commending both Abbot Ford and Dom Leo Almond to the Parish of St Benedict's, and hoped that time and the ability of these monks would ease the pain of Dom Gilbert's departure.

Dom Gilbert Dolan could proudly count his accomplishments as parish priest in Ealing. The census of 1904 revealed that the congregation numbered approximately 550 people.[78] Seven conversions, nineteen baptisms, and four marriages occurred during the same year. The parish also had three confraternities: the Altar Society, Children of Mary, and the Guild of Ransom.

The 1905 Visitation Report for the Archdiocese of Westminster also recorded the extent of Dolan's successes. This report supplied answers to questions dealing with the religious services, the sacraments, collections, governance of the church property, and the care of the vestments.[79] Concerning pastoral care, Dom Gilbert noted that 'the district is divided between the two of us, and an endeavour is made to visit every house at least once a month'. It also pointed out that the Ealing mission contained an orphanage, the convent of the Holy Child Jesus Sisters, and Twyford Abbey, a community of Alexian brothers. The Ealing monks ministered to the first two institutions. Dom Gilbert's remarks on the social composition of the congregation demonstrated that St Benedict's corresponded to the social structure of Edwardian Ealing. The majority of twenty-two families were of the 'villa rank', and he reckoned that only four belonged to 'the working class'. In addition to several widows, spinsters, and professional men, the parish had an unusually high proportion of 140 Roman Catholic servants and governesses.

On his arrival, Abbot Ford began to exhibit the enthusiasm and energy he possessed when he pioneered the establishment of Ealing during the last century. A greeting from Archbishop's House welcomed Abbot Ford to London and expressed Archbishop Bourne's wishes for 'good health and many consolations in pastoral and other work'.[80] Like his predecessor, financial problems and considerations of expansion dominated Ford's tenure at Ealing. Like Dom Gilbert, he also sought advice from Downside in his struggle to raise money from the Ealing congregation to reduce the debt. And he was complimented by an official of Downside's Mission Fund. 'I must congratulate you on your success at the Interest paying,' Dom Bede Cox told him in January 1908, 'since it is quite a cheerful turn in the Ealing life.'[81] During 1908, Abbot Ford sought to increase the number of regular subscribers and planned 'to ask two or three members of the congregation to act in helping the work of collecting'.[82] He tried not only to tackle the problem of the interest, but also the reduction of the capital debt. His efforts did not go unrewarded. For example, he estimated that the interest due for 1908 amounted to £213, and he proudly recorded that £187 had already been collected.

Although he had always been chary about the extension of the church, Abbot Ford now began to campaign for its completion. His argument sounded similar to that of Dom Gilbert Dolan: the rapidly increasing congregation needed more space. According to a memo written in January 1908, Abbot Ford estimated that the parish numbered over 650. He noted the healthy attendance at Sunday mass, approximately five hundred people, but complained that 'there is a bad custom of coming in after the service has begun, and in not a few cases when a considerable part of the Mass is over'.[83] In addition to expansion, Ford revealed his plans to enlarge the altar and to refurbish the sanctuary with wrought iron and hangings. Other statistics backed up his dreams. His archdiocesan visitation report recorded twelve baptisms, thirteen marriages, and three conversions for 1907.[84] He also noted that the number of domestic servants had jumped from 140 recorded in 1905 to over 256 within two years. 'There is no reason,' he pleaded with Abbot Butler, 'why we should not be considering the question of enlarging the church as a matter which may be called practical in a few years.'[85]

Abbot Ford's biographer notes that 'as he had done at Downside, so now at Ealing he set himself at once to enlarge the church'.[86] In order to collect the necessary funds, 'he got together a representative meeting of the Catholics of Ealing, placed his plans before them, and pointed out the best manner in which funds could be raised'. During 1909, Abbot Ford's drive to finish the parish church got some unexpected support from an anonymous article in *The Tablet*. The writer, identified as a 'Confrater of the English Congregation', described in glowing and highly romantic terms the recent celebration of St Benedict's Day in Ealing. After praising the liturgy, plainchant, and the homily, the author drew attention to the unfinished condition of the church. And his conclusions were obvious. 'At Ealing the monks have built not a church, not even a chancel, but a section of a nave with a temporary wall at each end,' he sadly informed the readers.[87] 'If you want a monument of Benedictine patience or thoroughness,' the article concluded, 'step inside this nucleus of a church and look around.'

But almost immediately after Abbot Ford arrived in Ealing, his health began to deteriorate, and this caused grave concern at Downside. Moreover, Abbot Butler had to face other problems caused by a shortage of manpower at his monastery; a monk stationed at St John's, Bath, became ill, and Butler considered transferring Dom Leo there. In a letter to Abbot President Aidan Gasquet, Abbot Butler discussed the re-assignment, but remarked that it would create 'a vacancy at Ealing which . . . will be difficult to fill'.[88] According to Butler, Abbot Ford 'is still in a fragile state of health, and though we may hope he will be able to administer Ealing, he cannot be relied on to do that work that has to be done there'. In this letter to Gasquet, Butler's feelings on the Ealing mission also emerged. 'I need not point out to you,' he reminded Gasquet, 'the magnitude of the interests at stake at Ealing – financial, monastic, and religious.' Abbot Butler characterized the type of monk he wanted to administer Ealing: 'he must be a man of some standing, strong and healthy, able to do all the Mission work and to take the services and to preach to a cultivated Congregation at a moment's notice'. He suggested, therefore, that a Downside monk who had been loaned to Belmont be recalled and sent to Ealing. Abbot Butler told Gasquet that in proportion to its numbers Downside had already supplied too many monks for congregational duties.

Aidan Gasquet replied and apparently agreed with Butler's proposal to recall one of his monks for re-assignment at Ealing. But the Downside Abbot changed his plans. Dom Leo agreed to go to Bath, but he informed Butler 'that it would be a mistake for him to leave Ealing'.[89] Dom Leo had two reasons to question his superior's policy. In the first place, Ealing had just recently gone through a traumatic change of command. Secondly, he told Abbot Butler that 'it remains to be seen how Ab[bot] Ford will get through the winter'. Abbot Butler did not transfer Dom Leo to Bath, and he informed the Abbot President that 'Fr Leo takes a not very hopeful view of [Ford's] physical condition . . . [and] this is a very serious aspect of the situation'.

Abbot Butler's diagnosis of Ford's stamina proved correct. In April 1909, he expressed his concern for Abbot Ford's delicate condition to Dom Leo: 'I fear we cannot disguise from ourselves the fact that it is quite possible – nay, likely – that Abbot Ford will not be able to resume charge at Ealing'.[90] As soon as it became clear that Abbot Ford could no longer function as the superior at the Ealing foundation, Abbot Butler requested a meeting with Dom Leo. Dom Leo replied to this alarming letter and told his superior that Abbot Ford seemed better and healthier, Butler, not surprisingly, was overjoyed: 'Please God he may be able to go on at Ealing after all'.[91] Still, Abbot Butler took no chances; at the end of the month, he informed the Ealing monks that he was sending Dom Cyril Rylance to Ealing. Dom Sebastian was overjoyed. Dom Cyril's appointment would save the school budget over £150 per annum in a salary the headmaster would otherwise have to pay out for the services of a lay master. In addition to his services at the school, the new Ealing monk would also have some parochial duties such as preaching and hearing confessions. This appointment was no doubt occasioned by Abbot Butler's apprehension over Ford's health. 'My last latter from Ab[bot] Ford is more cheerful,' Butler informed Dom Leo, 'but whether he will be able to continue in charge at Ealing, or whether he and Fr Cyril would be able to work it alone for a month, must remain quite doubtful.'

It appears, however, that Abbot Ford's health continued to give ample cause for concern. Anxiety and exhaustion seemed to be the symptoms. In early May, Abbot Ford took a holiday in Rome. During his stay, he had a papal audience with Pope Pius X, and, according to his biographer, asked for the Pope's approval for the extension of the church at Ealing, which Pius gave on 11 May 1909.[92] This seemed to be the elixir Abbot Ford needed. On his return to Ealing he began to campaign among the parishioners for the financial support for his dream. Assured of their generosity, the work on the enlargement of the church began immediately. Ford's biographer suggested that he got 'a new lease on life and vigour, and he was able to take his part in the parish in the functions of the church'.[93]

But Ford faced more immediate economic problems: the liquidation of the debt to the Mission Fund along with the interest. As the debt decreased, more money could be collected for the church, but the conditions were not favourable. Because of the repayments to the Mission Fund, the average parish income from 1911 to 1915 amounted to approximately £887, while the expenses stood at £2,407.[94] In 1910, for example, the total income to the

Ealing mission was £667, and £129 had been collected towards the debt.[95] The school, on the other hand, experienced a favourable balance of payments. The average yearly receipt for the same period stood at £2,407, compared with expenses which amounted to only £301. But Ford pleaded that the church finances were not as bleak as the books revealed. Unlike the practice during the Gilbert Dolan era, the accounts of the school and the parish had recently been combined. Ford explained this and argued that 'expenses in connection with Missions and Schools are so interdependent, they cannot be separated with any degree of accuracy'.[96] Using this logic, the average yearly income for 1911–15 amounted to a profit of £3,000.

However, the Ealing books may be interpreted, the new extension to St Benedict's began to materialize slowly and steadily. Ford's health, however, again seemed to decline. Consequently, Dom Sebastian directed the campaign to complete the construction. In January 1911, he told Abbot Butler that pressing school duties had monopolized all his spare time, but he was willing to tackle the problems associated with the extension of the church, 'now so urgently needed'.[97] He informed Butler that he was 'going to set to work to collect, not in pounds but in pence'. 'From servants, children and from people too poor to pay in pounds I am now going to begin to collect from all some small amount each week.' In addition to proceeds from concerts and other parish activities, Dom Sebastian believed that the fund would gradually climb. He set his goal at the collection of 500,000 pence (£2083). Abbot Ford's estimation lacked the optimism of Dom Sebastian. In stark contrast to the cheery *Downside Review* report of 1913, which announced 'from Ealing we have good news' and told its readers that 'the growth of the congregation has called for an extension to St Benedict's church there, to which three new bays are to be added',[98] Ford became a prophet of doom. In 1914, for example, he pointed to 'the dangers connected with the money market,' and suggested to Abbot Butler that construction on the church should be halted.[99]

But others continued to dream about Ealing's future. Abbot Butler was one of these people; he abandoned all caution when he announced to Abbot Ford in December 1912 that he intended to have the Ealing mission raised to the rank of a dependent priory. 'In regard to Ealing,' he informed Ford, 'my wish and my endeavour will be to create such a situation there as will make it possible for Ealing to become a "Priory" *secundum Constitutiones*.'[100] Consequently, Butler began to work to insure the quality of manpower at his future priory. He finally decided that Dom Leo was needed at Bath, and he assigned him there in 1912. But Abbot Butler appointed Dom Benedict Kuypers to take his place at Ealing. While Ford was absent during the winter of 1913, Abbot Butler informed the community that 'Fr Sebastian will be superior of the school and what directly concerns it'.[101] At the same time Dom Benedict became the superior of the mission and the community.

The Ealing mission ceased to be an experiment or a romantic dream which sought to implant Benedictines in the nation's capital. Finances appeared healthy. During 1913, the yearly income rose to £1,073 and the contributions to the building fund amounted to £412. Moreover, the interest on the debt had been reduced by nearly £150. Butler continued to dream about priory status for his monks, and the continued growth of the parish testified to the bright future of the Ealing Benedictines. In 1907, for example, the Ealing mission reported to Archbishop's House that approximately 513 adults attended mass on Sunday.[102] Commenting on the size, Ford noted that it was 'good in proportion to the total number of the congregation which is about 750'.[103] 'On the other hand it must be remembered that in this congregation the children too young to attend mass is very small and that there are scarcely any persons prevented by the conditions of extreme poverty'. He again isolated one area for improvement in this optimistic report. 'While the attendance is good, there is a bad custom of coming in after the service has begun, and in not a few cases when a considerable part of the Mass is over.' But human frailty did not entirely account for this bad habit. According to Ford, 'it is a pity that we have not a bell which could be rung for a minute or two before the services begin'. Moreover, he continued, 'we have not even a good clock in the church'. This report also revealed that the Benedictines baptized twelve children and blessed ten marriages. The enrolment at the Sunday catechism numbered twenty-six, and Ford proudly boasted that none of the children attended non-Catholic schools.[104]

The 1911 Visitation Report had revealed that the growth of the parish had reached a plateau.[105] It reported that approximately 513 adults attended Sunday mass, and estimated the total number of parishioners at 750. In 1914, however, Abbot Ford reported a significant improvement in numbers, and told Archbishop's House that the total population of the parish numbered close to 1,000.[106] A record high twenty-four baptisms during the same year also testified to the further steady growth of the parish. Moreover it was estimated that 650 attended Sunday mass. Butler's dream of a completed church to house this expanding congregation, however, did not occur until the outbreak of hostilities on the Continent in August 1914.

Like the steady development of the parish, the Benedictine school also survived its humble beginning and blossomed into a respectable and financially solvent endeavour. Commenting on the opening of the building which would temporarily house the new school, the *Catholic Weekly* captured the sense of excitement and optimism. The paper noted that 'solid proof of their zealous labours is now at hand in the opening of a very handsomely appointed and commodious school'.[107] This accomplishment represented 'a great improvement upon the makeshift school . . . at the monastery in Blakesley Avenue'. During the same year, 1904, Dom Sebastian had sought the advice of Abbot Ford, who was still the superior at Downside. Although he continued to counsel Dom Sebastian, Ford told his headmaster that he was 'burdening . . .

[himself] unnecessarily in sending reports every *fortnight*'.[108] 'Every month would be enough,' the Abbot told him.

Nonetheless, Abbot Ford did express his opinions and did exert his influence even in the smallest matters concerning the school. In 1904, for example, he questioned Dom Sebastian on the wording of the proposed school prospectus. Ford suggested that the short distance from public transport should be emphasized. In the descriptions of Geography, Modern Languages, and Science, Ford advised Dom Sebastian that 'you want to use the terms which the business man will understand, and to state the particular parts of the subject which he will look for'. Ford also wanted the rules and regulations for the day-students spelled out in clear language, and again he sent Dom Sebastian some suggestions. 'As the school grows you will find it will become necessary to have such rules,' he advised. 'You can understand them now without difficulty just for the very reason that they are not yet much if ay [*sic*] all needed; you will find it very difficult to impose them later.' On the other hand, Abbot Ford believed that the prospectus should eschew all descriptions of the methods, philosophy, and 'enlarged statements of the course in any subjects'.

While Abbot of Downside, Ford also settled differences of opinion and addressed the tensions which naturally arose between school and parish. Concerning space in the new building, for example, Ford intervened and settled the problem. 'I have written to Fr Gilbert,' he told Dom Sebastian, 'and have, I hope, made things clear, to wit, that the new building is the school, to be used only for school purposes.'[109] Questions dealing with everything from the qualifications of a lay master, space for the students, and even plumbing were referred to Downside for advice and consultation. Dom Sebastian also sent a brief description of every potential student to Abbot Ford. When the headmaster heard a rumour that a family with one or two boys planned to move into Ealing, he begged Abbot Ford to write the father and try to convince him to send his sons to St Benedict's school.[110] Ford agreed, and recommended Dom Sebastian's school to the father. 'The school has now gone into a good building with plenty of room and accommodation,' the Abbot wrote, and 'besides our priests are good masters are engaged for modern languages and other work'.[111]

With this slavery to detail and the intimate partnership between headmaster and Abbot, the Benedictine school firmly implanted itself within the fabric of the suburb. In 1904, when the school moved into its new quarters, the enrolment had already reached thirty-two, and a former student reminisced that the school occupied 'two or three rooms in the semi-basement of the building'.[112] As yet there were no playing fields or playground, and the small concrete area between the church and school building served as both. In 1905, Dom Denis Goolden joined the teaching staff of the school.[113] A Downside Old Boy, he went up to Christ's College, Cambridge, and took honours in the

Classical Tripos. After ordination, he was assigned to Ealing to teach classics, an appointment which lasted nearly twelve years. During the same year as his appointment, the school experienced a sudden and unexpected jump in enrolment: nearly fifteen students from the short-lived St Charles, Bayswater, entered the Benedictine school.

The next several years also saw the physical plant of the school expanding. In 1906, the tenant living in Orchard Dene (5 Montpelier Avenue) moved. Needing more space, Dom Sebastian quickly transferred the administration, classrooms, and boarders into this spacious Victorian house. The *Downside Review* recognized the significance of this move and told its readers that 'the change seems in every aspect to have been one for the better'.[114] 'Dom Sebastian is to be congratulated upon the success he has achieved during the five years the school has been in existence,' the article continued, ' and upon the steadily increasing numbers which are a sure sign of efficiency.' With this change of venue for the school, the parish Fathers soon moved out of 39 Blakesley Avenue across the street to the former school, now called the 'Priory.'

Playing fields were next added to the school's possessions. The monks purchased the main portion of the Perivale playing fields, twelve acres, for £1,500 in June 1906. During the following year, Dom Sebastian asked Downside for permission to purchase an additional two acres and a wooden pavilion at the same site. But Abbot Butler had some reservations about asking the Downside Council for this additional funding. 'The question is,' he told Dom Sebastian, 'have we the money?'[115] Butler pointed out that 'already we have sunk in Ealing, out of house and mission funds, over £30,000'. The Abbot told the anxious headmaster that he had 'not the courage or nerve for finance on this magnificent scale'. Nonetheless, he told Dom Sebastian that he would present the proposal to his Council. And Abbot Butler must have been persuasive. Provided that Ealing's solicitors could get a mortgage, the Downside Council approved the purchase of the land and dwelling for £700.[116] Abbot Butler ended his letter with restraining encouragement: 'As soon as it can be done Ealing school should be put on a sound commercial basis'. 'But,' he added, 'I have been advocating the view that it would be a mistake to throttle the school – so don't be alarmed!' In 1910, therefore, the construction of a new gymnasium, and a cricket pavilion in 1913, increased the sports facilities at Ealing.

Dom Sebastian's school also enjoyed high-level ecclesiastical approval and sanction. In 1905, Archbishop Francis Bourne joined with Abbot Ford, Dom Sebastian, and Abbot President Aidan Gasquet to celebrate prize-giving at the Benedictine school. Bourne told those gathered that he agreed to attend the festivities 'to testify as publicly as he could to the importance of the work in which they were all engaged . . . [and] as a sign of the . . . gratitude he felt to all the Catholics in Ealing'.[117] He praised the Benedictines for their efforts and

assured the parents that they had every reason to be proud of their local
Catholic school. Nine years later, in 1914, Aidan Gasquet, by then a Cardinal,
also attended a prize-giving at Ealing, and the local press gave extended
coverage to the event. After an address by Abbot Ford, Cardinal Gasquet
commented on his work in Rome, the revision of the Latin Bible, but he did
not minimize the educational apostolate and the accomplishments of his
confrères in Ealing. 'We are living in very strenuous days,' he told the
assembly, and 'to neglect the opportunities of education means the spelling of
failure altogether'.[119] After noting the intellectural accomplishments of the
Roman Catholics in America, he congratulated the monks and concluded by
telling them that 'as Catholics, [we]are bound by our allegiance to our religion,
to do the utmost in this matter'.

Not only a growth in numbers and publicity, but a series of accomplishments marked the life of the Benedictine school prior to the Great War. In
1908, for example, the fashionable journal, *The Whitehall Review*, published
a complimentary pictorial essay on the Ealing school. The original dream of
a proper and respectable public school situated in the equally fashionable
suburb appeared to have been realized. 'Situated in an exclusive residential
neighbourhood,' the article began, was a relatively new school, but it could
'claim parentage from the oldest and most respected traditions of Catholic
education.'[119] Its educational credentials could be judged by its sudden climb
in enrolment, from three to seventy in six years. The story clearly demonstrated what class of people the school wanted to recruit, and it emphasized
the preponderance of roses, gardens, and trees in Ealing. Moreover, 'among
the London suburbs it claims to rank with the prettiest, the healthiest, and the
most select'. The description of the school furnishings also appealed to the
upper-middle class: 'Having been a high-class residence, it is fitted up in a
refined and complete manner . . . the rooms are bright, spacious . . . and are
fully and suitably furnished'. A 'capable' matron took care of the needs of the
boarders. Parents were also reminded that the Benedictines encouraged a
family spirit: the boys and their masters took their meals together in the
dining-room of the school's refectory. Day-students were also invited to the
mid-day meal.

The true test of the worth of a school was not the social class of its clientele
or recognition by exclusive magazines, but the results of public examinations.
By 1908, Ealing attempted to prepare its students for the Oxford Local
Examination, Preliminary, Junior, and Senior, for the London Matriculation,
and for the Royal Navy. In its short life, the Benedictine school did have a
solid claim to respectability. During the first six years, 23 out of 29 candidates
who sat for the competitive public examinations succeeded. In 1913, for
example, the *Downside Review* announced another fruitful year. According
to the article, 'the school did credit to itself and to Dom Sebastian Cave, its

headmaster'.[120] At the July Oxford local examinations, eighteen candidates secured a pass, and of these six passed with honour.

Quite early, Ealing had recognized the importance of science in its curriculum. In 1910, a science laboratory was built and the services of a qualified master obtained. Dom Sebastian could not hide his pride. He once boasted to Abbot Ford that his school was better equipped than any school in the area. Financial solvency presented another litmus test for success, and the Benedictine school received full marks. In 1911, Dom Sebastian told his superiors that 'we have between 60 and 70 boys and of those 14 are boarders – they alone bring in close to £1,000 a year'.[121] From 1911–15, the yearly average expenses of the school were estimated to be £301, while the receipts for the same period were £1,821: a yearly profit of £1,520. In 1914, the school showed an enrolment of seventy boys, but another happening cast a pall over this triumph. The same year also saw the death of Ealing's premier mission priest, Dom Gilbert Dolan, who died on 10 April 1914.

Unpredictable external factors, however, tended to interrupt the growth of the parish and school. Complaints and the threats of a neighbourhood petition against the school because of alleged noisy conduct evaporated after the school moved from 39 Blakesley Avenue to its new quarters, but the tenant who occupied Orchard Dene when the Benedictines purchased it provided more headaches. Until he left in 1906, he made constant demands for extensive improvements, such as hot water service, modern sanitary arrangements, and even a ground-floor billiard room. The stormy relation between the Benedictines and the Society of the Holy Child Jesus of Mayfield lasted longer and proved more tense. The nuns arrived in Ealing and opened their school in Castle Hill House on 14 January 1901. The five nuns welcomed one boarder and five day-students. A sixth sister soon arrived, and on 25 May, the first mass was said in the convent chapel and the Blessed Sacrament was reserved. Like its Benedictine counterpart, the growth of this school was slow, but steady. The initial contact between the monks and the nuns appeared cordial and friendly. In 1903, Dom Sebastian told Abbot Ford the relationship between the two religious communities could be described as warm, and he pointed out that a friendship had developed between himself and the Mother Superior. She had many contacts and even tried to recruit a few boys for the Benedictine school.

But the friendly contacts soon disappeared. In 1904, the convent school numbered 24 day-scholars and 20 boarders, and the close proximity of the boys in their new building, twenty-five yards from Castle Hill House, terrified and alarmed the nuns. They had already complained while the boys were housed in their old residence, and once in their new house, the Benedictine boys allegedly terrorized their female counterparts. The Mother Superior informed Abbot Ford that 'one of our little boys had his forehead cut open by a brick from the above building . . . [and] on another occasion a large piece of stone or brick was thrown amongst the girls'.[122] But other dangers lurked; the possibility of romantic trysts between students of the two schools frightened the nuns. 'Then again notes have been passed over the wooden palisade,' the same nun informed Ford, 'and meetings arranged.' She described her feelings on the situation as: 'altogether very disagreeable'. Illicit rendez-vous *per se* were not the only reason for concern and worry. She told Abbot Ford that she also feared that 'our parents might object to our school on this account'. Sister Maria claimed that she had experienced difficulty in persuading certain 'mothers to place their elder daughters with us'. She ended this letter with a thinly veiled threat: 'I must ask your forgiveness for writing as I do . . . but as it may mean our having to relinquish our work at Ealing, I feel bound to tell you what we think'.

Abbot Ford responded quickly to this possible crisis. Not only were the nuns rent-paying tenants, but from the beginning they had played an instrumental part in Ealing's long-range educational programme. Couched in the language of tact and diplomacy, Ford responded: 'I have anticipated the difficulties to which your letter refers,' he begun, 'and I think I have prevented their recurrence by establishing a neutral "buffer state" between the two playgrounds.'[123] He sent her a ground plan of the monks' property, which he asked her to return, and marked out the proposed neutral zone, 'an enclosed garden for the priests which would make the buffer continuous with your fence'. Other arrangements could be made, and he assured the Mother Superior that 'some definite rules [will] be drawn up for the regulation of matters in play hours'. Ford then informed Dom Sebastian of the problem, outlined the creation of 'an enclosed "garden" between the convent and the boys' playground', and asked him to compose some rules governing the area'.[124] He also told another monk what he planned to do, and expressed a hope that 'by having some fixed rules affecting the boys and girls' play hours, we ought to be able to avoid the difficulties of the past'.[125]

Abbot Ford's solution did not impress the nuns. According to sister Maria, 'we cannot make ourselves happy – even with the proposed amendment of the "buffer" state'.[126] She continued her criticism of the Benedictine boys and emphasized the romantic nature of some of the meetings between the boys and girls and pointed out some sexual implications. 'There are windows from the "Priory" overlooking the girls' playground from which conversations can easily and privately be held,' she wrote Abbot Ford. More importantly, 'there are trees which the boys climb and watch the girls . . . , and altogether the close proximity of the boys and the temptations to human nature have a serious aspect for us.' Again, Sister Maria threatened Ford and explained that 'we shall be sorry to relinquish our work at Ealing'. She tried to justify her concern: 'our first experience with girls is our only apology'. Abbot Ford responded with a modification to his previous plan. The boys 'cannot have access to the rooms where the windows overlook your playground; and the garden is going to be cleared of much undergrowth and two fences put up'.[127] He also told the Mother Superior to avoid the temptation to anxiety of suspicion. 'We have provided against the boys troubling the girls,' he assured her, but he also queried, 'what about the girls troubling the boys?' Abbot Ford ended his short note with a touch of educational philosophy. He promised to visit the convent soon, and remarked that 'later you will come to my view that the boys and the girls should be brought up together'.

This crisis passed, and the two schools existed in a spirit of friendship, co-operation, and isolation. But after nearly ten years at Castle Hill House, the Society of the Holy Child Jesus decided to leave Ealing. In March 1910, Mother Mary Frances, Superior General of the Order, broke the news to Abbot Cuthbert Butler. 'It is with real regret I write to tell you that we find it necessary to withdraw our nuns from Ealing,' she told the Abbot.[128] If the monks failed to find another community of nuns to staff the school, she promised that 'our sisters will continue to work until such arrangements can be made to relieve them'. She feared leaving 'the Mission without a school for the Catholic girls'. The only reason which prompted this sudden move was that 'circumstances made it necessary to close the Convent'.[129] This piece of news saddened Abbot Butler. He wrote to the superior at Ealing and told her that 'when last at Ealing I heard some rumours that prepared me for your letter, though was led to hope that probably they would not take shape'.[130] Butler told her that certain details would have to be worked out with Abbot Ford, who unfortunately would be away in Europe for several months. Abbot Butler also thanked the Mother Superior for allowing her nuns to remain at Ealing until other arrangements could be made for another community to take over the school. And a new community was quickly found. Forced to leave France because of the renewed persecution of religious orders and the growing wave of secularism, the English Canonesses of St Augustine accepted Abbot Ford's invitation to live at Castle Hill House and continue a school for girls, and it soon opened for seventeen students.

One individual, however, tried to dissuade these nuns from moving into Castle Hill House. When Father Richard O'Halloran found out that the Canonesses of St Augustine had arrived at Castle Hill House to continue the girls' school, he wrote to the superior and informed her that he was 'the Parish priest in union with the Holy See and the Archbishop of Westminster'.[131] He claimed that the Benedictine monks were 'irregular intruders', and that 'the priestly ministrations of the Benedictines are *illicit* and without any authority from Rome'. He suggested that the nuns 'refuse to accept their priestly offices' and seek advice from Rome.

Father O'Halloran continued to represent the greatest threat to the stability, reputation, and success of the Ealing Benedictines. In spite of ecclesiastical suspension and condemnation by Archbishop's House, his Mattock Lane church not only survived, but even showed signs of expansion. A religious census of London churches taken in 1904, for example, revealed that 65 people attended O'Halloran's Sunday morning service, and 43, the evening.[132] O'Halloran's rebellious activities also became infectious. Under his direction, St Cyprian's Catholic Church, Longcott, in nearby Gunnersbury, was opened in 1903 in opposition to the tactics of Archbishop's House. The *Daily Chronicle* reported that a Roman Catholic priest had recently taken over this mission, and it pointed out that this was 'the second mission in the . . . diocese of Westminster that has openly proclaimed itself in revolt' and hinted that other secular priests contemplated similar moves.[133] The local Ealing paper later reported that Cardinal Vaughan had simply transferred the priest in charge of this breakaway church, and thus quelled any schism. It also noted that Father O'Halloran's 'Secular Mission' had not been closed, and moreover, three secular priests had joined O'Halloran at Mattock Lane.[134] In addition to the existence of satellite churches and open support from other disgruntled clerics, Father O'Halloran planned to enlarge the apostolate of his church. If the Benedictines could succeed in establishing a school, then O'Halloran believed that his mission must also have one. In the spring of 1903, he announced his plans to establish a school at Mattock Lane. It would open in the autumn. The Ealing press also continued to report the happenings at O'Halloran's church as faithfully as the events of other local churches. In 1905, for example, the *Middlesex County Times* commented on the celebration of Corpus Christi at Mattock Lane and noted that 'at the early mass large numbers of the parishioners received the bread of life in Holy Communion'.[135]

Father O'Halloran could not avoid trouble, and his name became associated with issues not connected directly with the neighbouring Benedictines. During 1903, he authorized a parishioner, Miss M.E. Webb, to act as his agent and to solicit funds on behalf of the Mattock Lane church. In January, this woman accused an unnamed man of behaving 'in a most ungentlemanly manner', using 'the most insolent language towards her', and witholding 'her letter of credential and authority'.[136] Father O'Halloran threatened legal action unless the man returned the documents, but the individual's solicitors took action first. They sent the letter of authorization from Father O'Halloran and his threat to Archbishop's House. The solicitors then sent a firm and uncompromising letter to the cleric. They denied that their client acted 'in any ungentlemanly way to Miss Webb' and argued that 'she would be liable to prosecution for obtaining money under false pretences'.[137] O'Halloran's credentials and status as a Roman catholic priest became the point of contention. In a letter written to Miss Webb, the solicitors repudiated the charges of rudeness levelled at her by their client and also emphasized O'Halloran's questionable ecclesiastical status. Moreover, they continued, 'The Rev. R. O'Halloran is nothing more than a suspended Catholic Priest . . .

[and] under these circumstances to collect subscriptions on the ground that his church is a Roman Catholic one and that he is a Roman Catholic priest is to obtain money under false pretences'.[138]

Predictably, O'Halloran responded to this challenge, and he dragged Cardinal Vaughan and the Ealing monks into this controversy. Father O'Halloran rushed off two hasty letters to the solicitors. In the first, he forcefully claimed that he was the *bona fide* Roman Catholic priest of Ealing, attacked the integrity of their client, and referred to Vaughan as that 'crafty Cardinal'.[139] He closed this letter with the trademark of his stormy campaign against Cardinal Vaughan and the monks: 'Remind your client that we live in England, not in Spain or Portugal . . . [and] here a Cardinal cannot do what he wills'. Written the following day, O'Halloran's second letter continued his diatribe. Again, he testified to the integrity of Miss Webb, smeared the intentions of their client, and referred to Cardinal Vaughan as 'a fraud'.[140] 'All the world knows *what* a perfect humbug Cardinal Vaughan is in reference to myself,' O'Halloran thundered. 'I am as much Roman Catholic Rector as he is Roman Archbishop of Westminster.' He also informed the solicitors that he planned to forward the correspondence to Rome to serve as an example of the libellous campaign being conducted against him in the London area.

This potentially dangerous situation quickly burnt itself out in an exchange of letters. The solicitors replied to Father O'Halloran's two letters. To call himself a Roman Catholic priest and 'to obtain contributions from people in their belief that they are aiding a "Roman Catholic" Mission, is to obtain money on false pretences.'[141] They openly welcomed a court case, but Father O'Halloran prudently refused to accept the challenge. Responding to their query about O'Halloran's standing in the Roman Catholic Church, Archbishop's House told the solicitors that 'His Eminence says that at present there is nothing further that he can do, and that matters must take their own course'.[142] This letter also clarified the official position on O'Halloran's status as a clergyman: 'I do not think O'H. has been formally excommunicated – but it is possible that he has incurred excommunication *ipso facto*'. Father O'Halloran, however, fired the last shot in this skirmish; his hatred of the Cardinal triggered the outburst. He branded Vaughan as a 'liar' for maintaining that he was not a Roman Catholic priest.[143] Moreover, 'Cardinal Vaughan is the biggest *humbug* that was ever covered by a Cardinal's hat – and history records many Cardinal humbugs.'

Another incident, also related to O'Halloran's feud with Vaughan and the monks, gained some national notice. In 1902 Father O'Halloran and an ex-Roman Catholic priest, Arthur Galton, emerged as leaders of a movement styled 'Revolt From Rome'. The philosophy sounded similar to O'Halloran's blasts against the Ealing Benedictines: the rights of the secular clergy in England were being abused and violated. Moreover, the religious orders constituted the biggest threat to the independence of the secular priests. And the secular press glorified in another scandal associated with the Ealing priest, Richard O'Halloran. According to the newspaper reports, revolution teemed within the ranks of the secular clergy. O'Halloran and Galton argued that approximately 150 priests throughout the country supported the aims of this movement. Critics pointed out the apparent close association between these two individuals and the Old Catholics in England. Responding to this allegation, O'Halloran and Galton pointed out that their clerical revolt was not directed against the venerable and historical office of the papacy, but the alleged 'Italian' control of the Roman Catholic Church. The Roman Curia, they argued, had consciously orchestrated a policy opposed to the interests of the secular clergy in England. And the priestly supporters of 'Revolt From Rome' had vowed to act as a corporate body. In order to protect their rights, therefore, stories of the establishment of a so-called 'subsidiary episcopate' began to surface. The rumour mills had already picked Father O'Halloran as this alternative bishop. When called upon to comment on the reality and significance of this new development, Archbishop's House claimed that it had no knowledge of a 'Revolt From Rome'. Whatever its force or the size of its membership, the movement quickly disappeared. O'Halloran's specific problems with the Ealing monks did not occupy the centre stage of 'Revolt From Rome', but the parallels were clear and unmistakable.

A respite suddenly developed in the querulous relationship between Father O'Halloran and the Ealing monks. Stories which even purported that O'Halloran had surrendered to Archbishop's House over the conflict with the monks found their way to Downside.[144] But in reality Father O'Halloran refused to concede anything to his next door rivals; however, he continued to negotiate with the President of the English Benedictine Congregation, Aidan Gasquet. He did not use the press as his soap box. Although he had previously received little satisfaction from Gasquet, Father O'Halloran initiated this new round of talks in 1903. As usual he did not mince words: 'I notify you that I have lodged a formal application before the Vicar Capitular to set aside your title to Ealing Mission on the ground that it rests on fraud [and] that I am the valid rector'. He probably hoped that Aidan Gasquet would cooperate to bring the 'title to the test before an Ecclesiastical Court', and he appealed to the 'Christian Character of the whole Benedictine Order' to resolve the embarrassing impasse. If O'Halloran believed that he could resolve the conflict peacefully, his abrasive language wrecked any chance of success. He lashed out against Gasquet and told him that his 'grievance is greater than your order in that you both slandered and robbed myself and this secular parish of our Catholic good name and our money.'

O'Halloran immediately fired off another letter to Downside. This time, however, his tone was more suppliant; he asked Gasquet to support him in a 'demand that Rome should grant an independent commission to convene in London – on the spot – and thus put an end to this dreadful scandal which is distracting the Church in this diocese'.[145] He told Gasquet at Archbishop's House had previously agreed to an independent investigation, but soon afterwards unknown 'sinister influences were brought to bear' and the Vicar-General refused to produce certain valuable documents which would prove his contention. According to O'Halloran, the Vicar-General informed him 'that Propaganda refused the investigation and demands an unconditional surrender'. Father O'Halloran clung to his claim that he was an 'incorporated secular of Westminster' and the lawfully appointed priest of Ealing. He pleaded with Gasquet to work for a fair settlement. But again his grating choice of words, reminiscent of the 'Revolt From Rome', destroyed any chance for a peaceful outcome: 'I appeal to you – the Superior General of a numerous, wealthy, and powerful religious order – not to take a mean advantage of the isolated position in which every secular priest is placed – to capture my mission and income by brute force and not by the justice and equity of canonical process'. This letter also represented another phase of O'Halloran's separation from the Roman Church; he abandoned his previous claims of loyalty to the Holy See. 'I cannot be deprived of these rights by the arbitrary will of any man,' he boldly informed Gasquet, 'not even by the Pope – except by canonical trial – if I refuse to surrender voluntarily.' 'Not all the thunder of the Vatican will touch my conscience or cause me to budge one inch in my external conduct in the exercise of my priesthood.'

The simplicity, directness, and brevity of Gasquet's reply must have infuriated Father O'Halloran. He apologized for not responding immediately and told the Ealing priest that he had been away from Downside. But he offered O'Halloran little comfort or solace. 'I fear that I cannot in any way help you to regularize your position at Ealing,' he wrote, because 'it is essentially a matter for you to settle with your Bishop.'[147] Throughout September and October, Father O'Halloran bombarded Aidan Gasquet with letters, often weekly, and begged him to intervene and settle the Ealing debâcle. O'Halloran's arguments began to run thin: the monks possessed no valid title to Ealing; he was a secular priest unlawfully deprived of his rights by a vindictive prelate; forces were at work at Archbishop's House which sought to frustrate his attempts at justice; and his plea for an impartial and independent investigation continued to go unheard. A detailed history of the Ealing debate and lengthy quotations from papal decrees and canons were intended to convert Gasquet, who could heal the wounds at Ealing by helping him get justice. Gasquet's replies revealed his solution to the problem; the entire question belonged under the jurisdiction of the Archbishop.

A new element, however, did emerge. Realizing the weakness of his position and painfully aware of the successes of the Benedictine monks, Father O'Halloran proposed another solution. 'There is the more peaceful way of compromise,' he suggested to Gasquet. 'This is a large district [and] the population here has been increased by thousands since the quarrel began in

1896.'[148] 'There is room enough for two missions and work for many priests.' Gasquet remained unmoved by these arguments, and the last letter from this round of correspondence came from his pen. He prudently avoided any discussion of the Ealing situation with Father O'Halloran, and again pointed out that it was 'so plainly a question between the Archbishop and yourself'.[149]

Father O'Halloran also tried to pursue secret talks with officials at Archbishop's House, but the result was similar to his conversation with Aidan Gasquet. In October 1903 O'Halloran wrote to the new Archbishop, Francis Bourne, and asked for an interview 'to see if we could bring about peace'.[150] Bourne refused to meet him. O'Halloran also sent a letter to Archbishop's House and asked that this be forwarded to Rome. According to his account, this request was also denied. Later in the month, however, Monsignor Fenton invited Father O'Halloran to a 'private and unofficial talk'. O'Halloran recalled that this Monsignor, the Vicar-General, told him that 'the meeting was sanctioned by the Archbishop', and this authorized him to make the following proposal, namely, that the rebel priest should consent to a transfer to a diocese in England – which is neither Westminster nor Middlesbrough'.

Father O'Halloran's recollection of the meeting revealed his growing paranoia and his resolve to fight for his patrimony in Ealing. He told the Vicar-General that 'the late Cardinal was a most dishonourable man' and that his own priestly reputation had 'been so damaged by the Benedictine monks and so vilified by Cardinal Vaughan .that nothing can induce me to accept any proposal which would lead the public to believe that I was in the wrong'.[151] The character of the English hierarchy became the topic of the meeting: 'I have found that English bishops were mean, crafty, unreliable and dishonest'. Consequently, he told the Vicar-General that he had to 'refuse any offer which will not recognize my permanence as Rector of the Ealing Mission'. Moreover, he argued, 'transfers from one diocese to another have not been happy'. He believed that there were only two solutions to the problems at Ealing. The ecclesiastical authorities could divide the area between the Benedictines and his mission at Mattock Lane, or convene a trial before a recognized ecclesiastical court.

Monsignor Fenton told O'Halloran in reply that Archbishop Bourne would raise no objection if he approached Rome and petitioned for a court of inquiry to hear his complaint.[152] Consequently, Father Richard O'Halloran wrote to the Cardinal Prefect of Propaganda Fide and asked for a canonical trial. Nonetheless, O'Halloran felt that Archbishop's House minimized the importance of his requests, and he expressed his anger at this alleged snub to Aidan Gasquet. 'Thus the authorities *fool* men's lives,' he complained, and he refused 'to *cloak* the dishonour of the late Cardinal by going to a third diocese.'[158] By the autumn of 1903, therefore, it appeared that O'Halloran's attempt to negotiate a compromise with Archbishop's House had failed.

Moreover, Father O'Halloran's sudden desire to avoid publicity and his willingness to work through ecclesiastical channels was abruptly shattered by remarks made by Vaughan's successor, Archbishop Bourne, during his March 1904 visit to Ealing. Here the new Archbishop castigated Father O'Halloran and urged the Roman Catholics of the area to avoid him. The day following this inopportune sermon, O'Halloran sent a strong protest to Cardinal Merry Del Val, the English-born Secretary of State. As in the past when he mounted his soap box, O'Halloran used the columns of the local press to air his complaints, and he sent the *Middlesex County Times* a copy of this letter, which it printed. O'Halloran told Merry Del Val about Archbishop Bourne's remarks concerning his alleged position along with the Archbishop's statement that Roman Catholics who attend his Mattock Lane church have sinned. Consequently, he entered an official protest against Archbishop Bourne with the Secretary of State 'for having stated what is not true, and [who] committed an outrage on my faith, dignity, and position as a Catholic priest'.[154] Father O'Halloran asked Cardinal Merry Del Val to register this protest with Pius X. Moreover, he again repeated his wish for an ecclesiastical investigation and trial: 'I ask your Eminence ... to bring the sad condition of this Ealing mission, torn by schism, before the personal knowledge of the Holy Father, and to let him know our desire for a Canonical Inquiry'. The same edition of the paper also printed a petition from members of O'Halloran's parish to Archbishop Bourne which charged him with favouritism towards the monks. It inveighed against the Archbishop's open association with the Benedictine monks and the support extended to their mission. O'Halloran's supporters urged Bourne to cancel any future visits to St Benedict's so that he might be able to judge the merits of the case impartially.

The Benedictines quickly responded to this latest outburst in the press. Dom Gilbert informed Abbot Ford of this attack. He also sent copies of the newspaper story to Archbishop Bourne, Cardinal Merry Del Val, and Aidan Gasquet. Dolan, it appears, wanted legal action taken against Mattock Lane. He told Abbot Ford that a lawyer friend had advised that someone make 'an application to the courts to obtain an injunction to prevent O'H calling himself Roman Catholic Rector of Ealing'.[155] He also told Ford that many Irish bishops and numerous superiors of convents had written to Archbishop Bourne urging him to silence O'Halloran. Archbishop Bourne, however, did not agree with Dom Gilbert's desire to use the power of the courts against Father O'Halloran. In a letter written to Dom Gilbert, he urged caution. 'Personally I should not like a legal action against F. O'Halloran,' Bourne advised, since 'I gathered from you that his supporters are few in numbers, and it is better to ignore him as much as possible.'[156] 'Notoriety would be a gain to him,' Bourne concluded.

And O'Halloran continued to plead his case in the pages of the *Middlesex County Times*. In April 1904, the paper printed the correspondence of the previous year between Father O'Halloran, Gasquet, and Archbishop's House in which he unsuccessfully tried to work a compromise.[157] He also sent the paper his petition to Rome asking for a formal inquest, and emphasized that it was dated 22 October 1903. In a display of anger, he declared that 'no answer has yet come from Rome', and he reminded the readers that while waiting for the reply Bourne had visited Ealing and denounced his church in Mattock Lane as 'schismatical', and his status as 'suspended'. In addition to the press, O'Halloran also approached an unnamed fellow priest and denounced the Benedictines; he claimed that he alone possessed the valid title to Ealing. In this letter, O'Halloran reviewed his past and asked the priest to use his connection in Rome to help his cause. O'Halloran also brought up the question of education. He argued that the monks broke up the 'poor schools' of the area, and consequently 'poor Catholic children have been sent to Protestant Schools'.[158] After the Benedictines 'captured the schools . . . [they] broke them up – confining themselves to a High School for the rich'. This tactic failed; the cleric sent this letter immediately to the Ealing Benedictines.

Father O'Halloran must have sensed that he was losing his battle with the ecclesiastical authorities and the Benedictines, for through the next several years, he kept on the offensive and reprinted all the old documents, reviewed the well-known history of his struggles, and still clung tenaciously to the belief that he had been robbed of his rightful claim to Ealing. But during the flurry of these articles, Rome finally acted. Not surprisingly, the authorities dismissed O'Halloran's case. After a long three-year wait, Propaganda Fide wrote and thanked Archbishop Bourne for the information concerning the O'Halloran affair, and expressed a relief 'that the troubles excited by him are gradually vanishing . . . due to a lack of support and means'.[159] The Cardinal Prefect also noted that Father O'Halloran had frequently addressed petitions to the Holy See. Propaganda then directed Archbishop Bourne to advise Father O'Halloran 'to leave off his rebellion and disobedience and to go away from Ealing, using to this purpose the work of some good priest who knows him'. Bourne was told to remind O'Halloran of Propaganda's earlier decision in 1897 which declared that he did not belong to the Archdiocese of Westminster. Moreover, Rome told the Archbishop to inform the Ealing priest that if there was a problem about the expenditure of his personal funds, the Westminster Curia should examine the case. Propaganda Fide, in other words, refused to make a decision. In fact, it informed Archbishop Bourne that if Father O'Halloran 'turns to a better attitude, we can see what to decide about his case'. Archbishop's House conveyed this information to O'Halloran, who interpreted it as a victory for his crusade. He wrote Dom Aidan Gasquet that 'Rome has condemned the conduct . . . [of Cardinal Vaughan] in exceeding his power in this Ealing dispute'.[160] The onus rested with the Benedictines. 'It is now for you and your monks to decide whether or not you will support Cardinal Vaughan in disobeying Rome and keeping members of my flock in open rebellion against me their lawful pastor.'

Another issue soon pitted Father O'Halloran against the Benedictines, and again the public press provided the venue. As a response to the school established by the monks, Father O'Halloran believed that it was imperative that his mission also have one. Consequently, O'Halloran started a school in 1904, but it quickly drained needed funds from his mission coffers. In the same year, he tried to have his school placed on the rates, but the Council of the Evangelical Free Churches urged the Ealing Educational Committee to reject his motion.[161] The Committee took no action, and O'Halloran withdrew his petition. By 1910, however, he again determined to have his school supported by the rates. Moreover, O'Halloran wanted his facility classified as a *bona fide* Roman Catholic institution. Ealing's religious problems, therefore, would be dramatized in the chambers of the local educational committee.

After Father O'Halloran again approached the Ealing Educational Committee, the long and slow process began. In February 1910, the Committee ruled that it could not incur any expense for 'the proposed Roman Catholic School in Mattock-Lane until the Board of Education placed it on the Grant List'.[162] Moreover, the local authority stated that it would maintain the school only as long as it remained on the List. By October, certain alterations and improvements required by the Board of Education had not been completed, but the local press reported that 'most of the work had been done'.[163] A committee of local Roman Catholics, however, interrupted the work of the Ealing Educational Committee. A deputation from the Ealing and Hanwell branch of the Catholic Federation, led by Mr Hobson-Matthews and Mr Dean, attended one of the meetings of the Education Committee. Hobson-Matthews said that the group represented the Roman Catholics of the borough, and wished to address 'a matter which touched their public interest as ratepayers'.[164] He argued that his people did not oppose the construction of any elementary school or its maintenance from the public purse. But, he continued, 'they objected to this particular school being regarded as a Catholic school, inasmuch as the application for its establishment did not proceed from the Catholic authorities.' Roman Catholic parents, consequently, could not in conscience send their children to this school. 'They . . . asked that in justice, the committee would not allow this school to be classed as a Catholic school.' Also present, Father O'Halloran asked to be recognized after this deputation left, but the chairman refused him permission to speak and pointed out that any communication to the Committee could be conveyed in writing.

Father O'Halloran immediately took his grievances to the local press, which was always eager to report religious controversies. A committee from Mattock Lane voiced their objection to the statement of Hobson-Matthews. They argued that it was absolutely necessary for every parish to be blessed with a school, and they took offence at the indictment that they were not loyal Roman Catholics. In the same edition, O'Halloran castigated the Benedictines as the people responsible for the anti-Catholic charges. 'The Ealing Catholic

Federation is a political organization presided over by the Benedictine monk, the Abbot Ford, O.S.B.,' O'Halloran maintained. Hobson-Matthews later tried to refute Father O'Halloran. He admitted that Ford was the chairman of the Catholic Federation but also pointed out 'that Catholic parents cannot in conscience send their children to any school over which the Rev. Mr O'Halloran exercises any sort of control'.[165] Even *The Tablet* got involved and printed a letter from Hobson-Matthews which outlined the history of the Ealing dispute, and posed the essential question: 'Who is to decide whether a given school is "Roman Catholic" or not?'[166] He answered that recognition by proper Catholic authorities was needed and, as a suspended priest, O'Halloran had forfeited his claim to the heritage of Roman Catholicism.

In December 1910, the Educational Committee seemed to favour Father O'Halloran. It informed the Catholic Federation that the committee had no power over the proposed name of O'Halloran's school and that the attendance officer of the local authority would not require parents to send their children to a particular school. Both sides squared off and dragged up the old arguments, histories, and documents to prove their respective cases. The *Catholic Herald* vehemently condemned O'Halloran. In January 1911, it declared that marriages at the Mattock Lane church were not sacraments: 'a marriage ceremony performed by a suspended priest is null and void in the eyes of the Church, just as a marriage performed in a registry office alone, is null and void'.[167] The paper reminded parents who contemplated sending their children to Father O'Halloran's school that they could not receive the Sacrament of Confirmation.

During the following month, the same paper also alleged that in 1899 Father O'Halloran had been consecrated an Old Catholic bishop, that is, a bishop in the breakaway Old Catholic Church.[168] Angered by these allegations, supporters of the suspended priest took their case to Rome, and the authorities reacted harshly. A letter from the Sacred Congregation of the Council informed Archbishop Bourne that some parishioners had approached Rome seeking justice for their priest. Consequently, the Congregation directed the Archbishop to inform Father O'Halloran of the following decision:

> since the aforesaid priest actively persists in this contumacy and rebellion against ecclesiastical authority, and despite the warnings and paternal exhortations of the Sacred Congregation of Propaganda Fide, has for a long time remained under the censures thus incurred, no Catholic may lawfully make common cause with him, much less acknowledge his spiritual jurisdiction.[169]

Father O'Halloran's last chance at legitimacy, therefore, depended on the findings of the Educational Committee, which had repeatedly postponed its decision because of O'Halloran's tardiness in bringing the school up to required standards. But finally, in September 1911, a decision was reached; O'Halloran's request was denied. The report questioned whether Father

O'Halloran could successfully remedy the deficiences at his facility. Moreover, it noted, the financial well-being depended on his personal income, and not the Roman Catholic Church. In reference to O'Halloran's claim that the school was Roman Catholic, the report stated: '. . . I cannot ignore the fact that, on the evidence before me, he is not in accord with the authorities of the Roman Catholic Church'.[170] Because of a possible public scandal, it continued, parents might refrain from sending their children to this school, and 'for this reason there is some uncertainty as to whether the present numbers can be maintained'. The finding also questioned the accuracy of the number of students contained in the official school register. For these reasons the Ealing Educational Committee denied Father O'Halloran's wish to have his school maintained or supported by the rates.

In a manner now predictable, Father O'Halloran violently attacked this decision in the pages of the Ealing press. In a long letter written to the Secretary of the Board of Education and published in the *Middlesex County Times*, he claimed that 'the whole inquiry was a farce'.[171] 'It was a belated farce,' he complained, and 'brought about by the wire pulling of the monks, who did not produce one rate payer at the inquiry.' He openly alleged that the Board of Education had given into pressures exerted by the Ealing monks: 'Your actions show not equitable administration, but religious persecution at the instigation of the Benedictines'. The disappointed priest maintained that approximately three hundred people had signed a petition in favour of his school. On the other hand, he argued, because of the 'instigation of the Benedictine monks, who hold no mandate from the Pope to destroy our school, whose ecclesiastical claims to enter Ealing rest on deliberate fraud' the findings of the Ealing Educational Committee 'is not just governmental administration'. 'We must have our schools,' Father O'Halloran pleaded, 'we cannot in conscience send our children to non-Catholic schools.'

This struggle to have his school sanctioned by the civil authorities marked Father O'Halloran's last great struggle against the Ealing Benedictines. A few skirmishes, however, did arise. In 1913, for example, the Vatican dispatched an agent who interviewed Cardinal Bourne and Father O'Halloran to gather more information on the Ealing schism. As a result of this visit, O'Halloran published an open letter which alerted his supporters to the words and actions directed against him by the monks. 'Meanwhile it is my duty to warn you against all misguided persons who seek to lead you astray by their fanaticism or ignorance of Christian teachings and Catholic principles.'[172] During the last week of 1913, O'Halloran again appealed to Abbot Butler. The rhetoric sounded familiar: the monks 'have a church here in opposition to me the lawful priest'; their claim rests on fraudulent documents; and his title came from 'the *Supreme* authority of the Holy See and General Councils'.[173]

After nearly two decades of contentiousness and appeals to the authority of Rome, the Vatican finally acted in a decisive and definite fashion. In April

1914, the Sacred Consistorial Congregation formally excommunicated Father Richard O'Halloran.[174] The notification cited the priest's scandalous actions which had created the public schism in Ealing. However, he still continued to minister to the dozen or so members of his small but loyal congregation until his death in 1925.

CHAPTER V

Between the Wars:
A Dependent or
Independent Ealing Priory

Despite ominous noises from Labour, and from Ireland, the growing international tensions and the rumours of war arising from the Continent, the summer of 1914 smiled on the Ealing foundation. On 4 July, the Benedictine Cardinal Aidan Gasquet presided at the school's annual prize day. Speaking of the school's educational programme, he remarked that Abbot Ford and the Benedictines could feel happy because of its accomplishments. According to the first edition of the school's new paper, *Ealing Catholic School Magazine*, the Cardinal 'said that he thought that Ealing School had just reason during the past year to be proud of its achievements, for the test of the work done in a school was the position it took when brought into competition with other schools, and in the past year . . . Ealing school had gained the second place in all England for French at the Senior and Junior Oxford Local Examinations'.[1] The magazine also commented on theatres, sports, and the formation of a choir, which provided 'good music for the Church services'.[2] Moreover, the enrolment had mushroomed to seventy students. Financially, however, the school failed to make a profit or break even.

The parish also blossomed during the last months of peace. In his triennial report to Archbishop's House for 1913, Abbot Ford reported that the total Catholic population had increased to 950 people.[3] He estimated the average number of adults who attended Sunday mass at approximately 650 people, and he stressed that the monks had baptized twenty-four infants. When compared to the last financial report in 1911, which recorded a loss of £222 for that year, the mission had become stable. Ford proudly pointed out that the mission of Ealing had realized a profit of £240. The enlargement of the church also testified to the growth of the Benedictine parish. On 9 July 1913, 'Abbot Ford at Council urged [the] necessity of finishing the substantive portion of the Church'.[4] Ford argued that the size of the church was inadequate and presented a tangible obstacle to the growth of the mission. And he presented the Downside officials with a plan. Ford suggested 'that the payment of interest borrowed for [the] church from the Economus [5] might be held in suspense for five years, so that the whole energies of [the] collectors might go to the Church Building Fund . . ."[6] The Downside Council agreed 'that Abbot Ford should be allowed to proceed with the enlargement of the church', but the feasibility or wisdom of collecting no interest for five years caused concern. A solution, however, emerged: 'the only way of giving effect to the above decision of the Council is that Downside (Monastery) advance the interest yearly to Economus on behalf of Ealing, the money to be recovered from Ealing after the five years'.

Abbot Ford immediately began to plan for the construction. The architect, F.A. Walters, altered the original plans for the sake of economy, but potential contributors were assured that 'the alterations . . . neither reduce the accommodation nor affect the design of the building.'[7] Ford continued to appeal to the generosity of the parish for the needed funds, and money was pledged. A great deal of progress was made on the structure before the shooting at Sarajevo shattered European peace. Construction did not stop, however, after August 1914. The contractor refused to halt work, and moreover, the Asquith government wanted 'business to continue as usual'. And building epitomized the spirit of patriotism. In December 1915, therefore, the *Downside Review* announced that 'the large extension of St Benedict's Church, Ealing . . . has been completed and opened for use', and this only marked another step towards a grand monastic church.[8] 'When completed the church will have a length of over 200 feet, but at present only about half of the total length has been erected.' Another event, however, dampened the spirit of the Ealing mission during the early months of 1914; Dom Gilbert Dolan died on Good Friday at Little Malvern. A sentence in an obituary captured the character of the monk who had struggled to ensure the success and stability of the Benedictines in Ealing: 'He was a man of great ideals, and though his enthusiasm sometimes made him very impractical, yet they were contagious, and inspired many of those with whom he came in contact with lofty ideals'.[9]

The peaceful and smooth operation of the Ealing foundation along traditional Benedictine lines presented difficulties: lack of manpower, illness, and the tension between school, mission, and the monastic life tested the durability and resourcefulness of the monks. In 1909, Dom Leo Almond had informed Abbot Butler that several members of the mission needed a well-deserved holiday and others had been recently troubled by sickness;[10] Dom Sebastian, for example, 'had a troubled term, owing to the measles, and has not been quite well lately'. Dom Leo also told his Abbot that he was searching for a foreign or possibly a neighbouring priest to help ease the burden during the summer holidays, but finding clerical help always presented a problem to the under-staffed mission. Abbot Ford's health continued to present problems as, according to Ford's biographer, 'he was obliged, under doctor's orders, to spend two or three months each year in southern Europe'.[11] Consequently, 'this deprived his small community of his presence among them, it held up important work, and of necessity it imposed extra burdens on the few fathers at Ealing, who had already too much to do'. His fragile health and frequent absences worried many. 'I hope Abbot Ford is not so unwell as to necessitate his abandonment of work here,' Dom Leo wrote to Downside.[12] 'He had bronchitis after the influenza.' In addition to sickness and the paucity of able hands, the outbreak of the Great War placed additional strains upon the Ealing Benedictines.

Recent wars had remained distant from Great Britain. Fought in some remote or romantic part of the Empire, the anguish and suffering seemed to be defused by the magic of newsprint. Local and colonial conflicts occupied centre stage in the history of hostilities. The action of the assassin Princip drastically changed the rules of this game. The Great War was literally a world war of total conflict. The enthusiasm and excitement which greeted Great Britain's entry into the war quickly turned to horror when reports of the mounting casualties, incompetency, and the conditions of trench warfare on the Western Front reached England. The First World War abruptly changed the style of life of upper-class Ealing.[13] Fund-raising campaigns, a Tank Day in 1918 which netted a quarter of a million pounds, volunteer service in hospitals, enrolment in the National Reserves and the Special Constabulary, and the help extended to numerous refugees by the inhabitants of the suburb characterized Ealing's war effort. Some citizens of Ealing agonized over the possibility of enemy air raids, but not a single bomb fell on their borough. Whitestile Road, Brentford, was the nearest casualty of air attack.

The conflict on the Continent did not exempt the Benedictine community, but it did not alter and disrupt their lifestyle as radically as the 1939–45 War. With the exception of the new addition to the church, parochial life continued as normal as possible under wartime conditions. As in the case of other schools and universities, the war left visible and sad scars upon the monks' school. It also contributed to the lost generation of English youth. 'Although the School was only twelve years old when the Great War broke out,' the school magazine later eulogized, 'it took a heavy toll of our boys, and no fewer than twenty-one gave their lives for their country.'[14] The war years also saw a drop in the enrolment and the appointment of a new headmaster in 1916. In the midst of the hostilities, the Benedictines at Ealing and their superiors at Downside debated the future of the London community.

As a young monk, Cuthbert Butler had already taken a keen interest in the potential of Ealing. As Abbot, he continued to dream of a strong and independent monastic community in the London suburb. Abbot Ford's illness presented an opportunity to scrutinize Ealing and to draw up plans for its future. Ford's 'health broke down completely, and he felt obliged in 1915 to write to Abbot Butler asking to be released of his charge' as superior at Ealing.[15] In his letter to Butler, Ford also expressed the view that the time had finally arrived to make Ealing a conventual priory. And in Abbot Butler's mind, 'this seemed to be the occasion to consider carefully the condition of things at Ealing, and a Committee was appointed by the [Downside] Council to go into the matter and report.'[16] In March 1916, therefore, Abbot Butler asked the following Benedictines to investigate and report: Abbot Ford, Wilfrid Corney, Bede Cox, Sebastian Cave, and Bruno Hicks. This committee met at Ealing on 5 July 1916. According to Ford's notes, Abbot Butler had already composed his own report, the 'Ealing Comprehensive Statement', and this was distributed to the membership several days before the meeting.[17]

The scope and extent of the Abbot's statement was accurately reflected in its title. Including his proposal for the future of Ealing, he presented detailed descriptions of the following areas: the extent of and the terms of the ownership of the property at Ealing, the amount of money already expended on the mission, the recent extension of the church, Ealing's source of income, the 'Ealing Account with Downside', and the future prospects for the school. In Abbot Butler's opinion, Ealing's property holdings and the question of ownership represented bright spots. Financially and legally, the Benedictines were secure. The cost of establishing Ealing, however, might have appeared staggering. He estimated that £37,000 had already been invested; funds generated by the Ealing mission had helped to liquidate nearly half of the sum, while Downside had contributed the remainder. Including the overdraft of £1,900 for the new church, the liabilities in 1916 amounted to over £20,900. However, subscriptions continued to help the cause of economic well-being. Since 1909, the ordinary income from the mission averaged only £700 per annum, but nonetheless, Ealing had succeeded in paying the interest, nearly £370 per annum.

It was not so much the money expended or the debt which troubled Abbot Butler, but rather the financial arrangement or agreement between Ealing and Downside. According to the Abbot, 'the current relations with the Monastery Income Account are by no means satisfactory'. Moreover, 'the monastery [Downside] bears landlord's expenses in regard to the houses and properties, and pays the interest on the mortgages'. Downside had not received a penny of rent from Orchard Dene, which was occupied by the school, or from Perivale, the playing fields. Butler explained that 'all these accumulations of landlord's expenses, all cash payments, all arrears of rent and interests are lumped together as "Ealing Estate",' and in 1915 the total amount stood at £3,016. The situation merited serious examination. Did the school help to defray the cost which Downside shouldered? Abbot Butler's statement answered in the negative. After working expenses, Butler explained, Dom Sebastian paid an average of £850 per annum into the Ealing purse, out of which Ford paid 'the rates and taxes, lights and provisions, providing dinner for about 50 boys and all meals for a dozen boarders'. 'According to his [Ford's] Mission sheets,' Butler pointed out, 'the money received from Fr Cave fell short of expenditure in respect of the school by a considerable sum, as much as £250 sometimes'.

With this dismal prognosis, Abbot Butler queried, should Downside jettison Ealing? The Abbot argued that Ealing actually represented a monastic gold mine: 'there can be no practical doubt that our Ealing properties . . . will ultimately become very valuable; so that whatever the outlay on them may be . . . it may be recovered and more than recovered'. Moreover, he reasoned, 'if we hold them long enough, the Ealing properties will be a sound asset for anything spent at Ealing'. The possibility of a proper and vigorous monastic life also seemed within reach, and Abbot Butler declared that 'Ealing is now in a position that it could become a "Dependent Priory".' But the vineyard needed more labourers. Two monks should be assigned to work exclusively on the parish, and employment for six monks could easily be found in the school.

'Moreover, the extension of the Central London Tube to Ealing Broadway is nearly completed, and then the journey to [the] British Museum or Record Office will be hardly more than half-an-hour from door to door; so that anyone engaged in historical or research work could without inconvenience live at Ealing.' If the heavy financial liabilities could be met, there could easily be enough work to support even a dozen monks at Ealing. Abbot Butler painted a bold and grandiose picture of Ealing's future:

> Indeed, with the Church and the property, and the buildings, and the School, and the growing congregation, and the situation, which will before long become thoroughly London, the future of Ealing ought to be as Haverstock Hill, or Stamford Hill, or Wimbledon, a strong religious house, and there is nothing extravagant in the idea that Ealing Priory should in time become an independent, autonomous Benedictine Monastery in London.

The 5 July committee meeting at Ealing was long, and the members considered every aspect of Butler's report in great detail. Abbot Ford seemed annoyed at what he believed was Abbot Butler's attempt to control and dominate the meeting, but Butler remarked that his report was only meant to guide and give direction to the discussion.[19] Ford then immediately questioned the accuracy of some of Abbot Butler's financial statements. Butler responded and stated that he would re-check his figures after he returned to Downside. Abbot Ford, consequently, argued that the financial condition of Ealing was not as bleak as Abbot Butler suggested. Moreover, Ealing's future economic growth did not depend on the property, since the suburb might not expand as much as Abbot Butler predicted; increased income from the school and parish, on the other hand, would meet all financial emergencies. In respect to the remarks about manpower, Abbot Ford reminded the committee that he had already pressed for an additional priest to work on the parish several years ago. He also pointed out that the existing residence for the priests could only house five monks. If the community be increased, then additional space must be found.

In general, however, the committee agreed with Abbot Butler's estimation and description of the Ealing situation. At the end of the meeting,

> the view was strongly held that if Ealing eventually becomes a real, autonomous Benedictine Monastery in London all the expenditure on it will have been very worthwhile; that this is the time to carry out our original undertaking to Cardinal Vaughan to make Ealing a conventual house; that Ealing should be put in possession of the various properties we hold there, and that as soon as it can be done Ealing should receive subjects for itself, and be established as an independent Conventual Priory.[20]

This committee, therefore, adopted two proposals for the future of the Ealing mission: every effort should be made to establish Ealing as a dependent priory under the jurisdiction and supervision of Downside; and second '. . . it should be developed as rapidly as possible into an independent Conventual Priory', separate from Downside. The Ealing committee formulated six resolutions to be placed before the Downside Council later in the month.

This group suggested that Ealing 'be put in possession of the various Ealing properties, with the obligations of paying the interest on the various mortgages'. 'This would mean that in our Monastery Balance Sheet £12,800 Capital Assets, being the cost of the Ealing properties, would be removed.' Also, 'the £9,800 mortgages on the properties would be removed from the Capital liabilities'. Downside should consider the difference, £3,000, as a gift to the London foundation. Moreover, the 'Ealing Estate Account', that is, the so-called 'landlord's expenses' which included such items as arrears in rent, should also be remitted. The title to Glastonbury House, a gift from a private individual, should be handed over to Ealing. The Ealing community, however, would be responsible for the interest on the various outstanding mortgages held by Downside. Ealing would also be liable for the debt of £6,200 owed to the mother house, but on the other hand, it would not be responsible for the interest on the sum: Downside would undertake to pay the interest, £215, to the Economus account for seven years. At the end of this period, it was hoped that both the debt and interest would be extinguished or reduced to such a relatively small figure so as not to burden the new priory. 'On this basis,' Abbot Butler told the Council, 'it is believed that Ealing would be financially workable, and that its financial position could be gradually strengthened and consolidated.'

The findings of the committee also emphasized that Ealing could become financially independent. Their report told the Downside Council that the income from the school and mission 'has proved sufficient in the past few years not only to meet the expenses of School and Mission, and pay [the] interest £109 on the priory, but also to put up the Gymnasium £1,500, kitchen £300, and do very considerable repairs'. But economic caution should not be forgotten: a thirty per cent and forty per cent increase in living expenses was projected; Ealing would still have the responsibility for repairs at Castle Hill House and Glastonbury House; and the community would also bear the cost for the development of land at Perivale. Nonetheless, the committee reasoned, 'the growth of the congregation, and with a sufficient and efficient staff of priests, the receipts from the Mission and from the personal work of the priests, will very considerably increase; and if the school is kept going it may at any time develop'.

Finally, the Council was reminded of the requirements which had been stipulated by *Diu Quidem* and the Constitutions of the English Benedictine Congregation which governed the establishment of any new priory: a community of at least six monks under a Prior appointed by the Abbot of the founding monastery, the recitation of the Divine Office in choir, and the observance of the *vita perfecta communis*. The committee strongly endorsed the following statement. 'Such a Priory would be at first a Dependent Priory, but it is proposed that, as soon as permission can be obtained, subjects should be professed for Ealing, and that every effort should be made to develop it as rapidly as possible into a self-standing, independent Benedictine Monastery.'

The Downside Council approved the recommendations of the Ealing Committee and the London foundation became Ealing Priory. But Council believed that 'until Ealing shall become an independent Priory, it cannot be put in full possession of the Ealing properties'.[21] It felt, however, that 'in order to make the beginning of an independent existence for Ealing, it should be responsible for the administration of the properties there'. The Council also discussed methods of increasing donations and subscriptions to pay off Ealing's capital debt. The re-organization of the school also came under consideration. The Downside Council questioned the feasibility of the current system where school and mission were administrated by an authority independent and separate from each other.[22] One plan advocated giving the monastic superior at Ealing control over both the parochial and educational establishments, a system which had operated at Downside before the abolition of the two provinces in 1899. This, some believed, would bring more order into the system and eliminate some of the tensions and rivalries which had developed between school and parish. Further, this would mold the organization of Ealing along the lines of a bona fide priory. The Downside Council saw the wisdom behind this plan, and gave its approval.

The Council also supported the goal of future independence for the Ealing community, and it suggested that it might be wise to explain this at the next conventual chapter, 'so that the community as a whole may be fully aware of the policy which is being pursued, and their sympathy and support secured for it'. Downside's encouragement and backing for this venture must not be lukewarm: 'to put it at the lowest, the outlook for Ealing in 1916 is enormously brighter than was that of Downside in 1814 . . . and the wonderful success which has crowned their efforts should give us courage to go forward in this venture with equal confidence and hope'.

New blood was required to give force to these recommendations, which the Council approved. The name of the new Prior and questions concerning the membership of the new dependent priory became the business of the Downside Council. Abbot Butler, however, had ideas on both. Earlier in the month, Butler had contacted Dom Roger Hudleston about the possibility of living at Ealing. Dom Roger replied in the affirmative. 'I can now say definitely that I *should* like to go to Ealing and help in its development in some capacity,' he wrote Abbot Butler, but 'preferably *not* as a schoolmaster only.'[23] 'My chief interest is in its becoming a normal monastic house with its own community, and for that end I am quite prepared to devote myself and all that I am worth in whatever way you decide to be best.' The two also discussed some changes in personnel, especially Abbot Ford. Dom Roger approved of Ford's departure from Ealing, but he also maintained that 'the retirement of Abbot Ford ought to be accompanied by that of Fr Sebastian if the new regime is to have a really fair chance, and that the present opportunity for such a fresh start ought certainly not to be let slip'.

Dom Roger's suggestions made good sense. Dom Sebastian Cave had served as headmaster at Ealing for nearly fourteen years. He had struggled to start the school and could take pride in its successes. The sharing of power or authority between the parish and school aggravated a tense situation. And Abbot Ford's frequent absences had also become a source of discontent and irritation. By 1916, Dom Sebastian was complaining formally about Abbot Ford; the situation at Ealing had become intolerable. A letter to Abbot Butler expressed the sense of disorganization and monastic inefficiency which Butler and the Council hoped to rectify. In the first place, Dom Sebastian complained about the manpower shortage. Another monk was urgently needed. Part of the blame must be placed on Abbot Ford and his fragile health. According to Dom Sebastian, 'the Abbot, the head of the mission, has been away for nearly four months and is not back yet'.[24] The parishioners always ask about his return, but 'he no sooner turns up from a four months holiday abroad than he must be off again to recuperate'. Cave confessed that 'we are all very sorry for the Abbot's illness and weak state but business has to be done and there must be someone here to do it who understands the affairs of the place'. Moreover, the laity, he continued, have begun to grumble and speculate: 'it only makes the congregation wild and is much of [the] reason for gossip that Dom Sebastian would no longer be Headmaster at Ealing.'

Abbot Butler had finally reached a decision on the membership of Ealing Priory: Benedict Kuypers, Edward Green, Cyril Rylance, Roger Hudleston, Denis Goolden, and possibly Bede Camm. Both Abbot Ford and Dom Sebastian were to be re-assigned. But the office of Prior still remained vacant. The Downside Council debated the merits of the following monks: Cox,

Almond, Birt, Rawlinson, Cave, Kuypers, Pearson, Camm, Caffrey, and Hudleston, and eventually favoured the appointment of Dom Wulstan Pearson. On 28 July, Abbot Butler sent each new member of the new priory a letter which outlined his dream for the future of Ealing and polled each monk on their choice for the office of Prior. Butler enclosed a copy of the report of the Ealing Committee, and told the monks that 'it may be taken for granted that Ealing will be dealt with on these lines'.[25] He took this opportunity to inform the community that Abbot Ford had resigned and that Dom Sebastain would also be leaving, 'but it's better that neither be said at Ealing yet'. He announced the names of the new Ealing community and revealed the candidates for the job of Prior. 'The final opinion of the Council was clearly in favour of Fr Wulstan Pearson,' Abbot Butler told them, 'but so far he has no knowledge of this, [and] I wish to sound the community before making the appointment.' Consequently he asked each member if Pearson would be an acceptable superior, and if not, he asked for the names of others to fill the office. Abbot Butler also wanted their comment on the following: 'It is considered desirable [that] the Prior should be as Rector of Wimbledon or Stamford Hill, i.e., should combine in himself fundamental functions of Headpriest and Headmaster, his position being much like that of the prior here in olden times'.

The prospective Ealing monks agreed with the decisions reached at the Downside Council, and approved of Butler's redefined duties of the Prior and gave their assent to the name of Dom Wulstan for that job. Dom Edward Green, for example, replied and told Abbot Butler that 'Fr Wulstan would make an excellent superior and I should be very glad to work with him again, as I did so many years at Downside'.[26] Dom Cyril Rylance was more blunt. He believed that Dom Wulstan outdistanced all other candidates 'as head of [the] mission or the whole place'.[27] Moreover, 'of all the other names discussed only two others were *possible* to my mind'. Not everyone wanted Dom Wulstan as their superior. Dom Denis Goolden initially lent his support to the appointment of Dom Wulstan, but later revealed that Abbot Butler's choice did not enkindle much enthusiasm in him. Although he believed that Dom Wulstan would make a fine headmaster, Dom Denis did not think 'Fr Wulstan would make a good superior for this place although if he is appointed I personally would not have any difficulty in working under him'.[28] The responses of the other community members have not survived, but it was clear that the Ealing community, like the Downside Council, wanted Dom Wulstan Pearson as their first Prior. Moreover, the Ealing monks voiced general support for combining the duties of the headmaster and the 'head priest' in the office of Prior.

Abbot Butler had to convince Dom Wulstan, who was stationed at St Mary's, Liverpool, to become Ealing's superior. Butler wrote to him on 7 August 1916 and informed him of the departures of Abbot Ford and Dom

Sebastian from Ealing, and revealed the names of the new community. The Abbot then addressed the question of the Prior. 'It was I may say the unanimous feeling of the Council, accepted with approval and pleasure by the members of the Ealing community that you are the man to work the place.'[29] Abbot Butler's charge was succient: 'Accordingly, I hereby appoint you PRIOR OF EALING'.

The Abbot then outlined the shape and thrust that he wanted the office of prior to take. The Prior of Ealing would function as the headmaster and head priest; 'the practical experience of the Jesuits is worth learning from in the working of such establishments'. Abbot Butler probably anticipated some hesitancy on the part of his candidate, and he told Dom Wulstan that the job represented an 'important and responsible position [and] you will have the good will and confidence of us all . . .' He concluded on a positive and affirmative note: 'I have no doubt you will find it congenial, as you will have . . . school work, and there is . . . an element in the mission you will deal with better than anyone here now.'

Shocked and stunned, Dom Wulstan replied in a whimsical but serious manner. 'Fr Leander used to love dropping bombs,' he told his superior, 'but the one you have just exploded is a real high explosive.'[30] He thanked his Abbot for the confidence he placed in him, but argued that 'the scheme is so vast and the ideas so new that I must have a day or two to pray about them and think over them before replying to you'. On the following day, Dom Wulstan wrote a long and passionate letter begging Abbot Butler to reconsider this appointment. Expressing his surprise at the Abbot's letter and telling him that he had given the matter serious thought, Dom Wulstan came to the following conclusions: 'I am quite clear in my own mind that I am not the man for such a work and therefore beg of you to appoint someone else'.[31] Dom Wulstan than gave his reason behind this decision. He maintained that he was not equipped to deal with any future postulants or novices the priory might receive. Youth had always respected him, but 'all I did inspire in them was a sort of respectful fear'. 'If a group of boys was together talking and laughing my joining them was enough to break up the whole thing in a very few minutes.' Secondly, he did not have the necessary monastic experiences to guide a fledgling foundation; school duties and work on the missions had taken him away from the regular monastic observance. 'I should be a fraud and guilty of the greatest rashness if I undertook to . . . guide others in the highest of the acts, that of the Monastic Life.'

Dom Wulstan continued to search for excuses. He told Abbot Butler that 'the Head of a House like Ealing aspires to, should be . . . known in London and of some position too.' Noting that Abbot Ford excelled in that aspect, he confessed that he knew 'nobody and nobody knows or would know anything about me.' Considerations of finances presented another impediment. 'I know nothing about the first principles,' he complained. 'In about six months the whole business would be in such a muddle. . .' His brother's drinking problem created another serious obstacle. Dom Wulstan explained that in the past his intoxicated brother had sought him out several times in Liverpool, but this did not create a scandal. 'But in a place like Ealing it would be quite different and though the good people there would not consciously take up a different position to me . . . I should not like it to be the subject of conversation at five o'clock tea.' Dom Wulstan concluded by pleading that 'there are many more reasons' why he wanted to decline Abbot Butler's offer, and he told the Abbot that his assignment in Liverpool 'has been the happiest working years of my life'.

Abbot Butler responded and addressed Dom Wulstan's request, which he described as 'very proper' and which 'does credit to you [in] all sorts of ways'.[32] The Abbot told him that he would present the case to the Downside Council, but reminded him that 'if after this I still think it right, I will call on you to submit yourself to my judgement'. Butler again reminded him of the strong support he enjoyed from the Council and the Ealing community, and pointed out that 'the quite ideal person is not to be found for any office, Abbot downwards – we can only hope for the one who for the whole is the best, positively and negatively.' Abbot Butler concluded his letter and assured Dom Wulstan that he was sensitive about his brother's drinking problem and the embarrassment it might create. Dom Wulstan replied and thanked the Abbot for his time and consideration: 'If the Council will only place themselves in my place they will advise aright'.[33]

But the response from Downside smashed all hopes of a compromise. Abbot Butler told Dom Wulstan that he read his letters to the Council and asked for their opinion. 'Their judgement,' the Abbot reported, was 'unanimous and unhesitating that you are clearly the right one for the post; and that being so, that the trouble about your brother being so should not stand in the way of your undertaking the important work to which you are destined.'[34] Abbot Ford attended this meeting, and, according to Butler, stated that the congregation at Ealing was fair and 'even the worse would make no difference in the relations of the congregation to Dom Wulstan.' Abbot Butler's final word on the matter contained elements of gentle encouragement. 'And so,' he concluded, 'perfectly clear intellectually, but with much emotional distress at putting this strain upon you, I confirm my former letter, with full confidence God will work it . . . right for you.'

Dom Wulstan accepted his new appointment with resignation, and told his Abbot that 'in obedience to your order I shall be at Ealing by the end of the week'.[35] But the new Prior could not hide his unhappiness. 'The more I think of it,' he revealed, 'the more I am puzzled at the appointment.' 'Four years ago you told me, and the Council did also, that my work was evidently on the Mission in a big city.' His anxiety at the move became more apparent. 'I am puzzled . . . because after twenty years of teaching and close connection with boys the idea of renewing this does not appeal to me in the least.' However, he realized that not even a final plea could change the mind of his superior at Downside.

> I shall go to Ealing . . . with the full determination with God's help to make things go. If I do not succeed I promise you it shall not be my fault as far as I can help. And if I do not succeed I only beg of you now not to leave me out there but to move me at once.

The *Downside Review* informed its readers of Ealing's new status as a Benedictine priory and announced the name of its new superior. 'Our Mission at Ealing has now been made a properly constituted dependent priory of Downside,' the announcement read, and 'Dom Wulstan Pearson who did so much for Downside during the years he was Prefect, has been appointed prior.'[36] The article listed the membership of the new priory and noted that 'as may be expected, it was necessary for Downside to make some sacrifice for her offspring; and although we do not begrudge what we give, we mourn what we lose.' Downside had lost two members of its teaching staff, Dom Edward Green and Dom Roger Hudleston, and it also had to replace Dom Wulstan at Liverpool.

Born in 1870 in Preston, the new Prior was educated at Douai and Downside, where he was solemnly professed in 1894 and ordained a priest three years later. He began his clerical career as a teacher, and 'for nearly twenty years he taught in the school with remarkable success'.[37] Remembered as an accomplished teacher and a stern disciplinarian, he became First Prefect in 1902. After this long tenure at the school, Dom Wulstan was sent to St Mary's, Liverpool, where he served for nearly four years. At Liverpool, 'he took up his duties as if he had come straight from a seminary – he wanted to learn, not to teach, though it was obvious in a very short time that he was a real master, and an ideal pastor.' These qualities, therefore, commended him as Prior. He arrived at Ealing in September 1916.

The appointment of a new superior and monks also meant the departure of two Benedictines whose lives had been intimately connected with the establishment of this London foundation. Tired and in weak health, Abbot Ford had already asked Abbot Butler to remove him as the superior of Ealing in 1913, and Butler agreed three years later. Ford left Ealing in September 1916, and journeyed to Italy to live with his old friend Aidan Gasquet, who had been created a Cardinal in 1914 by Pope Pius X. During the same month, Dom Sebastian Cave left Ealing for a new assignment at Whitehaven. His successes with Ealing's school were universally recognized. 'He developed a school of seventy boys of all ages out of a handful of four taught in a drawing-room, and the foundations of that school . . . have been sound and strong enough to take the weight and stresses of the buildings built upon them.'[38] He left Ealing 'with a heavy heart,' and 'a string of weeping boys', who accompanied him to the station, attested to his popularity. The school magazine later remarked that 'he did not often revisit Ealing, and seemed burdened with some sadness of regret, that showed still after the lapse of many years and the detractions of responsible work far afield, and revealed how deeply he had felt the parting'.

After the change had taken place, Abbot Butler approached Archbishop's House and notified Cardinal Bourne that Ealing had become a dependent priory of Downside. On 17 August, he wrote to the Cardinal and told him of Abbot Ford's retirement and the appointment of Prior Wulstan as his successor. Butler then addressed the essential and crucial element of change at Ealing. The Abbot wrote 'that the church is completed [and] it makes sense to be the time to carry out the original idea of Ealing and make it a "dependent priory" of Downside, in which a regular community life will be observed'.[39] Consequently, 'the Superior will have the title of Prior.' Abbot Butler expressed a hope that Ealing would develop into a centre of religious life and exert a strong influence throughout the area. Two days later, Bourne replied and thanked Abbot Butler for the information about the reshuffle at Ealing. Cardinal Bourne gave his blessing: 'I quite approve of the suggested arrangements'.[40]

Abbot Butler, however, wanted more from the Cardinal about Ealing's recent elevation to the rank of a dependent priory and the future goal of independence. In November, Butler again wrote to Cardinal Bourne and discussed the status of Ealing. For the time being, he told the Cardinal, Ealing would remain dependent on Downside, but the priory should be encouraged to develop into an independent priory and 'should be allowed . . . as soon as possible, to become independent and live its own life as a normal Benedictine monastery. . .'[41] He explained that dependent priories always strive to become independent of their founding monasteries. Moreover, independence was 'the only dignified status, the only one worthy of London and of the Archdiocese, that it could hold'. 'But,' Abbot Butler argued, 'it will greatly strengthen the position at Ealing if we say that it is our Ealing policy.'

Abbot Butler then anxiously awaited an affirmative statement from Archbishop's House concerning the future independence of the priory in Ealing. Less than a week after his initial letter, the Abbot sent Cardinal Bourne a document concerning the nature and status of Benedictine priories, and remarked that he hoped this additional information 'brought it out into quite clear light'.[42] That document, 'On Dependent and Independent Priories', pointed out that, in the case of the former, the Abbot of the founding house appointed the superior and that the community remained under his jurisdiction.[43] The latter, the independent priory, elected its own superior, enjoyed autonomy, and professed its own members. Butler also noted that this distinction had never arisen in the Dominicans or Franciscans, and he emphasized the historical and canonical aspects of the Ealing situation. *Diu*

Quidem, he continued, governed or legislated for the existence of dependent priories in the English Benedictine Congregation: 'a Dependent Priory is already a canonical Religious House, and its development into an Independent Priory is only a matter of Benedictine polity which does not introduce any change into its essential nature as [a] Religious House'.

Believing that there might be a problem, Abbot Butler tried to argue that the eventual independence of the Ealing community would not constitute the foundation or establishment of a new religious house in the Archdiocese of Westminster. 'Cardinal Vaughan's original permission, to which the consent of the Chapter of Westminster and the H. See was obtained,' had approved of the existence of a proper Benedictine monastery in Ealing, he reminded Cardinal Bourne, and consequently the transition to an independent priory would 'not introduce any legal alteration in the status of the House in its external relations to the diocese, but only in its relation to the Benedictine Body and especially to Downside'. Hints of possible opposition must have reached Butler at Downside, and he struggled to demonstrate that independence did not signal a change in the relationship between Archbishop's House and the Benedictines. He ended his letter with an appeal to earlier archiepiscopal actions: 'it appears that the development of Ealing into [an] Independent Priory . . . is not tantamount to the foundation of a Religious House, for that Ealing already is [a] Dependent Priory, in virtue of Cardinal Vaughan's actions which has never been retracted. . .'

Abbot Butler's fear had some basis; Cardinal Bourne did have doubts about the wisdom or propriety of Ealing being raised to the dignity of an independent priory. In December, the Cardinal invited Abbot Butler to Archbishop's House to discuss the wider implications of the Ealing question. Commenting on the meeting to Dom Wulstan Pearson, the Abbot believed Bourne 'was most kind and sympathetic, but put difficulties and considerations that occurred to him against Ealing becoming [an] autonomous House'.[44] Moreover, according to Abbot Butler, the Cardinal 'said that in any case consent of the Diocesan Chapter would be necessary as previous consent was only for [a] "Dependent Priory".' Consequently, Butler told Dom Wulstan to avoid the word 'independent' in reference to Ealing, and he also urged the Ealing Prior to visit the Cardinal after the forthcoming Christmas holidays. Butler also asked Abbot Ford to intercede with Cardinal Bourne.

The actual wording of the original document or rescript, Abbot Butler believed, might break the impasse created by Cardinal Bourne's apprehensiveness, and consequently, Butler initiated a mad rush to find the now valuable piece of paper. The Downside Abbot asked Dom Roger Hudleston to locate a 'box of bundles for diverse missions sorted and tied up in Ab[bot] Ford's time'. Dom Roger replied that he had 'never seen the copy of the papal rescript about Ealing . . . but no doubt it is among the Ealing papers at Downside'.[45] He told Abbot Butler that the document might be housed in one of Abbot

Ford's rooms at Downside. He also suggested another possible location: 'in the tall mahogany cabinet next to the entrance to [the] Bathroom wing on your floor'. Dom Roger claimed that 'there are a big lot of mission papers in pigeon holes, and of these a large no., I think two or three holes full, refer to Ealing.' The document could not be located, and the Benedictines would not possess a copy for nearly two decades.

Writing from Ealing, Dom Roger tried to calm his Abbot's fears about Cardinal Bourne's motives. He remarked that the Cardinal had every right 'about securing every point with him' about Ealing's future as an independent monastic house.[46] And Dom Roger did not think that Cardinal Bourne 'is in any way opposed to us'. He believed, rather, that 'the Cardinal takes it for granted that all necessary permits . . . were obtained by Cardinal Vaughan in 1897, and so does not interest himself in Ealing as a *new* foundation at all.' In spite of some pressure and constant queries from Downside, Archbishop's House waited for nearly two years before it gave its opinion on the future of an independent Ealing Priory; the disruptions and urgencies caused by the war, especially the question of military chaplains and conscription, took precedence.

In September 1918, Cardinal Bourne finally invited Abbot Butler to London for a meeting about Ealing. After an exchange of letters, 7 November was agreed upon as an acceptable date. When the two prelates met, Cardinal Bourne brutally shattered Abbot Butler's dreams. The Cardinal explained that 'the question of [an] independent Priory had never been considered by Diocesan authorities'.[47] Moreover, he 'deprecated' the concept of independence 'as contrary to [the] interests both of OSB and Diocese'. The Cardinal then attempted to explain that Ealing could not properly conduct a novitiate or educate students. Independence would also make the 'possible useful change of Priests difficult'. Not realizing what had already happened two years previously, Cardinal Bourne told Abbot Butler that he 'would welcome [a] fully constituted *dependent* Priory' in several years.

In the opinion of some Benedictines at both Downside and Ealing, however, questions of manpower at the London priory were more important than a debate about its future independence. Late in 1916, Dom Roger Hudleston raised the alarm. 'Ealing really *does* need more men,' he informed Abbot Butler, 'but I fancy you have heard that said before.'[48] Early in the new year, the same monk told the Abbot that Ealing had been experiencing a bad streak of sickness, and this, consequently, placed additional burdens on the healthy. Dom Roger realized that his plea for assistance might fall on sympathetic but deaf ears because of the war. Chaplains to the forces were needed on the Continent, and some Downside monks eagerly volunteered for service. 'I don't want to make a fuss,' he pleaded with Abbot Butler, 'but before you send any more of the Downside community as chaplains I would beg you to consider whether Ealing has not as good a claim for men',[49] Dom Roger reminded

Abbot Butler that he had previously acknowledged the necessity of at least eight monks stationed at Ealing. The work load demanded the service of two additional monks. 'Of course,' he wrote, 'you will say "but during the war it is not possible".' Dom Roger tried to force Butler to re-consider: 'If Downside can spare three or possibly five men – I really don't see why *one* at least if not two of them cannot come here.' The Ealing monk recognized that 'the prospect of going out to France or elsewhere as a CF is more exciting than that of coming to Ealing as a monk or schoolmaster,' but he continued to urge Abbot Butler to ponder 'diverting one or two . . . who are leaving Downside for war-work as chaplains to home-work here'. The expenses involved in hiring laymen for work in the school, moreover, could not be considered a prudent alternative.

Prior Wulstan emphasized the seriousness of the issue by asking Abbot Butler for a temporary dispensation from the recitation in choir of Prime, one of the offices sung by monks in the morning. He gave sickness and the additional heavy burdens on his monks as the reason. The Abbot granted this request. In another letter to his Prior, Abbot Butler addressed the problem of understaffing. Butler tried to re-assure Prior Wulstan that he 'would be glad to do what can be done.'[50] But it was the war effort that strained Downside's resources. 'At the same time I feel the need for Chaplains is the supreme call now,' Abbot Butler maintained, and he related how 'Fr Dominic gave a pitiable account of things in France.' Butler told Prior Wulstan that he could probably spare Dom Ephrem, who could say masses and 'help to lighten the burden and could do visiting in the parish.' The Prior accepted the offer of Dom Ephrem, who planned to arrive at Ealing during the summer. Unlike Dom Roger, Prior Wulstan told the Abbot that he felt 'very strongly with you about the chaplain question and I feel that we ought to do everything in our power to help'.[51]

Dom Roger, however, continued to voice an approach different from his Prior and Abbot Butler. He could not understand how so many monks could be spared for work as army chaplains while Ealing had to suffer. He thanked Abbot Butler for sending Dom Ephrem, but he candidly admitted that he would rather have someone else. Dom Roger apologized for appearing ungrateful, and confessed that 'we want a man who can take his place socially in the parish, who can also give some help in the School, and who is really willing to do anything that may be asked of him'.[52] He doubted whether the Abbot's candidate could meet the demands and challenges of Ealing; a more experienced monk would fit the bill. These arguments failed to sway Abbot Butler, and the appointment was not changed.

And problems continued to plague Ealing. For a time after his arrival, Prior Wulstan had assumed the position of headmaster, but after a term, the 1916 plan which combined the offices of 'head priest' and that of the headmaster was altered. Dom Denis Goolden took over the important post as headmaster.

In the spring of 1917, the health of this new headmaster 'broke down', and Prior Wulstan appealed to Downside for relief. Abbot Butler replied that he could not contemplate a replacement until the summer. He suggested the name of a possible candidate, but also pointed out that this individual 'could only be Head . . . [and] the [other] burdens would have to be taken off his shoulders by younger men'.[53] But Butler had to take quick action. Consequently, he appointed one of the Ealing monks, Dom Roger Hudleston, as the successor to Dom Denis as headmaster. During the summer, the Abbot also realised that he must re-assign Dom Denis; he left in July 1917 for the mission at Gorey. His replacement, Dom Basil Bolton, arrived in September. Dom Basil came with high recommendations: 'I'm sure he will be a help and a comfort to you – sympathetic, good, earnest, and keen up to his limit'. The trials and headaches associated with staffing and directing Ealing had also drained Abbot Butler, however. After the last rounds of requests and appointments, he threw up his hands and expressed his frustration to Prior Wulstan. 'I suppose,' he confessed, 'humanly speaking, it was [a] mistake to start a Priory during the war, but it was [the] case of striking spark while [the] iron was hot.' The opportunity might have been lost forever. Butler began to philosophise on his eagerness for the priory. Temporary or stopgap measures were out of the question. One must also consider the 'final abandonment of the idea', the Abbot revealed to Prior Wulstan, but he then forcefully declared that 'this is impossible, unjustifiable'.

Not surprisingly, the Ealing Prior also questioned the wisdom of constituting Ealing as a canonical priory. 'I have come to the conclusion that the starting of the Priory idea during the war was quite a mistake.'[54] 'We are admittedly short of men,' the Prior continued, and 'it would have been far wiser and more discreet to have manned the place as a school and mission than to fill the house with men.' Moreover, he begged his Abbot to articulate or clarify Downside's plans for Ealing. 'If it has to go on as a Priory I do think that you ought personally to let it be known what your wishes and ideas are. . .' The Ealing Prior mentioned that Dom Cyril Rylance had hinted about leaving Ealing, and this would mean another monk or additional expense to hire a layman to fill his slot.

The new year, 1918, did not see any solutions for the shortage of Benedictines at Ealing. On 2 January, Prior Wulstan responded to rumours that the recently arrived Dom Ephrem was scheduled to be sent to the mission in Bungay. The Prior needed this monk at Ealing. To find a lay substitute for the school would constitute yet another heavy drain on the fragile budget. In spite of this plea, Abbot Butler assigned Dom Ephrem to the Suffolk mission. The Abbot's letter of appointment revealed that the strain of the war and the demands of Downside's numerous commitments had forced him to make this hard decision. Butler revealed that he was 'determined to bring to an issue the questions raised . . . as to [the] conditions of manning the missions'.[55] The

Ealing headmaster echoed the need for more monks. Speaking for the Prior, Dom Roger invited Abbot Butler to visit Ealing to discuss 'the question of disproportion of work and number of men to do it [which] is becoming increasingly acute'.[56] The school could easily expand, but more qualified monks must be found. Dom Roger, however, soon created another problem for his beleaguered Abbot at Downside. After he had begged for additional men for Ealing and had questioned the policy of sending numerous monks to the Continent as chaplains, he asked Abbot Butler for permission to resign as headmaster in June 1917.[57] In an open letter to the parents of his students, Dom Roger announced that 'Abbot Butler has now granted my request'. For those who knew the contents of his past correspondence with the Abbot and his arguments for an increase of Benedictine manpower at Ealing, Dom Roger's new career might appear as a paradox. Abbot Butler, he told the parents, 'has sanctioned my applying for a commission as a Chaplain to the Forces'. He also announced that Dom Edward Green would take over as headmaster, and that the teaching staff would be strengthened by the arrival of Dom Dunstan Pontifex.

But Prior Wulstan's dissatisfaction and his demands for a transfer eclipsed the urgent demands for help at Ealing. Happiness and contentment always eluded Ealing's Prior. Early in 1917, for example, Prior Wulstan told Abbot Butler that he still hoped 'that you may see your way to move me'.[58] The instability of the community tended to make matters worse, and the Prior did not hide his dissatisfaction from the monks at Ealing. After Dom Ephrem's transfer, one of the Benedictines found the Prior 'quite alarmingly gloomy'.[59] 'As you know his heart is in work like that at Liverpool and he never wanted to come here,' this monk told Abbot Butler, 'so that if he feels he is not being supported in the way he ought to be by Downside, it is morally certain that the hopes you have of finding in him the solution of the long standing "Ealing difficulty" will be disappointed.' Nonetheless, Abbot Butler seemed convinced that Prior Wulstan possessed the strengths and abilities of a good monastic leader. And Butler also had the responsibility of a priory to take into consideration.

Responding to another request from Prior Wulstan for a post on the missions, the Abbot told him that he wanted 'to avoid a mere stopgap arrangement, appointing as Superior someone else "to carry on" who is not the right man'.[60] Abbot Butler tried to reason with the Ealing Prior. A short-term or temporary appointment might harm the growth and spirit of the community, or it might mean 'somebody's life would have to be deranged'. The Abbot's approach seemed a bit patronizing. 'My dear Father, you worry too much,' Abbot Butler wrote in August, and 'you are doing your best and not failing, in [the] judgement of anyone but yourself.'[61]

Abbot Butler's alleged lack of sensitivity finally forced Prior Wulstan to express his frustration and anger. In August, he sent a long and emotional letter to Downside. One could immediately detect a homesickness for Merseyside. 'I can't help but feel . . . that I was taken away from a place where I was supremely happy by these men, some of whom will now want to clear off,' he began, and 'I am never happy in [the] house' at Ealing.[62] He admitted that he enjoyed what parochial work he did, and urged that the priory should become more involved in parish work. Parochial work, and not the monastic routine, should be the primary responsibility or work of Ealing Priory. Prior Wulstan also suggested that the comfortable and wealthy received more attention than others, that is, 'those who don't give dinners'. The Prior ended this letter to Abbot Butler with a forceful and succinct plea: 'Couldn't Fr Benedict then take charge and free me?' The Prior again emphazied that he preferred the duties of a parish priest to the style of living of the priory. 'I sometimes wonder how much longer I can carry on,' he wrote in December.[63] 'I must confess my main interest is to be out of it all.' And he pleaded with his monastic superior to be assigned to parochial work anywhere, even at Ealing. 'If you would like me to stay here and help on the Parish and [the] general work of the House I am ready to do so,' he admitted, but 'honestly I think it would be better not.'

Prior Wulstan Pearson's anxiety also had a philosophical or ideological basis, one which had rocked and would continue to threaten the calm of the English Benedictine Congregation. How much emphasis should English Benedictinism give to the parish work of its monks? The Ealing Prior had strong views: 'I don't think Ealing ought to stand in the way of the proper manning of our Missions'.[64] These constant complaints from Ealing succeeded in disturbing Abbot Butler, who responded in strong and harsh terms. 'I cannot but say that the persistence with which you press your wish surprises me,' the Abbot scolded him, and he told Prior Wulstan that his 'remonstrance before the appointment was perfectly right and so was . . . [the] appeal in the summer, after six months experience'.[65] Then Butler lost his patience. 'But when I then definitely . . . called on you to stick to the post till the end of the War, with virtual promise to release you then, I do think you might have taken it from St Benedict that so is best, not only for Ealing, but for you. . .' Abbot Butler reminded him that shortages and the demands created by the war were trying. Being the Prior at Ealing 'is certainly less of a strain than anyone of the millions of men in the trenches are bearing,' he cajoled, and 'I must say I don't think it is quite worthy of you.' Prior Wulstan's response seemed apologetic and meek. He agreed that a monk could not be selective about his work; candidates 'should not be received unless they are willing to undertake any of and all of our work'.[66] His final word also reflected a spirit of compromise and acceptance. 'Let us have stability and fixity of policy . . . that we may go on with with our work in peace and confidence.'

Relations between the Ealing Prior and the Downside Abbot became less acrimonious and heated. Abbot Butler sincerely hoped that Dom Wulstan would remain in charge at Ealing, and he praised the wonderful work he was doing among the parishioners. 'I ask myself . . . what interest at Ealing is the one [that] will suffer if you go out of it,' Butler wrote. 'It is certainly the parish and the pastoral work, the thing you are above all else keen upon.' The Abbot tried to convince him that the high level of pastoral work depended on his willingness to remain as Prior. The other monks did not have the necessary 'driving power' to manage a successful parish. Even flattery, however, failed to calm Dom Wulstan's troubles. After another of his requests to be relieved of his responsibilities at Ealing, a tired Abbot Butler told the Prior that 'it would be an unjustifiable upsetting of another man's life to make him Prior in the uncertainties as to whether it would be only for nine months'.[67] It suddenly appeared that Prior Wulstan accepted his fate as the superior of Ealing; the stream of appeals to Abbot Butler stopped.

The Prior's discontent, the internal struggles, the urgent need of manpower, and the deprivations caused by the war could not obscure the real success and growth of Ealing Priory. The area of economics and finances saw great improvements. Convinced that Abbot Ford's accounting techniques were 'unworkable', Abbot Butler informed Ealing that he planned to institute the following change in procedure: 'Ealing will be treated as a single financial unit, without attempt to separate Priory and school'. Butler, however, did not want to penalize Ealing in matters financial. He did not minimize the amount that Downside had contributed to start the London foundation, but the Abbot also believed that 'if we want Ealing to go, we must treat it with great generosity' in respect to the debts and mortgages.[68]

The Ealing monks also laboured to raise money to make the priory solvent. Early in 1917, Prior Wulstan initiated a campaign, and circulated a brochure throughout the parish. In an accompanying open letter, he apologized 'for such an appeal . . . when everyone's resources are being severely taxed'.[69] In this pamphlet, the Prior sketched the history and accomplishments of Ealing Priory, and stressed the generous contributions made by Downside. The goal of this fund drive, he stated, aimed to eliminate the capital debt on the priory, £12,800, and its yearly interest, £510. He congratulated his congregation for their support in helping to reduce the amount still owed for the enlargement of the church, and hoped that annual subscriptions could eliminate the mounting interest on the capital debt. Prior Wulstan emphasized that 'all donors who give, or leave by will the sum of £1,000 will be ranked as Founders of the Priory, and for each of them a series of thirty Gregorian Masses will be said at death, besides an annual Mass during life and a special anniversary Mass of Requiem in perpetuity'. The leaflet ended with a letter of encouragement from Cardinal Aidan Gasquet and Abbot Cuthbert Butler.

The drive achieved some success. The church extension overdraft was finally paid in 1918. 'I write to congratulate you and to thank you,' Abbot Butler wrote Dom Benedict Kuypers, who directed this drive, 'both in the name of

Ealing and my own, for every one of the burdens of Ealing removed is [a] load off my shoulders.'[70] 'It's certainly a triumph to have done it, and in War time, quicker than expected,' Butler continued. And the Abbot gave him another charge: 'to make [a] beginning of clearing [the] old debt on [the] church, about £6,000.' 'I know we can rely on you to do what can be done to keep [the] pot boiling,' he concluded, 'and that you will do it more effectively than anyone else.'

Another possible source of income, Castle Hill House, also came under abbatial consideration. The Canonesses of St Augustine had moved out shortly before the war, and consequently the premises failed to generate any income. During the conflict on the Continent, the dwelling housed approximately seventy Belgian refugees. After these people had secured permanent dwellings, someone expressed a keen interest in occupying the house as a tenant. The Benedictines had two options: carry out some minor renovations to meet the demands of the possible occupant; or to take over the premises and remodel it for the use by the priory. The question of repairs to Castle Hill House had wider consequences for the Benedictines; it revealed that the Downside community did not share Abbot Butler's plans and enthusiasm for Ealing. In December 1919, Butler wrote to Dom Benedict Kuypers and sadly told him that he had 'not been able to get others to rise to my own ideas of what is reasonable generosity and backing for Ealing'.[71] The Abbot confessed that he 'quite foolishly failed to carry the Conv[entual] Chapter with me in May in matters of repairs to Castle Hill House'. Abbot Butler, however, never failed to express his deep support for Ealing: 'I . . . am responsible for all these interests . . . [and] am torn in all directions – but in this matter my heart, and my head too, is with you'. At the end of the month, he again expressed his appreciation for the work and dedication of the Ealing monks to reduce the debts. Butler apologized again for his failure to convince Downside to spend the funds on Castle Hill House, but he explained that the demands upon the monastic purse had grown out of proportion. In spite of this setback, the house began to produce some revenue for Ealing Priory; a tenant, the Lambert family, soon occupied it.

The school also showed positive signs of growth despite the rigours and demands of the war and the instability of its staff. In his 1916 statement, Abbot Butler reported that the school, now housed at Orchard Dene, educated about seventy students, but it appeared that the enrolment had reached a wartime plateau. Commenting on the health of the school in 1917, the headmaster, Dom Roger, sounded optimistic. The enrolment stood at 65 boys, of whom 17 were boarders, 'Seven old boys left,' he noted, but 'fifteen new ones have come, so the school is now on the increase.'[72] Dom Roger's report also noted that more monks were needed, but ended on a positive note: 'still we shall survive'. By the end of his first year, the headmaster began to clamour for more space for his growing population; he suggested to Abbot Butler that the school take over Castle Hill House in addition to Orchard Dene. 'The bare fact is that I have had every available bed filled since I became Head Master,' he wrote.

When Dom Roger resigned as headmaster in 1918, Dom Edward Green took over the job; but his health began to fail noticeably, and one of the monks, Dom Dunstan, informed Abbot Butler that 'his continual physical weakness and illness is having a bad effect on the school'.[73] 'I want therefore to say that it does seem to me,' Dom Dunstan continued, 'that a really competent headmaster is urgently needed "here and now".' Abbot Butler chose a replacement. In September 1919, Dom Dominic Young, who had recently returned from the army, was appointed. His tenure of nearly twenty years at this post greatly contributed to the stability and growth of the school. Educated at Downside and Christ's College, Cambridge, the new headmaster enjoyed the educational background necessary for his new job at Ealing. Within three years, he increased the enrolment to nearly a hundred students, of whom 25 were boarders, and began to search for additional space.

The parish also thrived during the first years of Ealing's life as a Benedictine priory. The statistics for 1918, for example, measured substantial growth, but also reflected the realities of war. Prior Wulstan estimated the total Roman Catholic population of Ealing to stand at approximately 1,613: 376 were men, 682 women, and 555 children. Parish life flourished in other ways. In addition to a comprehensive programme which prepared children for First Communion, St Benedict's served three area convents and schools. Because of the growing Roman Catholic population of the area, the monks also begun to lay plans for the future enlargement of the church.

During the 1920s and 1930s, several important additions and subtractions took place in the membership of the Ealing community. In the summer of 1922 Abbot Cuthbert Butler resigned as Abbot to live at Ealing Priory where he remained until his death in 1934. The tensions between the demands of the missions and, according to David Knowles, a movement on the part of some of the Downside monks 'to secure for the monasteries a larger community and for the individual monks at least a possibility of permanent residence under the conditions of claustral life' contributed to Butler's decision to resign.[75] In the past, Downside could adequately fill the vacant gaps in the missions from the ranks of its growing community, and monks had always volunteered for a tour on the missions. The climate suddenly changed. 'In the first place, the growth of the school and of the whole establishment, together with the increase of liturgical observance, demanded a resident community of a size far in excess of that imagined twenty years before.'[76] The demands of Ealing for more monks contributed to this confusion. In 1910, Abbot Butler had already outlined his policy: 'that it be accepted that our first aim should be to increase the resident working community'; and 'that it be recognized that the time has come to begin lessening our sphere of missionary activity'.[77] Naturally, this decision caused some controversy within his community. Moreover, the war and the temporary stoppage of novices aggravated this problem. Butler's re-election in 1914 seemed like a vindication of his vision, but by 1922, according to Knowles, 'Abbot Butler had lost his power of initiative owing to a mixture of compromise in deliberation and irresolution in action'.[78]

One of Abbot Butler's last abbatial actions concerning Ealing reflected his wish to lighten the workload of the monks there. In January 1922, he successfully petitioned Rome for a five-year dispensation from Matins and Lauds for the Ealing Benedictines. The various commitments had overpowered the handful of monks stationed at Ealing Priory. In the mind of Abbot Butler, 'their work in the parish and in teaching in the school is such that I conscientiously declare that for them to attempt to say Matins and Lauds in choir would be a very heavy burden, and indeed in the circumstances . . . hardly possible'.

Scholarship and the promotion of the principles of Roman Catholicism became Butler's apostolate while stationed at Ealing. When Abbot Butler announced his arrival to Cardinal Bourne, the ex-superior made it clear that he was 'not to be the Superior at Ealing'.[79] 'It is the Abbot's [Leander Ramsey] wish that I be quite free to return to the old work of research and writing, which is very congenial to myself.' A biography of Bishop Ullathorne would be his first project. In addition to academics, he also told Bourne that he hoped 'to throw myself into the Catholic Forward Movement'. Abbot Butler's love and aspirations for the future of Ealing Priory, however, never waned. His notes from the 1926 Conventual Chapter at Downside testify to this dedication. In respect to finances, he told the Chapter that the property at Ealing had become 'completely unencumbered'.[80] Moreover, 'it is certainly worth a great deal more money in the market than the £13,000 it has cost Downside'.

The priory's economic health did not monopolize his interest. Ealing must become an independent Benedictine Priory. 'The natural future of Ealing. . .,' he believed, 'would be to become at no distant date an independent House, a Conventual Priory, able to profess subjects for itself.' Ealing could easily find work for twelve monks, and he took the opportunity at the Chapter to warn 'the Abbot and Community that, should the number of effectives fall below eight, it would not be possible to keep things going at the present level'. More monks meant a more powerful and significant presence in the capital. 'An increase would . . . make possible a fuller presentation of Benedictine life and observance,' he argued. 'There is no reason why a quite good standard of Benedictine life should not in time be produced at Ealing.' His final statement to the members of the Downside Chapter might have sounded naïve and visionary. 'I have said that I believe in the near future Ealing may become [an] independent Conventual Priory; but I believe its ultimate destiny is to become a Benedictine Abbey in London.' In a 1928 memorandum, Abbot Butler returned to this theme. He mused that 'there is no reason why a good standard of Benedictine life should not in time be produced at Ealing'.[81] 'The natural future of Ealing, if given scope, would be to become at no distant date an independent House, a Conventual Priory, able to profess subjects for itself.'

Ealing Priory was honoured to have such a scholar and churchman as Abbot Cuthbert Bulter in residence, but in 1924 another event brought the priory even greater prestige. In December, its first Prior, Dom Wulstan Pearson, was appointed the first Bishop of the recently formed Diocese of Lancaster. The *Downside Review* reported that ecclesiastical gossip had hinted that the new Bishop might be a Benedictine, 'but his (Wulstan Pearson) was not among the names that rumour had given us in advance'.[82] The appointment even took the Archbishop of Liverpool, Fredrick William Keating, by surprise. Writing to Downside, the Bishop-elect told his Abbot that the Archbishop of Liverpool 'was rather upset, as he had no idea of anything going on till he received the "Bull".'[83] 'However,' Pearson continued, 'he was very kind to me and told me that it would make no difference and that he would do all he could to start me well.' Prior Wulstan appreciated the problems associated with being named the first Bishop of the new northern diocese. He wanted to visit Lancaster immediately after his appointment became public 'to break the ice there, and there is a lot of ice about'. The possibility of suspicion and jealousy between the secular clergy and the religious orders haunted him. 'A Benedictine is not wanted,' he confided to Abbot Ramsey. Wulstan Pearson was consecrated as Bishop of Lancaster on 24 February 1925, and his departure from Ealing meant that a new Prior had to be found.

The Ealing Community numbered eight monks: Benedict Kuypers, Edward Green, Basil Bolton, Abbot Butler, Maurus Vanthiel, Cyril Rylance, Dominic Young, and Dunstan Pontifex. Dom Benedict Kuypers, who had arrived at Ealing in 1912, emerged as the premier candidate. Several days before Prior Wulstan's appointment became public, Abbot Ramsey wrote and congratulated him. The Abbot also told the new Bishop-elect that 'it is simply impossible to replace you in the true sense of the word'.[84] 'It looks very much as if we ought to make the best of Father Benedict,' he continued, and he asked Dom Wulstan whether 'Father Benedict would be able to carry on the Priory in a satisfactory manner, or whether you think the idea of appointing him should be dismissed'. A question of poor health, not ability, presented a question mark. Abbot Ramsey directed Dom Wulstan to consult with Abbot Butler, and then send the outcome of their deliberations to Downside.

Prior Wulstan hesitated, and his response to Abbot Ramsey was more diplomatic than helpful. He remarked that the Ealing community liked Dom Benedict and his contributions had helped in matters financial. But if appointed Prior, 'he must be given a bit of rope'.[85] Another letter suggested that Abbot Ramsey should consult the entire Ealing community about the choice of their new Prior. 'If you appoint Fr B. "over the heads" of the community here,' he warned, 'it will not be a success.'[86] Dom Wulstan tried to stress the point that Dom Benedict might be the best choice, but Ealing had to be heard. Whether Abbot Ramsey visited the priory and polled its members is not known, but Dom Benedict Kuypers became the community's second Prior in 1925.

That year also witnessed the death of an individual whose life and career had been intimately and emotionally entwined with the Ealing Benedictines. After a week's bout with pneumonia, Reverend Richard O'Halloran died on 13 October 1925. The excommunication by Rome in April 1914 had brought peace and silence to the religious atmosphere of Ealing. Diatribes from his pulpit and attacks against the monks in the local press had ceased, but Father O'Halloran remained at his Mattock Lane residence in active retirement for nearly twenty years. In spite of the Roman prohibition, he continued to say mass 'for himself and his congregation, which steadily dwindled as its members were removed by death . . . [and] there was no influx of new life to compensate for the loss'.[87] One popular legend states that the new Ealing Prior, Dom Benedict, asked Archbishop's House for permission to visit O'Halloran and to bring him the sacraments before he died, but this request was refused. The old rival of the Benedictines died unreconciled to his old church.

After Father O'Halloran died, Prior Benedict viewed the body and telephoned the diocesan authorities for instructions, especially regarding the Blessed Sacrament.[88] Because of possible legal consequences, Cardinal Bourne told the Prior that the Eucharist could be removed only if the person in charge, O'Halloran's housekeeper, consented. Prior Benedict decided to wait until after the funeral to approach the woman. Before the interment, the housekeeper visited Archbishop's House and pleaded for a priest to officiate at the burial of her ex-employer, but this request was denied. Several laymen, therefore, conducted a prayer service at his old Mattock Lane mission, and the same people also presided at a graveside ceremony in nearby Hanwell. After the funeral, Prior Benedict visited the housekeeper. She expressed her willingness for him to take the Blessed Sacrament, but she also hoped that the Cardinal would answer her prayers and send a priest to conduct services at Mattock Lane. Archbishop's House, not surprisingly, refused. After some negotiations between the housekeeper, the diocesan authorities, and Prior Benedict, the Eucharist was removed and the church finally closed.

If the success of an enterprise can be measured by mortar and bricks, then the Ealing parish continued to exhibit signs of phenomenal growth. The completion of the abbey church now seemed a real possibility. The elimination of the church debt through the efforts of Prior Benedict and the urgent need for more space because of the increase in the parish population led the Ealing monks to dream. And the 1923 visitation returns encouraged them: total Roman Catholic population of Ealing borough, 1066; attendance at Sunday mass, 819; and average numbers of communions on Sunday, 249.[89] Five years later, the report again served as a barometer of steady growth. The estimated Catholic population now stood at 1,135, and the estimated number attending Sunday services, 850.[90] Abbot Butler also noted this healthy expansion of St Benedict's parish, and he told Downside that the enlargement of the church had become an urgent need.[91] Prior Benedict Kuypers volunteered to undertake this project. 'This proved the great passion of his life and was crowned before his death by the final completion of the whole structure.'[92] Prior Benedict had directed the earlier additions to the church which were completed in 1915, and he had also been responsible for the construction of the War Memorial in 1928.

With the mortgage cleared in 1925, and with the help of the legacy of Mrs Matilda Schwind, which amounted to nearly £25,000, the work on the church began in earnest during August 1931. The school magazine, *The Priorian*, announced that 'the long awaited development of our church has at last begun, and at the time we write [December 1932] the foundations are practically completed'.[93] The article announced that the addition would consist of four and one half bays, the west front of the nave, an organ chamber in two storeys, and sacristies for altar boys. 'It is expected that when due allowance has been made for the choir and its stalls, comfortable seating for at least six hundred people will be available in the nave.' The local paper also reported on the progress of the work on the church, and told its readers how 'operations were begun this week in cutting down trees and clearing the garden between the temporary end wall of the Church and the road and in making out levels.'[94] Subsequent editions of the school's magazine kept the people of Ealing informed about the project, complete with pictures and impressions of the completed product, descriptions of the columns, capitals, the roofing, and carpentry.

The church was finished in 1934 at an estimated cost of £31,000, of which about £25,000 had been bequeathed by Mrs Schwind, and the first liturgy in the completed structure took place on Whit Sunday, 1934. The *Downside Review* described the church as 'very spacious, among the largest Catholic churches in London', and consequently, 'both community and congregation will have ample accommodation'.[95] Cardinal Bourne visited Ealing in the afternoon and gave his archiepiscopal approval. Another significant change in the fabric of St Benedict's occurred four years later: responsibility for running the parish was separated from the office of the Prior; and Dom Dunstan Pontifex was appointed parish priest in February 1938.

Urgent demands for space forced the school also to expand. In 1922, for example, the enrolment stood at one hundred and the Preparatory School finally moved from the priory building and occupied two classrooms in Castle Hill House. One of Dom Wulstan's last acts as Prior was the purchase of East Down, 56 Eaton Rise, and some adjacent property. Eaton Rise soon developed into the main school building; while Orchard Dene became the residence for the boarders, who were increasing in numbers. In 1929, the Benedictines acquired Glendyne, 54 Eaton Rise, with a hope to develop it as part of the school's facilities. Moreover, the reputation of the Ealing school had become well established. In 1930, the *Downside Review* reported that 'in the recent Certificate examinations Ealing Priory School achieved remarkable results'.[96] This, consequently, contributed to an increase in students. In 1931, for example, the enrolment soared to 168 with 49 boarders, and this forced the monks to build a school refectory next to 54 Eaton Rise. In the following year, the number of students climbed to 175, and this steady growth forced the headmaster to embark on a building programme.

This project represented the last major undertaking in the long tenure of Dom Dominic Young as headmaster of Ealing's school. In the spring of 1936, construction of a building began to join the two houses already occupied by the school on Eaton Rise. 'At long last we are really building something that has hitherto been only a castle in the air, a dream and hope of the future,' *The Priorian* joyfully announced. The magazine told its readers that 'we have sorely needed a school ... where rooms would be the right shape and size, offering less temptation to the wearied heart of the scholar to seek refreshment by gazing raptly through broad window panes or nestling in some nook just around the corner'.[97] Dom Dominic, however, left Ealing before the blessing of the new school extension in 1937, but he left another legacy: during his term as headmaster approximately forty students entered the priesthood or monastic life. His successor, Dom Austin Corney, watched with pride as Archbishop Arthur Hinsley solemnly opened the new building on 6 February 1937. The *Middlesex County Times* reported that the extension had been constructed in an 'up to date style and provides for the maximum amount of light and air'.[98] The article detailed the ceremonial blessing, the prize-giving activities, and printed extracts from the Archbishop's address which urged students 'to live up to a grand old tradition' learned at the Benedictine school.

In the years before the 1939–45 War, therefore, the Benedictines' school had matured and achieved numerous successes: a large physical plant, a sizeable enrolment, and strong showings in public examinations. But the school also witnessed other developments which contributed to its standing among Roman Catholic schools. By the 1930s a school magazine, a cadet corps, athletics and sports, and an Old Boys Association strengthened the fibre of the school. An outstanding staff had also been assembled: Austin Corney (the nephew of Wilfrid and Vincent), Rupert Hall, Basil Bolton, Ambrose Agius, David Knowles, Fabian Pole, Gervase Hobson-Matthews, Andrew Snelgrove, and Clement Hayes. The last year of peace also saw the passing of the individual who had been most influential in the development of the school: Dom Sebastian Cave, founder and past headmaster (1902–16), died at Redditch on Easter Sunday, 17 April 1938.

Although not as grand as in the case of the church or the school, the priory building also underwent some renovations and additions during the decades prior to the war. To provide more space for the monks, another storey was added to the building in 1929. The friends of the monastic community were told that 'the Priory has been greatly improved by the recent additions, which gave another eight rooms with lavatories and bathrooms'.[99] 'The interior is very simple,' the article continued, 'and each room has central heating and hot and cold water laid on, a great convenience and a saving of domestic labour.' Despite some important changes in monastic leadership, the community achieved a stability which eluded it during its early years. During the 1920s and 1930s, four Abbots ruled Downside: Leander Ramsey (1922–29), John Chapman (1929–33), and Bruno Hicks (1933–38), and Sigebert Trafford (1938–46). Another Downside superior and pioneer of the Ealing foundation, Abbot Hugh Edmund Ford, died in 1930.

Ealing Priory also had several Priors during the same period. Superior of Ealing since 1925, Dom Benedict Kuypers died on 31 August 1935, the anniversary of his golden jubilee of monastic life. His obituary emphasized his role in the expansion and construction of the church, but it also noted that 'Father Benedict was first and foremost a splendid type of the Christian Gentleman'.[100] The full-page coverage of his funeral by a local newspaper reflected his popularity in Ealing. Dom Edward Green, who had arrived at Ealing in 1916, was appointed the next Prior by the Abbot of Downside. He did not remain long in office; Dom Mark Pontifex succeeded him in the spring of 1938.

During these changes of leadership, Abbot Cuthbert's old vision of an independent Ealing Priory did not disappear. But the original rescript, which would lend support to the argument, had still not been found despite some frantic searching. In July 1932, an official at Downside wrote to Archbishop's House and confessed that 'we cannot find here any copy of the Papal Rescript authorizing us to make a foundation at Ealing, although it is certain that such a document was obtained'.[101] The letter hypothesized that Cardinal Vaughan had probably kept the prized document, which was consequently housed in the archives at Archbishop's House. The Downside monks asked for a copy of the rescript for the monastic files. Within a week, the long-lost document finally reached Downside Abbey. And after reading the rescript, the Abbot's secretary suggested that Ealing was no longer bound by the original conditions or stipulations. He noted that 'practically all of them have been since set aside by the Cardinal, or by his predecessors'.[102] 'Of course the abandonment of the scheme by which the monks of Ealing were to supply a choir for Westminster Cathedral rendered the original conditions useless, which no doubt is the reason they were set aside.' The discovery of this document, therefore, freed Downside of any conditions or limitations Archbishop's House might insist upon concerning Ealing's future. Independence became a real possibility, but others within the Downside community began to debate the wisdom of an independent Ealing.

Like Abbots Butler and Ramsey, their two successors dealt with questions concerning Ealing's status as a monastic community. This interest, however, arose because of certain difficulties which had always troubled Ealing during its short history. Was Ealing primarily a monastery or a mission in the traditional sense which Downside understood? In addition to this tension between the monastic and parochial interpretation of religious life, the relation between parish, priory, and school had never been adequately addressed, let alone solved. The perennial shortage of monks to operate these three departments exaggerated the problem. In August 1932, Abbot John Chapman visited Ealing to examine some of these difficulties, but no solution or remedy came from the visit. One Ealing monk believed that it might be 'better to leave these things alone and leave us to get on as well as we can until a more definite movement comes'.[103]

The same monk, Dom Basil Bolton, who had arrived at Ealing in September 1917, composed a lengthy memorandum on the nature of his priory, and it captured the difficulties of the 1930s. For the first time, a member of Ealing addressed the question of Ealing's future and analysed the possible courses of development. Dom Basil immediately put his finger on the cause of Ealing's confusion and turmoil. The priory 'is . . . in a process of transition,' he maintained.[104] Looking at its history, he pointed out that Ealing had been founded as 'a *parish* worked by a small community observing common life and reciting the Office'. Was Ealing a monastic institution in the traditional and accepted sense? According to Dom Basil, with the addition of responsibilities for the running of a school 'the monastic side was stagnant'. 'The Office was not attempted,' and life at Ealing resembled 'that of [a] secular priest.' Not until 1922, he noted, did Abbot Ramsey impose 'the obligation of the full Office ex issu Abbatis'. Yet, burdensome outside obligations still took their toll. This Ealing monk told Abbot Chapman that 'under the stress of circumstances Office is performed at times with only two in choir . . . though it has never been omitted'. If numbers were increased, however, 'the full obligation could be undertaken, even throughout vacations'.

Dom Basil pleaded with his Abbot for more monks 'to really man it [Ealing] as a Benedictine monastery'. Again, he captured the essence of the problem: 'We are ready to become a monastery'. 'Hitherto we have been a parish and school with monastic duties superimposed, now we can become a monastery that carries out external works in parish and school.' However, he urged caution in this direction and told Abbot Chapman that 'we must not rush at it'. Dom Basil believed that 'the men who form the community should have their hearts in it' and he also suggested that Benedict Kuypers should be replaced as the superior, because 'We shall need a man of monastic training and good ideals, who will lead and inspire the community in the monastic life, as well as the merely priestly and religious.' As for the community spirit, he described it as good, and what frictions did exist could be solved by the re-assignment of personnel and a re-definition of jobs. In spite of this criticism. Dom Basil saw no pressing emergency threatening Ealing: 'we rather need more strength and men'. The so-called 'Ealing Situation', he maintained, was 'due not to failure, but to success, and to the development and growth that has been made and has now made a monastic resettlement possible.'

Dom Basil also outlined the current views or options concerning the future of Ealing Priory, and he began by stating that it was 'a complex question, for it is not a new foundation that can be started de novo on clear lines, but an already existing institution that requires direction according to ideals that have been developed since its commencement'. If Ealing were a school or parish exclusively, the problems would be minimal, but 'it is something of an anomaly: it has grown and is now flourishing as a parish and school run from a conventual base'. The crucial factor, he believed, had already been voiced at Downside: 'Can it live prosperously as a Benedictine monastery after developing in this rather unorthodox fashion?'

After this reflection, the Ealing monk told his Abbot that Downside faced three choices concerning the future of Ealing Priory: abandon it; grant Ealing the ecclesiastical status of independence; or continue life there as a dependent priory, that is, the status quo. He immediately dismissed the first option since this meant 'destroying a flourishing institution', The other alternatives proved more difficult, and his thoughts revealed the difference of opinions within the Ealing community and at Downside. Dom Basil first addressed the problems involved in monastic independence. 'Ealing has not yet been tried out,' and consequently it 'would seem very rash to cut it adrift before it has really been ascertained whether it can float.' Secondly, he argued that the priory needed a 'strengthening and building up' directed by a 'monastically minded superior'. Moreover, it still remained a question mark if Ealing could financially support a large community. But 'the most serious objection,' he believed, was 'the confined site and limited enclosure'. Also, would Archbishop Hinsley 'consent to a novitiate and an independent house?'

Along with the majority of pre-war Downside, Dom Basil favoured the third proposal, 'to continue on the present status and solidify it', but he also outlined some objections or criticisms of the way Ealing was currently operated. He believed that those who wanted to make Ealing independent created the tensions there. Dom Basil's second point proved more fundamental: 'At Ealing the rather undefined and unsatisfactory status of a dependent priory, which is experimental'. He explained that since the Abbot of Downside was the 'real Superior, the Prior is liable to feel hampered'. An Ealing monk, for example, might appeal to Downside when dissatisfied, and the local superior could be overruled. On the other hand, the Prior enjoyed certain advantages over his immediate superior in Somerset: the Abbot's term was fixed by law, but the

Ealing Prior could continue in office indefinitely; and the latter had more freedom from constitutional and canonical restraints than the Abbot at Downside. Those who wanted independence for Ealing pointed to the problems which then surrounded the stability of the Ealing monks. Dom Basil also noted this strange circumstance: 'besides the above, the fact that they can be moved at any time may tend to cause restlessness under difficulties'.

Nonetheless, since these arguments or reasons should not pressure Downside to grant independence to its London foundation, Dom Basil began to plead his case that Ealing remain a dependent priory for the time being. He told Abbot Chapman that the suspicion or animosity between Ealing and Downside had been exaggerated. Moreover, any dissatisfaction at Ealing had not been as contagious as some believed. Dom Basil even offered a cure for the anomalies associated with the office of Prior. The community could elect their own Prior, or the Abbot of Downside could appoint 'the superior to be elected for a definite period, say four, six or at most eight years, or until the term of his [the Downside Abbot's] own office'. Ealing could also have its own council without jeopardizing the relationship with the mother house.

Dom Basil's lengthy treatise to Abbot Chapman concluded with a final argument for keeping Ealing canonically dependent on Downside Abbey. He believed that 'the course of fully equipping a dependent Priory on trial for some years involves the least change, the least danger of a mistake, and the safest way to a satisfactory final solution by improving and supporting the status quo'. An independent community needed a stable supply of monks, a workable system of government, financial security, the facilities for receiving novices and training the junior monks. Ealing enjoyed none of these necessities. Should Ealing Priory fail, 'withdrawal will still be possible', but if it succeeded, 'independence can still – and in better circumstance – be envisaged'. Dom Basil summed up his position for keeping Ealing dependent on Downside and postponing independence: 'it will tend to enable Ealing to settle its own future more maturely, while at the same time also helping to increase the Downside community and make return for the sacrifice of men sent to it'.

But the difficulties inherent in Ealing's special relationship with Downside did not disappear with a letter from an Ealing monk or by shutting one's monastic eyes; Downside's policy dedicated to the status quo only exacerbated the problems which Dom Basil had described. Abbot Bruno Hicks, who succeeded John Chapman as Abbot of Downside, encountered similar difficulties with the Ealing community. On returning from the London Priory, Abbot Hicks told a junior monk at Downside that he had had a very difficult visit and 'I can't do anything with them'. After another visit in March 1934, the Abbot sent his evaluation of the priory to Prior Benedict Kuypers. He began by congratulating the Prior 'on the magnificent spirit of the community at Ealing and the great affection which they all feel towards you personally'.[105]

Abbot Hicks also made some recommendations dealing with the daily schedule, the monastic routine, and the furnishings of the church. The Prior, for example, should give weekly conferences, and 'except for those who are exempt by the Prior for some duty, permission should be asked to go out of the Enclosure'.

Abbot Hicks gave Prior Benedict another list, which he described as 'orders to be carried out as soon as possible'. Order and regularity must replace the haphazardness which he encountered at Ealing. A priest sacristan must be appointed. 'Women are never to enter the Sanctuary. Work there is always done by men.' Bells must announce conventual duties, monks must not visit another's room, and curfew and the grand Silence must begin at 10.30pm. Any exceptions or deviations from the established rules and customs must be sanctioned by the Prior, and these must be put in writing. Moreover, Ealing's liturgy must conform to the practices and rites of Downside. Abbot Hicks even legislated on the shape of the monastic dining-table in the Ealing refectory. After promising to send additional monks to Ealing, the Abbot explained the reason behind his stern commands. 'I am afraid that this is a large ORDER,' he wrote, 'but it is done to make Ealing, mutatio mutandis, another Downside.' Hick's plan to regularize life at Ealing fell short of its goal, but his successors would embrace his programme with a zeal and a holy vigour.

The Priorian of that year captured the anxiety and hope of the nation. 'The clouds of war loomed large and dark while this issue of the School Magazine was being prepared in the press, and it is with deep gratitude to God, and, under Him, to our Prime Minister, that we are able to appear in the serenity of peace.'[106] The Editorial stated that plans had been made to evacuate the children in the case of hostilities, but it is confidently reported that 'now all is happily normal again and school life carries on as usual'.

CHAPTER VI
Another War and Independence

Before the bombs began to fall on the borough of Ealing, Abbot Hicks had made some significant changes at Downside's London priory. Dom Austin Corney, headmaster of the school since 1936, asked for a re-assignment, and in 1938 Abbot Hicks appointed Dom Adrian Morey to succeed him. During the same year, Prior Edward Green's health also forced a change in leadership, and consequently Dom Mark Pontifex became Ealing's fourth Prior. Other re-shuffles also took place. Doms Walter Mackey and William Tate went on the mission; and Oswald Sumner and Rudesind Brookes took their places at the Priory. Dom Basil remained as Subprior, and Dom Dunstan as Parish Priest. Many believed that these changes would greatly strengthen the fibre of the community and improve the quality of the school. *The Priorian*, for example, reported that 'we trust it will prove a sound and effective reconstruction of the school, and will preserve all that was best in the old and . . . flourish with renewed life and vigour'.[1]

With his doctorate from the University of Munich, Dom Adrian seemed to be the obvious choice as the new headmaster, but his dedication and attachment to his Somerset monastery was also strong. When approached by Abbot Hicks about the possibility of moving to Ealing, he told his superior that 'in the natural order everything holds me to Downside, and it will be especially hard to give up my House at the point where I might begin to harvest the labour of the past four years'.[2] According to Dom Adrian's recollection, Abbot Hicks expressed some anxiety about conditions at Ealing, especially the financial well-being and the condition of the school.[3] Moreover, the Abbot believed that Ealing should receive the same generous treatment that Downside had shown towards Worth. At a meeting in the Abbot's quarters, Hicks told Dom Adrian that the school finances would be put under his control. Dom Adrian was also commissioned to remedy the obvious inefficiencies of the school, with special attention directed to the lacklustre performance of some relatives of the monks who were on the staff. But abbatial reform would also extend into the life of the priory; Hicks wanted to strengthen and to improve the monastic observance at Ealing. During this meeting between Dom Adrian and his Abbot, various names were discussed, and Dom Mark Pontifex emerged as the obvious choice for the job of Prior. A 'new deal' had been drawn up for Ealing: A Prior and headmaster, drawn from outside the ranks of the resident Ealing community, would captain the priory. Consequently Dom Adrian told Abbot Hicks, 'if you wish me to undertake the responsibility it is no doubt my duty to accept'.

After this interview, Dom Adrian and Dom Mark went to visit their future assignments during the 1938 Easter break. Dom Adrian found the surroundings 'depressing'. He noticed, for example, a disorganized and inept filing system, inferior examination results, and later related how he had asked to see the timetable, and was directed to the only copy available: an illegible, handwritten schedule hung on a wall in the headmaster's office. The accommodation for the boarders also horrified him. Because of the recent turnovers in the past of headmaster, Dom Adrian knew that it was imperative that he succeed, and consequently he outlined some strong recommendations which might help. He needed a professional staff, and Ealing fell short of the mark. 'The inefficiency of Ealing school has done, and is still doing,' he claimed 'great harm to Downside.'[4] 'Are we also morally justified in running a school in this way when other and better schools exist?' Dom Adrian compared the 1937 examination results of Ealing with those of Wimbledon, and emphasized the dismal results of the Ealing students.

Dom Adrian also believed that more monks must teach at the school, and he even named the four that he wanted. His list included two junior monks, and he argued that they could continue their study of theology under the guidance of Dom David Knowles, who was currently stationed at Ealing Priory. The new headmaster's rationale appeared convincing: 'I think that their inclusion in the list is more important . . . [because] the introduction of young blood would inspire the Ealing Community on its monastic as well as scholastic side, and at present it is disheartened'. But this plea fell on deaf ears at Downside. Youth also became the keyword for the lay staff, and Dom Adrian asked for permission 'to terminate if necessary the engagements of all save two in order to introduce younger, qualified substitutes'. This reorganization, he hoped, would help to secure recognition from the Board of Education. But more was at stake than academics. 'I should also endeavour to bring the school before the public notice by judicious publicity and by trying to take a fitting part in the Catholic life of London.' He ended his long letter by pointing out that Downside and Ealing had approximately the same enrolment, but the former enjoyed the services of nearly twice the number of monks.

Dom Adrian's urgent call for reform at Ealing's school reflected the opinions of others in educational circles. In May, he told Abbot Hicks that Ealing's reputation was abysmal. 'At the Board of Education,' he confessed, 'I was told that they regarded Ealing as one of the most inefficient private schools in London, which they would close if it lay in their power.'[5] Catholics in London also had a low regard for the school, and a number of the parents had expressed a dissatisfaction with their children's education. The headmaster's position sounded extremely alarmist: he prophesied that an increasing number of students would continue to leave because of the poor quality of instruction; and consequently the life of the school would be threatened by financial considerations. Even 'the general atmosphere of poverty makes the buildings unattractive'. The only panacea, 'as alternative to closing the school', 'appeared to be a radical re-organization'.

As in his previous letters, Dom Adrian cried out for extensive reforms. To improve the quality of teaching, and also an economic consideration, he again proposed the elimination of four masters. Three new masters would be hired, and this move would yield an annual saving of £600 a year. Consequently he gave notice to these teachers, effective September 1938. Although approved by Abbot Hicks, this change of personnel caused a great commotion and resentment among the staff and some of the monks. The poor physical condition of the buildings also demanded urgent repairs; if the school had to close in the future, these improvements would increase the value of the school, and Dom Adrian estimated that he must spend up to £1,300 during his first year. This large expenditure would refashion Ealing's image: 'it is not a grammar or secondary school, but provides a public school education on Downside lines adapted to the circumstances of the boys'. His grand dream became apparent. 'In other words,' he told Abbot Hicks, 'it does for Catholic boys in London in a humbler way what St Paul's and Dulwich do for others.'

Dom Adrian sketched out a series of proposals. To bring his school up to par with Harrow and Winchester, Ealing must secure the invaluable recognition from the Board of Education.[6] In concrete terms, this represented an additional expenditure of £200 for needed equipment and also a commitment to the construction of a school library. The grounds needed improvement 'in an attractive way, and this would entail a new playground'. A separate Prep School must be started, games fixtures must be improved, and the necessary introduction of rugby would involve new washing accommodations. Finally, he asked for, and received, permission to change the name of the school to St Benet's School. This was not cosmetic. 'The new name will more easily secure admission to the number of public schools for day boys.' he argued, and 'the aim should be to make Ealing the one Catholic school of that type.'

During the summer, Dom Adrian kept up pressure on the Abbot. He repeated his request for £1,300, itemized how the money would be spent, and told Abbot Hicks that he wanted to start spending the money at the beginning of the new term. Dom Adrian's prayers, however, were not answered; the proposals seemed unrealistic and financially unobtainable to the Downside officials. Abbot Hicks gave him only £1,000. By December, Dom Adrian had spent £600, and Abbot Trafford, the new Superior at Downside, stopped the balance. And moreover, the failure to recruit more monastic help for St Benet's also levelled his grandiose plans. Nonetheless, he continued to complain that he needed housemasters, a second master, and a games master to take charge of the young boys. In his mind, the last point presented a serious problem. 'In a school where about one hundred boys are of preparatory school age a very great deal will depend on the monk in charge of them and this has become even more apparent to me after meeting a few of the better type of parents,' he tried to reason with his Abbot.[7] Without the aid of more monks, the future seemed bleak. One reason was financial: 'I have already had to increase the laystaff to an extent I had not expected as several monks have been removed from the school, already understaffed, and their classes have to be taken.' Two days before the term opened, he again vented his frustrations. 'The whole staff here, monastic as well as lay,' he wrote to Downside, 'are working to far more crowded timetables than is customary at Downside.'[8] The message to Abbot Hicks was blunt: 'My chief problem is to run a school as large as Downside with a staff one third the size'.

The enthusiastic headmaster faced another hurdle. He believed that the Ealing community resented the Abbot's plans for educational and monastic reforms at the hands of a new headmaster and Prior. Many, he believed, wanted no change in the status quo. The boiling international situation, however, also helped to complicate Dom Adrian's vision of a proper public school at Ealing Priory.

Fascist Germany had long coveted Czechoslovakia, and some of the Prime Minister Neville Chamberlain's encouraging remarks during the Sudeten crisis seemed to imply that Britain would stand by the Czechs. As Hitler's demands became more and more aggressive during the summer of 1938, it appeared that the Sudeten would become the flashpoint for another war. The French began to mobilize, as did the British navy. On 28 September, the same day that Chamberlain made some ill-chosen remarks about a 'quarrel in a faraway country between people of whom we know nothing', the Ealing headmaster described the fear and anxiety which gripped the country on the brink of war. 'As evacuation of the elementary children is going on now,' he informed Abbot Hicks, 'I am afraid that it may be impossible to get [the] boys out if we wait too long.'[9] Students, therefore, were being dispatched to Downside for the weekend. Dom Adrian did not underestimate the danger, but he also understood the feelings of the parents. 'Apart from the seriousness of the situation it has been necessary to do this as a result of many requests from parents,' he explained, and 'a large number of boys have already been withdrawn.'

Not only parental panic, but officials of His Majesty's Government also suggested the evacuation of the London area. War, they believed, loomed imminent. Dom Adrian told Downside that 'we are advised to urge any parent who could send his child out of London during the coming weekend'.

Consequently he could not feel justified in keeping the boarders, and he made plans to send them home. Moreover, the Home Office had planned to close the government schools when the inevitable hostilities broke out, and advised other headmasters to follow their lead. At first, Dom Adrian wanted to close St Benet's, but later told Abbot Hicks that he 'would hold the boys back and see how things go'. And the government did more than just talk about evacuations. The Ealing Prior, Mark Pontifex, told Abbot Hicks that 'we have been fitted with gas masks and are arranging a refuge room according to instructions'.[10] The Prior also reflected the mood and fear of some of his countrymen: 'I have been optimistic up to now but my optimism is beginning to get a little dimmed'. His caution even extended to the possible closing of the school, which Dom Adrian wanted left open. 'We have discussed the situation,' he wrote, and 'I have also consulted others, and as parents want to know we are announcing that the school will close in case of war.' He also forecast that the major public schools, such as St Paul's, Westminster, and Eton, would also close. They never did, of course, although St Paul's was evacuated out of London for some time.

Dom Adrian's first months at Ealing, therefore, were not encouraging, but he viewed the situation with the stoic eye of a schoolmaster. 'The effect of all this on the school is most unfortunate and we have lost a number of boys by it.'[11] 'It has been an unfortunate beginning,' he noted. And trying to salvage some humour, he told Abbot Hicks that 'nobody can say that life is lacking excitement'. The day following this letter, 29 September, Chamberlain flew to his meeting in Munich which sealed the fate of Czechoslovakia. 'Peace in our time', however, meant that life at Ealing could return to normal, at least for the time being.

Rumours of war did not paralyse the necessities of monastic life in Ealing. On 20 September 1938, Downside Abbey elected Sigebert Trafford as its new superior, and he immediately informed Archbishop's House of a change at Ealing. Dom Stanislaus Chatterton, who had been in charge of St Mary's, Liverpool, replaced Mark Pontifex as Prior. The new Prior's first letter back to Downside reflected an optimistic forecast for the London priory. 'I am glad to report that I find everyone here in the best of spirits and all appear to be very happy,' he wrote.[12] The Prior also suggested that Dom Adrian seemed 'just a bit anxious'. In spite of the threatening international situation, he noted that the school situation looked healthy. 'The school appears to be well up in number,' he reported, 'and I don't think there is any cause at all for a pessimistic view of the situation.'

But in Dom Adrian's opinion, Sigebert Trafford's election represented a catastrophe. Abbot Hicks had supported changes at Ealing, and Dom Adrian soon realized exactly what plans the new Abbot had in mind for Ealing. The Abbot visited Ealing Priory after Christmas, 1938, and told the headmaster that he wanted to close the school in order to reduce Downside's commitment to and responsibility for Ealing. Ealing would then function solely as a parish. Dom Adrian believed that Abbot Trafford had always harboured anti-Ealing sentiments. After talk of an appointment to Cambridge, his monastic superior eventually wanted him to remain at Ealing as headmaster until the school's future could be decided, that is, to close down or to sell it to another religious order. Although he realized that he could not undertake any new project or exercise any initiative, and knew that his Abbot wanted to abolish St Benet's, Dom Adrian's vision of excellence for the school still survived. By March 1939, he had already made preliminary arrangements for inspection by the Board of Education. Always concerned about academic standards, the headmaster continued to agonize over questions involving teacher effectiveness and the university degrees of his schoolmasters. And he still begged Abbot Trafford for more help. 'This school is practically the same size as Downside and needs the same kind of teaching,' he pleaded.[13] 'Ealing has six laymasters and five monks; Downside has about thirteen of each.' But his plans were not heeded and, by May, the very existence of St Benet's seemed bleak. Following the lead of Abbot Trafford, some at Downside reviewed the economic status of the priory's school, and decided to back Trafford's desire to sell it and its property.

Abbot Trafford, therefore, approached the Christian Brothers, who had already expressed an interest. In May, the Superior-General of the order thanked Trafford and told the Abbot that he was 'grateful for your selection of the Christian Brothers to be the first to have an opportunity of considering your proposal'.[14] The Abbot wanted to begin negotiations concerning the acquisition of the property and the management of the school immediately, but the superior of the Christian Brothers told him that his order could not possibly staff the school until the 1940–41 school year. The Superior-General closed his letter and told Abbot Trafford that his vicar, Brother McCarthy, would visit Downside and discuss the proposal in detail. Abbot Trafford thanked the Superior-General for his keen interest, and also expressed his willingness to meet Brother McCarthy. The Abbot realized that the transfer could not take place immediately, and also understood the possibility of future difficulties. 'In fact, even if we come to an agreement it will be impossible to get the business through in time for you to start in the coming school year.'[15] Moreover, he confessed, 'I will have to put the matter before the Conventual Chapter'.

The closing of St Benet's and the sale of it to another order seemed close to realization. In June, Abbot Trafford wrote to the Ealing headmaster and confirmed that Brother McCarthy planned to visit Ealing soon, and reported that the Christian Brothers had to wait two years before they could staff the school. The Abbot told Dom Adrian not to worry, 'but to go on with the excellent work you are doing'.[16] Abbot Trafford also encouraged him to 'push on with the matter of getting the School recognized, with the possible

Government grant'. Dom Adrian's response revealed a sense of despondency or even failure. He regretted the two years' delay, and confessed that 'if the plan goes through I shall have acted for two years as locum tenens of Br McCarthy . . . and no ordinary person could feel enthusiasm for work done under such conditions or look forward to the unpleasantness of winding up'.[17] If the plan failed, moreover, initiative and planning for St Benet's would suffer. He ended his letter on tone of defeatism. 'More serious to me is the feeling I have that no blessing has rested on any work I have done in the community since my ordination,' he confessed, and 'that may seem pessimistic but no other member of the community, at least of my age, has had recent experiences like my own.' In the following month, the headmaster admitted that he had no objection to the Christian Brothers taking over the school, but maintained that Abbot Trafford did not understand his feelings. His months of hard work at Ealing did not seem appreciated, and he hinted that he might want an immediate re-assignment.[18] Dom Adrian later revealed that, not only did he feel extremely sad about the possibility of selling St Benet's, but the Ealing community viewed it as a blow to their integrity.

As plans for the transfer and closing progressed, conditions on the Continent made any deal impossible. During March 1939, Hitler took Czechoslovakia, and soon afterwards rolled over Bohemia and Moravia. Germany's non-aggression pact with the Soviet Union not only shocked British officials but gave ample proof of Hitler's intentions. Poland proved the flashpoint for the war which everyone knew had to come. On 1 September 1939, Hitler's forces invaded Poland, and two days later Great Britain declared war. The Christian Brothers' scheme, consequently, faded deep into the background, Downside having decided that Ealing's school would be closed in the event of war. But when this policy became public, Abbot Trafford faced some violent and dogged opposition from an unexpected quarter: parents and members of the parish bombarded Downside with letters protesting the closing of St Benet's One parent expressed her shock at the news. 'My husband and I were most surprised at the news of the closing of St Benet's,' she wrote Abbot Trafford on 2 September, the day before the formal declaration of war, 'especially as no provision is to be made for the day scholars'.[19] She continued and stated that Ealing was considered a neutral area, and 'therefore not included in the evacuation plans' drawn up by the Government. This mother pleaded to keep the school open, at least for the sake of her son. Abbot Trafford responded tersely: 'I much regret the necessity of closing St Benet's, but at the moment there is no other course open to me'.[20] He conceded that if there were a possibility of operating the school for a reduced number of day students, he would 'take any step possible'. The Abbot also remarked that, although Ealing had been designated a neutral zone, he claimed that he had information 'that it is highly probable that it will be made an evacuation area before long'. Remarking that the Ealing boarders would be transferred to Downside, Abbot

Trafford suggested that her child should also be sent to this monastery school, and he promised to view the financial consideration of this move very sympathetically.

Other concerned parents echoed the same theme. One stated that the closure would cause 'a great deal of perturbation, if not resentment, on the part of many parents and several of my friends [who] have boys at the school . . .'[21] This individual quickly pointed out that all the schools remained open during the last war. And the spectre of Protestantism also emerged: 'I have heard that in several cases if your school is closed the boys will be sent to Protestant Schools in the districts which are being kept open'. Another complained that his child's education would suffer 'at the most critical period of his career', and suggested operating St Benet's 'on a small scale' with a 'skeleton staff'.[22]

These letters and other pressures on Downside and on Prior Stansilaus Chatterton did produce results. Abbot Trafford replied to one letter and emphasized the financial difficulties involved in running a school with a low enrolment, and he again pointed out the fact that all boarders had been evacuated. But the Abbot did compromise: a limited operation would continue, but under the aegis of a new headmaster. 'The Prior came to see me last night with a proposal to keep open one House,' Abbot Trafford began, and 'this has my entire approval.'[23] Moreover, 'I have appointed Father Rupert Hall to act as Headmaster for the time being'. In response to another letter, the Abbot emphasized that this new arrangement applied only to day students.[24] He told another concerned parent that the school would remain open, but he could guarantee nothing beyond one term.[25]

Although Dom Adrian had serious doubts about keeping the school open at any cost, he had also expressed his wish to leave Ealing, and it appears that Abbot Trafford made his decision not to close Ealing's school and to appoint Dom Rupert Hall as headmaster independent of Dom Adrian. Trafford ordered Dom Adrian home from holiday in Belgium immediately and then informed him of the abbatial decisions concerning the future of St Benet's. On the same day that the Abbot informed several of the parents of his new plans, Dom Adrian wrote a letter to Downside which revealed his ignorance. He drew the Abbot's attention to the complaints from the parents over the rumoured closing and pointed out that he had already given the staff a provisional notice. The headmaster told Abbot Trafford that he had been 'kept very busy recommending boys to other schools and advising parents in their difficulties'.[26] He also made a comment about 'storing the furniture' and noted that 'this work of winding up is both exhausting and distressing . . .' Although Dom Adrian's departure might have been sudden and his tenure short, he had struggled to improve the standards of St Benet's in spite of manpower shortages, shaky finances, and most importantly, the instability of a year plagued by war fever.

The imminent invasion of Britain by German forces and the fear of devastating bombardment soon, however, subsided. After the emotional and psychological build-up, the invasion of Poland, and the British declaration of war, nothing much happened. During the 'drôle de guerre', or 'phoney war', Britons anxiously awaited Germany's next move. As the danger to London seemed to disappear, parents began to send their children back to their schools, and the priory school was no exception. Announced on 31 August, the government's evacuation policy was voluntary, and not mandatory. St Benet's opened on 14 September under the headmastership of Rupert Hall, who had been stationed at Ealing Priory since 1928. 54 students arrived for the first day of term, but the numbers soon began to swell. Within a fortnight, Prior Stansilaus Chatterton proudly wrote to Downside that 'there are at present 80 boys, and more likely to come.'[27] He estimated that the enrolment might peak at 100 by half-term, and he had been assured that other parents planned to send their children during the spring term. Classes and games continued as usual, but the boarders had been dispersed. The school never again admitted this class of student. Their old residence, Orchard Dene, provided the space for the war-time school; the buildings on Eaton Rise would soon be rented by the National Fire Service. Six monks manned the school: Rupert Hall, Basil Bolton, Fabian Pole, Dominic Young, Richard Davey, and Oswald Sumner. The priory suffered a decrease in membership due to the departure of four monks who volunteered as army chaplains: Rudesind Brookes, Gervase Hobson-Matthews, Philip Clarke, and Clement Hayes.

The school tended to dominate the life at Ealing during the early months of the war, and the monks struggled to ensure its survival. The life of St Benet's beyond the term still remained in serious doubt, and consequently the Prior sent a circular letter to the parents which announced that the question of the school would be discussed during the first week of December.[28] The decision would depend on the success or failure of St Benet's during the current term. Moreover, the Prior asked the parents to inform him whether their children would continue to attend in the spring; this would influence the history of the school. The circular tried to be realistic, and warned that if 'the final decision with regard to the reopening of the School should be an adverse one, this step will have been taken only with the greatest regret, and because the financial loss likely to be incurred would have been quite beyond the resources of the priory.' And the return of evacuated children to London augured well for the future of the school. By November 1939, the great exodus back to the cities had begun. 'By 8 January 1940, 900,000 of the nearly one-and-a-half million adults and children evacuated in September had gone home. In London and Liverpool only a third of all children were still away . . .'[29] And Dom Rupert Hall successfully pleaded the case against closing the school and argued for its life. He realized that Abbot Trafford's views and opinions would be important. Late in 1939, therefore, the headmaster asked his superior what circumstances or conditions would influence his final decision on the fate of Ealing's school.

Dom Rupert's lengthy letter tended to minimize the trials and attendant turmoil of wartime. For him, the school must continue. The headmaster's chief argument centred around an appeal to monastic and Benedictine pride. 'The school has supplied a great need in the past and done so very well,' he wrote Abbot Trafford.[30] Being a Benedictine school, Dom Rupert continued, 'it will always attract a large number of parents who cannot afford the fees that Downside or Douai demand'. If the school must close, Catholics would be at a loss to have their children educated, and if sold to another religious community or to the government, Downside 'will suffer a great loss of prestige for it will be a general confession of failure'. Moreover, many people had moved into the Ealing area because of the attractiveness of the Benedictine school. Again, the question of religion became an emotional but strong argument: 'there is hardly a school . . . in London which is open and so the need for Catholic education is paramount'. The threat of a generation of Protestant-educated youth could always touch a sensitive Roman Catholic nerve.

Numerous other arguments crept into Dom Rupert's defence of the priory's school. If the school closed, for example, he maintained that it would 'prove very questionable that we shall be able to retain the parish here'. Without the help of the teaching monks, the activities undertaken by the parish could not possibly continue. After the war, he prophesied, economic hard times would probably cripple the country, and consequently 'few people will be able to afford to spend as much on education as they have done in the past . . . So schools of the Ealing type will be increasingly more popular'. And if Downside did decide to keep the school, then the community there 'must make themselves whole-heartedly responsible for its well-being and development'.

Frustration and anxiety had coloured his experience at Ealing, and he blamed Downside. 'Successive Superiors have bandied us about, changed our personnel, called upon us for men, kept us short-handed, in fact treated us in a most cavalier fashion.' After repeating the accomplishments of the past and reiterating the great possibilities for the future, Dom Rupert argued one final point in conclusion: 'If it is considered to be for the good of Religion and the good of Catholic Education and the reputation of the Benedictine Community in England that our school is to continue, then questions of finance should not weigh very heavily in the scale against it'. Closure because of bad economics would constitute a grave scandal.

Abbot Trafford responded immediately to his headmaster's long letter, and he suggested that Dom Rupert provide him with the following information: the amount of money which had recently come into the school, and a list of the parents together with the amount each family paid. 'I cannot come to any decision on the immediate future of Ealing until I have this unfortuantely,' he told Dom Rupert, and 'when I have it I can discuss the whole matter with you.'[31] The Abbot refused to comment on the contents of the headmaster's letter which argued for the continuance of St Benet's, but he did point out an error in a related area, namely, the future of the parish and its relation to the school. 'It is no use mixing up the school and the parish,' he warned, and 'the question of giving up the Parish does not and will not arise.' Abbot Trafford ended his letter with a reminder that the Downside community had already invested large sums of money in the Ealing foundation, and this contributed to the current financial difficulties at the Somerset monastery.

The school remained open for a second term, and even showed an increase in enrolment. Prior Chatterton reported in March 1940 that 'there are close on 130 boys at present . . . [and] we have reached the limit now and have had to refuse several applications'.[32] But finances still remained a serious problem. Several letters concerning the accounts passed between Downside and Ealing, and Abbot Trafford did not hesitate to point out some questionable fiscal practices. In the spring, for example, he complained about some money expended on Castle Hill House. 'There is one rather alarming item,' he told the Prior, 'namely £545 spent on Castle Hill House.'[33] 'It is true that you get a good deal back in the way of income, but it seems to me at this juncture that it is not good to spend more on repairs than is absolutely necessary.' In the following month, he again questioned the wisdom of repairs to the house. Abbatial permission should have been sought. 'The priory would have paid its way easily,' he continued, 'but for the heavy expense on Castle Hill House.'[34] 'I am very sorry that the expense occurred and I had no idea that it was occurring.'

It was Dunkirk which reminded the Ealing community that the war on the Continent was real. Two Ealing monks who served as army chaplains, Dom Clement Hayes and Dom Gervase Hobson-Matthews, remained behind on the beaches after the makeshift armada from England had left. And the Ealing Benedictines anxiously waited to receive word of their fate. Dom Clement announced his return to the priory with a sense of monastic humour. According to one account, 'coming out of Vespers on that gloomy day [31 May] we saw a soldier sitting in the library, his tin hat on the back of his neck, rather untidy looking, his right elbow lifting a glass of beer to his lips'.[35] '"Here I am, boys," said he, and precious little else.' His confrère, Dom Gervase, however, was eventually reported missing, but his death was not confirmed for several months until the identification of his grave site in a French village. At Ealing since 1930, he had taught French and English in the school. *The Priorian* on January 1941 reported that he had decided 'not to use his own pass to escape . . . but to go back to the troops at Dunkirk and share their fortune'.[35]

As the hostilities inched closer to Britain during the spring of 1940, the Government continued to prepare the country for German attacks. Black-out instructions, the beginning of rationing, military conscription, and more new plans for the evacuation of the capital became accepted facets of English life.

The Nazi military seemed unstoppable; Norway, the Low Countries, and France had fallen to Hitler's armies. And England waited for the inevitable. Archbishop's House also began to prepare London's Roman Catholics. During May, Prior Chatterton received a letter from Bishop David Mathew which dealt with possible contingencies in the event of air raids. This letter asked two questions. 'Have you any priests on your staff who will not be required for the needs of the church or parish and who would be available to go out to other locations in the diocese where there might be need of priests to deal with heavy casualties?'[36] The second concerned the injured: 'Have you any car belonging to your house or to one of your parishioners which could be used for the purpose of taking priests to other parts of London to work with casualties?' This letter also told the Prior that an Air Raid Post had already been established at Archbishop's House to deal with messages and queries.

And with the threat of invasion increasing, the evacuation 'of children from supposedly dangerous towns, from Hull to Portsmouth and from London and the Thames-side towns had begun'.[37] In June, Cardinal Arthur Hinsley addressed the question of the fate of the schoolchildren. He informed Prior Chatterton that 'the Government has decided to begin the evacuation of children on Thursday next and continue it on the following six days until it is complete'.[38] The Archbishop related that 'it had also been decided that all the children shall be sent into the South West of England and Wales'. Chatterton was informed that this plan conflicted with others made by the London County Council, and consequently there might be some confusion. Archbishop Hinsley also stressed the importance that clerics go with the children: 'it will also more than ever be necessary for a priest to accompany the party in accordance with the arrangements already made'. 'Explain to the people the great importance which I attach to the presence of a priest with the children on the journey,' he concluded, 'and I am sure that they will overlook any inconvenience they may suffer.'

While Ealing prepared for air raids, black-outs, and the departure of the children, Abbot Trafford continued to agonize over the Prior's fiscal solvency. He told the headmaster, Dom Rupert, that his experiment of keeping two sets of books, one for the priory and the other for the school, had proved a failure. 'Therefore,' he informed Dom Rupert, 'I wish the arrangements at Ealing to be the same as those at Worth, namely that all expenditure is under the immediate jurisdiction of the Prior and no expenses of any kind whatever can be incurred without his permission, and he alone may sign cheques.'[39] Prior Chatterton would oversee all accounts, and he alone 'is responsible for the expenditure in any part of the establishment'. Dom Rupert, however, seriously questioned this 'one book' policy, and argued that it would be exceedingly difficult to judge the financial health of the school if its accounts were not kept separate. In respect to seeking the Prior's permission for expenditure, the headmaster told his Abbot that 'from the past experience here I believe that such an arrangement would not work well and personally I could not make myself responsible for the efficient running of the school under such an arrangement'.[40]

Abbot Trafford defended his policy, and maintained that the separation of the books had been merely experimental. It had not worked, and he opposed it on principle: 'the Prior must be the sole authority responsible to the Abbot, just as the Prior of Worth was'.[41] These economic reforms were far-reaching. Even minor repairs to the school must be approved by the Prior. 'There is no other way of getting the financial position straight,' Abbot Trafford argued, 'and I must have one person to hold responsible for expenditure.'[42] The problems at Ealing perplexed and disturbed the Abbot. 'The position at Ealing of course gives considerable anxiety,' and 'we cannot go on losing £2,000 a year'. 'A desperate effort must be made to get the place to pay.' The headmaster refused to accept his Abbot's limitations on his running of the school, and he reacted bluntly: 'I regret to say that I cannot agree to continue as headmaster on the conditions you lay down'.[43] He offered to resign his post. Dom Rupert told Abbot Trafford that 'there are various problems with the school which require an early solution, [and] it would be advisable to make a new appointment as soon as possible'. But Hitler's onslaught against London in September 1940 pushed these questions into the background.

To invade England, Hitler had to gain control of the air over the Channel. By August and September, the German air force had saturated London, and although he failed to gain that superiority in the air which he needed, the bombing of the capital and other industrial cities continued throughout the winter. Ealing had prepared for the war. During the Munich crisis, for example, trenches had been dug in the borough's parks and plans for shelters drawn up. The notion that an umbrella of neutrality protected Ealing was rudely dismissed in September 1940 when bombs began to fall upon the borough, first near Greenford Park Cemetery, and then around Edmonscote, Argyle Road, and the Mount Park area.[44] In early October the *Middlesex County Times* announced that Ealing had been declared an evacuation zone; areas north of the Great Western Railway no longer enjoyed the safety of neutrality. According to one account, 'there were nights when the glow of the great fires in the City and beyond mingled and melted in that of conflagrations closer at hand, when the smoke and din of battle enveloped Ealing'.[46] Statistics for war-time Ealing recorded the following: 746 high explosive bombs fell on the suburb; 304 people killed and 322 seriously injured; 443 houses demolished; and 11,671 damaged.[47]

Both school and priory life suffered during September 1940, and St Benet's struggled to survive. Dom Rupert told Abbot Trafford that 'an added difficulty in these times is ... the uncertainty of calling up'.[48] He pointed out that one schoolmaster had already left and an additional two might depart soon. This would increase the strain on the community. Moreover, the headmaster had to face 'the necessity to provide Air Raid Protection at the Playing Fields'. Prior Chatterton explained to the Abbot that 'the Raid Warnings are a bother in regard to School work as we cannot ignore them and carry on as usual'.[49] He also talked about the determination of some of the parents 'to carry on as usual'. They 'all know . . . that we are doing our best and I am glad to say that numbers are not very much down'. And he expected that more students would return. In another report, the Prior confessed that 'we are carrying on as well as we can under the circumstances, and during the day when there are Raid Warnings, the boys are able to carry on with their classes to a certain extent in the shelters'.[50] 'School work is very much interfered with owing to the constant raids and it isn't wise to ignore day time raids,' the Prior noted. He told Abbot Trafford that during the 'last week at lunch time a plane swooped over the Broadway and dropped some bombs which did a deal of damage'. One monk reminisced later how the students and staff took these interruptions in their stride. Games, for example, might take place during enemy action, and the gaze of the students would be fixed on a nearby dog fight instead of an the action on the pitch.

By October, enrolment had dipped to approximately eighty, but on the other hand, some interested people still continued to enquire about the school, and according to the Prior, 'those who are left do not seem to have any intention of running away'. But the bombs did cause some superficial damage. *The Priorian* reported that 'the school building showed some broken windows and a shaky chimney or two, and the gymnasium looked rather battered and forlorn, yet still standing up well'.[52] But the Battle of Britain threatened more than the smooth operation of a school; enemy action disrupted life in and around the priory.

A report from Dom Rupert captured the terror and determination of the monks during September 1940. 'The nights are a menace,' he wrote.[53] 'The sirens go about 8 or 9 and then the guns begin and, alas, the bombs too. It is surprising how cheerful we keep and that we are able to keep going.' The Prior kept the officials at Downside constantly informed of conditions at Ealing Priory. September, naturally, provided some horrific accounts. 'Air raid warnings throughout the day, and from sunset to dawn we are subjected to continual bombardment,' he related.[54] 'We are surrounded by heavy guns which make a fearful din all night, and to this is added the falling and bursting of bombs.' A dozen bombs had fallen in the parish, but only one or two near the priory buildings. On 21 September, the Prior noted that London lay 'under a heavy fog this morning and so that may mean a peaceful day, or on the other hand, the very opposite.' He explained his reasoning: 'Bombs appear to be dropped quite at random, and so the opportunity may be taken of the fog to come over and drop more just anywhere in the safety of the pall of fog'.

After acknowledging Abbot Trafford's kind and sympathetic response to his last letter, Prior Chatterton began to describe the escalating action over Ealing. 'From the moment darkness began to set in till dawn was breaking, we were subjected to constant bombardment, and with the roar of our own guns the night was an inferno,' he wrote on 26 September, and 'the night sky was very soon crimson red with the numerous fires.'[55] The bombs continued to fall about the borough in large numbers, but casualties remained light. The priory also continued to court luck; not even a single window had been broken. Daytime raids also became a normal part of daily life at Ealing. The Prior described one engagement as 'scores and scores of machines, all mixed together and all ends up'.[56] 'The sky was black with them.' On 28 September, the parish and neighbourhood suffered badly. A good deal of material damage resulted, 'but no casualties except one poor old lady got a black eye when the door of her room was torn from its hinges and flung in her face'.[57] Nearby Northfields, however, suffered much more damage. In addition to tending their own parishioners, the Ealing monks also cared for many homeless Catholics who flocked to the area, and the Prior described the plight of one family bombed out of three houses; he hoped the fourth would not be in St Benedict's parish. And the Ealing Prior could not resist commenting on German accuracy, which he described as 'hit and trust to luck'. 'It is really astonishing,' he wrote Downside, 'how many bombs fall in the middle of the road.' After a dreadful night of enemy action, he sent the following description to Abbot Trafford: 'Three within a stone's throw of us – and yet not hit – makes one wonder if they will *always* miss'.[58]

But the Benedictines' good fortune could not last forever. On the evening of 7 October two Ealing churches became the targets of enemy aircraft. Bombs exploded around the Anglican parish church, but it escaped serious damage. The Benedictine church did not. The *Middlesex County Times* reported that St Benedict's, 'a Roman Catholic Church noted for its beauty,' had been 'damaged by two high explosive bombs'.[59] 'They fell together and one of them, which fell against the outside of the north wall, destroyed the wall and the Chapel of the Holy Souls.' 'The organ chamber,' the paper told its readers, 'was also destroyed.' The second, a delayed action bomb, buried itself in the floor of the church near the high altar. The monks were ordered to evacuate the priory building, and they immediately hurried across to Orchard Dene. (One of the monks reported a lost sock during this hasty move, but it was politely returned the following day.) The bomb in the church exploded nine hours later and did considerable damage: the high altar and sanctuary were totally destroyed. Some statues were also damaged, but 'many of the other statues escaped injury because they had been placed on the floor so that they might escape the blast of an unexploded bomb which fell a little distance from the church some time ago'. The editorial in the same edition castigated the indiscriminate bombing of England's churches, and used the recent example of St Benedict's as its cue. 'In an age when autocrats are once again claiming to be above all the laws of man or God, this priory has suffered as Tintern or Fountains suffered from the totalitarianism of an earlier century.'

Almost immediately the Benedictines began to plan to restore the nave for public worship. Abbot Trafford inquired into the extent of the damage, and wanted to know if Ealing could expect any contribution from the government. Prior Chatterton replied that for the time being work on the church would be minimal: 'only what appears to be dangerous will be demolished, and only what is considered imperative for the preservation of what stands, will be done'.[60] He remarked that some money could be expected from the government, but the bulk would come from a fund-raising campaign in the parish. The Prior also reported that Castle Hill House 'has practically been split into two houses' due to some bombs which fell on Marchwood Crescent. Consequently extensive repairs on the house would have to take place after the war.

November 1940 provided a respite for the suburb, but the Luftwaffe returned in December and damaged Kenora, a house owned by the Benedictines and located on the priory grounds. Claims were sent to the authorities, and the Prior argued that £130 was needed immediately to make the house decent for occupants. And bombs continued to skirt the property. 'Bombs were falling within a few yards of the priory,' Prior Chatterton told his Abbot.[61] 'There were 58 fires in Ealing that night.' The year ended on a positive note: the work on the damaged church progressed well; and 'once back in the church', the Prior assured Abbot Trafford that he felt confident that the money to pay for the repairs would be found,

The war also wreaked havoc with the peaceful and scheduled routine of monastic life. Warned to avoid the upper floors of their residence during the night, the Ealing monks slept in the basement and library of the priory. 'Shrapnel is flying about all night and there is danger from that,' the Prior explained.[62] But the monastic regime could not be compromised. During the opening weeks of the war, Abbot Trafford ordered his Prior at Ealing to enforce silence in the monks' refectory. Prior Chatterton complained that 'this has not been carried out without a great deal of discontent'. He reminded the Abbot that 'our present hectic state does not conduce to strict monastic observance'. Nonetheless, the Prior described his community as 'keeping up well under the circumstances' despite a 'considerable nervous tension'. He optimistically told Downside that 'we are very cheerful in spite of it all, and certainly not downhearted.' One monk even described conditions as 'extremely happy'.

Black-out curtains controlled the life of the monks. 'We all retire to the cellar when the Warning goes within a few minutes of black-out time, and there remain till an hour before sunrise when the all-clear goes.'[63] The Prior described how the enemy aircraft 'generally finish up with a hectic burst of bombing about half past five'. The cellar, where the servants also lived, did offer some comfort and protection, and also became the stage for some black-out humour. The houseman, for example, stayed with the monks and generally looked after their needs, but 'with occasional lapses as when the butter was lost until the Prior went to bed under the stairs', where he found the missing food.[64] One monk related that a dartboard offered the community some recreation, and how the monks 'used it in the evenings when the aerial concert was getting tuned up.'[65] Commenting on the nightly air raids, the Prior once mused that 'when winter comes, if no antidote has been found in this matter of night bombing, I suppose we will be down there about four in the afternoon till eight or nine in the morning'.[66] At times, the monks chanted the Divine Office behind thick black curtains. Rationing usually meant 'grim food'. But in general, the community tried to carry on in a normal manner.

The Prior did realize the seriousness of the situation and the present danger to the priory. Some of the monks served nearby convents, but the Prior thought that war-time conditions warranted a change or alteration in this ministry. Concerning services at one convent, Prior Chatterton told the Mother Superior that if the hostilities continued, he 'could not dream of letting a priest go all the way up there in the hours of darkness with shrapnel falling all around him'. The Prior remarked that his monks would always brave the outside to attend to the needs of the sick and dying, 'but when it is a question of giving Mass to the Nuns, that will have to be arranged in such a way that the danger to the Priest concerned will not be imminent'. In fact, he strongly urged the monks to guard their safety. 'I have told the Community,' the Prior told Abbot Trafford, 'that no one should go out during the period of a Warning except on urgent business, and if one happens to be out near Blackout Time, he must return at once'. Yet the Ealing monks did not hide in the security of their monastery. Some put themselves in danger, and one monk was injured by a piece of flying shrapnel. Later in the war, the Ealing monks would don the tin helmet and become Fire Wardens for the area.

In spite of these warnings and precautions, one member of the community continued to live in his room at the top of the priory building; 'he maintained that it was safer than in the basement, as you could come down again if blown up'.[67] The same individual also continued to read nightly in his room by the light of the bulb in the wireless. And on returning to the priory during an attack, he was surprised to learn that a bomb had missed him by a scant three hundred yards in Queen's Walk.

Life during the Blitz also took its psychological victims. Although admittedly happy and cheerful, some nerves were strained at Ealing Priory. 'It is certainly a trying experience to lie in the darkness listening to the pandemonium, hearing the whistling of a falling bomb and wondering WHERE IT WILL FALL,' Downside was informed, and 'it is a relief to the tension to hear the explosion for one then knows that still another has passed over and with us at least all is still well.'[68] One monk became a bit tense and 'very nervy'. 'He will go round the house late at night to see that the black-out is all right etc though he knows this has been done.'

And bombs did continue to threaten the priory. Soon after the church was hit, the Prior reported that 'we got a nasty shaking in our dugout last night,' and this incident served as a commentary on the joys of the black-out: 'the electricity failed and we have been without light or heat for cooking since 8pm last night and I don't think we will have any current for two or three days . . . [and] we are living in perpetual candle light'.[69] In spite of these hardships, Prior Chatterton's estimation and admiration of the community never wavered. At the height of the action in September, he told Abbot Trafford that his monks would 'not hesitate to do anything'.[70] 'Thank God, we have a splendid lot of men here, and this common loyalty . . . means so much.' Even after the priory church had been severely damaged, he could still report that 'we are all cheerful and resigned'.[71]

For months, the priory building was threatened by an unexploded bomb that had landed across the road. On 1 October, a 1,222-pound bomb hit 5 Charlbury Grove, and the monks had to move to safer quarters. 'Since the bomb fell,' Downside was told, 'all have been out of our rooms both day and night [and] living at the passage in the back.'[72] In addition to the priory, Castle Hill House was also evacuated. The Prior captured the tenseness of the community: '. . . it is an anxious time at present, with this large bomb almost on our doorstep'. The Benedictines did not appreciate the dalliance of the authorities in disarming the device. 'Life will be much more bearable when that is done,' the Prior remarked, 'for we would be able to use our rooms in the daytime.'[73] No action brought another frustrated outburst from the Prior at the end of October, 'The bomb in Charlbury Grove has not yet been removed but I think we can surely say that it is a dud . . . I wish they would remove it.'[74] At the beginning of December, the bomb was finally defused. 'They had to dig 47 feet to get to it,' Prior Chatterton recorded, and when 'it came to the last stage they made us vacate our premises as they found the clockwork was still ticking away.'[75] He described, in great detail, the various steps in disarming the device. The Prior's closing comment expressed great relief: '. . . and so we have again escaped as it would have blown all the front of the priory to pieces had it gone off'.

If the future of the school had been seriously questioned before the war, that of the Benedictine parish always seemed secure. And during the hostilities, St Benedict's provided a necessary service to the area's Roman Catholics. No record of the actual population of the parish survives, but the Benedictines also ministered to numerous Catholics who fled to Ealing to escape the devastation of central London. Moreover, references in the Prior's letters to Abbot Trafford mentioned examples of the monks visiting the injured and comforting the bereaved. As far as possible, they tried to maintain a regular timetable for mass and the other religious services. The destruction of the church in October caused some inconvience and disrupted the flow of parish life. Services, consequently, were conducted in an alternative place. Prior Chatterton noted a sharp decline in the number of Sunday worshippers. 'Situated as we are in the Parish Hall, a large number of our people are now going to other churches, and many regular attendants, but not of our Parish, are also staying away.'[76] Yet he remained optimistic and believed that the flock would return and increase to its normal size after the damage to the church was repaired. The Sunday offerings also declined. But 'this is to be expected', the Prior informed Abbot Trafford; the people 'will all return to us . . . and so once back in the Church we will be able to go ahead'. Moreover, the parish was expected to finance, to a large extent, the rebuilding of St Benedict's. Prior Chatterton's prediction proved correct. After the war, the parish prospered and grew. In 1947, the average attendance at Sunday mass reached 1,720, and nearly a dozen guilds or fraternities functioned in the parish.[77]

The school had survived threats of closure and evacuation. Ealing Priory had weathered several near misses, and the monastic routine accommodated to the demands of the black-out. And the parish had temporarily lost the use of its church. However, an old plague, manpower shortage, sent hiccups through the community. In December 1940, Abbot Trafford recalled Dom Richard Davey back to Downside, and Prior Chatterton's reactions addressed the problems this move would create. 'It will be very difficult to fit things in here,' he confessed, and 'we may have to give up two of the Convents that we attend as Confessor Chaplains as it is difficult to find a priest free'.[78] The headmaster, Dom Rupert, would also have to find a replacement for Dom Richard at the school. The Prior offered to volunteer, but he already had a full schedule. Everyone's timetable was stretched: 'As it is, with the Parish Staff being obliged to help so much in the school, it has thrown quite a lot of extra work on me'. The parish would also suffer, and it 'would be left with three half-timers'. The Prior chronicled the extent of the duties at the local convents and the amount of work he was responsible for, but his arguments to find a replacement for Dom Richard proved unsuccessful.

With The Battle of Britain won and the plans for a German invasion of the island cancelled, life in England struggled to get back to normal. More mundane matters also began to grab the attention of Ealing Priory. The reconstruction of the church could not be postponed. Money had to be found, and the Prior expressed his confidence that the parish would raise the funds, as Abbot Trafford had expected. 'I have no hesitation in saying that they would be quite prepared to face up to a debt on the parish,' he told his Abbot, 'and would deal with it with great expedition.'[79] On 28 February 1941, the job had been completed, and the monks began to prepare for the re-opening. With the bombed part partitioned off by a temporary wall, 'the first services to be held in the newly-restored church took place on Sunday, 3 March 1941, when Bishop Mathew, after blessing the church, administered Confirmation to over a hundred children'.[80] By April, the church was fully functional again, and the Prior hoped that he would receive some compensation from the government. He estimated £45,000 for structural damages and approximately £7,000 for accessories. £960 had been collected from the parish campaign, and Prior Chatterton expressed confidence that he could count on the same amount to be collected annually. He also promised to keep expenses as low as possible.

Wartime conditions, such as rationing, continued to control life at the priory. Compared with the previous years, 1941 and 1942 passed quickly, but the reality of the conflict was made vividly clear by the publication of the casualties from the ranks of the old boys in the school magazine. Moreover, some reassignment of monks took place, and the Prior struggled to meet economic pressures. As a source of possible financial security for the future, the school still dominated the correspondence between Ealing and Downside. In the mind of the Ealing monks, the school could become a successful enterprise, and in 1941 Prior Chatterton shared his optimism with Abbot Trafford. He maintained 'that a day-school like Ealing has a good fortune after the war'.[81] 'It is the large Boarding Schools,' he predicted, 'that may have to suffer' because 'parents just will not have the means.'

But the war visited Ealing again in May 1943. Prior Chatterton informed Downside that 'we have just had another sort of trouble'.[83] 'Last night,' he continued, 'a bomb, a short distance from us, has caused a lot of superficial damage in the school'. The Prior reported that the explosion shattered almost all the windows and caused other minor damage. After a late start, however, classes resumed as usual. 'It is an open-air school, but fortunately being summer, that will not matter much,' he chuckled. The priory and church were not touched. Chatterton ended his report with characteristic stoicism. 'I suppose we will have to face this sort of thing now and so must be prepared for it. We have been left alone so long that we have come to consider ourselves immune.'

Another event, however, proved potentially more damaging than German explosives to the life of the Benedictine school. Dom Adrian had previously warned his superior of the need for improvement and upgrading at the school, and he had told Downside that the common opinion of St Benet's in educational circles was low. Some attempts were made at improvement. Two monks with Cambridge degrees, Dom George Brown and Dom Gerard Hayes, joined the staff in September 1942. The same move also brought Dom Kevin Horsey from Downside to work on the parish. But more was needed. To qualify for funding from the government and to ensure its reputation, St Benet's had to pass an inspection conducted under the eyes of the Board of Education and thus obtain the Recognition of Efficiency. The Board visited Ealing in May 1943, and the conclusions confirmed Dom Adrian's predictions.

Dom Rupert, the headmaster, informed Downside of the visit and confessed that he did not think that 'the Board would grant us recognition in our present state'.[83] The condition of the physical plant impressed the inspectors, however, as did the quality of the students. Along with good comments on their manners and neat appearance, they characterized the boys as 'intelligent and hardworking', but 'on these two points,' the headmaster quipped, 'we didn't enlighten them'.

But the negative points far outweighed the positive. 'They thought the teaching was outdated in most subjects and lacked efficiency and co-ordination,' Dom Rupert regretfully reported. The staff came in for more criticism: 'Various people in their [the inspectors'] estimation were teaching subjects they didn't know much about or employing wrong methods'. The headmaster related that they expressed a strong 'conviction in the immense possibilities of the school', but the teaching and curriculum needed improvement before governmental recognition. Dom Rupert gave his own estimation on the rejection. 'I think we must overhaul our methods pretty thoroughly if we are to satisfy these Johnnies, though really I don't suppose Downside or Ampleforth or most public schools conform to their requirements or suggestions.' In July, the official report came from the Board of Education, and it re-enforced the headmaster's report to Abbot Trafford. The Board of Education felt 'that while the school shows good promise for the future, the report reveals certain weaknesses in the teaching and organization which would hardly justify them in granting immediate recognition'.[84] But the report also stated that the Board was willing to conduct another inspection, 'assuming that the circumstances are favourable'.

Dom Rupert also sent Abbot Trafford a list of recommendations, which he termed 'impractical,' suggested by His Majesty's Inspectors. He pointed out that the chief weakness concerned the staff and the lack of 'guidance'.[85] With the exception of history, all subjects received critical comments. Not surprisingly, the inspectors singled out mathematics and science as those which needed the greatest improvement. Dom Rupert also recognized his own shortcomings, and he took full responsibility for the damning report, and told Abbot Trafford 'they would attribute much of the inefficiency they noted to the fact that the headmaster had not a University degree.' In his mind, the solution seemed obvious. 'Should you deem it prudent to make a change in my position,' he confided to the Abbot, 'you need not have the slightest fear that my feelings would be hurt.' Downside, however, could not address the recommendations of the inspectors or consider Dom Rupert's suggestion for two years. The war had not been won yet.

Ealing did not remain immune from further enemy action. On 23 February 1944, the Prior wrote that 'it was rather "hot" last night'.[86] Six houses in the parish were demolished, and an increasing sense of panic gripped the district. 'People are beginning to evacuate from here,' he told Abbot Trafford. And the

Prior shared their fear. 'I think . . . it is rather foolish to remain in London unless there is reason to do so.' Another attack caused great destruction and contributed to the growing fear: the police closed down the District Line; and people attending mass during the attack 'scrambled under the benches for safety'. The Prior prayed that Ealing would be spared in what he believed constituted a new offensive. 'Now that they have given us two or three days bombing,' he wrote in late February 1944, 'perhaps they will hit another district.'[87] His description of the community during this renewed action remained positive: 'we ourselves are grand'. Fearing the worst, the headmaster closed the junior part of the school during the summer, and Abbot Trafford offered comfort and a proposal. He reminded Dom Rupert that his monastery owned some property, Downside House, and offered it to Ealing for use as a Junior School. 'They could attend classes and have their meals here [Downside Abbey], sleeping at Downside House,' he suggested.[88] Payment of the current fees and a small amount for their meals would be required. Dom Rupert, however, did not accept the Abbot's offer; for the end to the war finally appeared in sight with the successful landings on the Normandy beaches and the liberation of France in the summer of 1944.

As the war in Europe began to wind down, the country struggled to return to peacetime conditions and began to face the numerous problems associated with reconstruction. And Abbot Trafford quickly resurrected an old plan he had cherished before the war. Nearly two months before the official and formal end of the 1939–45 War, the Abbot informed his confrères that the Downside Council had seriously considered the drastic manpower shortage which faced the monastery on 5 March 1945, and 'it was agreed by a large majority that it would be impossible for us to continue to maintain three Schools and three Monasteries simultaneously.'[89] Either Ealing or Worth, established in 1933, would have to be dropped or resources shared. But Worth had quickly become indispensable to the educational life of Downside: Downside's Prep School had already been successfully established there. Abbot Trafford's decision sounded painfully familiar to the earlier Christian Brothers scheme. 'After most careful examination of the position,' he wrote, 'I have decided to call the Chapter in order to ask its permission to arrange for a long lease or sale of the School property at Ealing and our withdrawal from work at Ealing School after the end of the coming Summer Term.' Trafford urged quick and resolute action in order to allow parents to make other necessary arrangements. The Abbot also wanted to avoid the hue and cry which his pre-war plan had aroused among the parents of Ealing, and he urged the monks to treat this information as confidential. He scheduled this meeting to decide the fate of St Benet's for 9 April 1945.

Again Dom Rupert Hall, the headmaster, emerged as the champion and chief advocate for the Benedictine school. He did not hide his anger or mince words over Abbot Trafford's plan. 'You will readily understand that we here are very perturbed by the proposal to withdraw from the School, and even, if necessary, to close the School.'[90] The headmaster argued that 'the shortage of manpower is temporary, but the giving up of the school (and the possibility of the parish too) is an irrevocable step'. As previously, he played the Protestant card. 'The greatest need of the Catholics in England today is Catholic schools and that is our best contribution.' Dom Rupert suggested possible solutions to the problems which Downside faced: 'reclaim some of our Army chaplains' due to be discharged; recruit help from the parishes; re-examine the size and commitment to Worth; and even approach the other English Benedictine houses for some temporary assistance for Ealing. He also pointed out another serious consequence if St Benet's were closed. 'Another aspect of the question is whether it is desirable to retain the parish if we give up the school,' he argued, 'for if we relinquish the land on which the School is situated, we shall find it impossible to develop the Priory as such.' He closed his letter and asked Abbot Trafford to visit Ealing and discuss his intentions with the community.

Abbot Trafford replied in a short and business-like manner. He declined the invitation to talk over the issue with the Ealing monks, and told Dom Rupert that he felt 'it would be better not to discuss the matter in any detail until it is actually put before the Chapter'.[91] The Abbot also corrected the headmaster on one point. 'I should like to say that there is no question of giving up the parish of Ealing,' he informed Dom Rupert. 'I certainly agree that it is desirable to retain it, even if the School has to be given up.' Dom Rupert, in Abbot Trafford's opinion, had confused two different issues, namely, the future of the school and the parish. And again the Abbot had to clear up this misconception. 'There is no intention of giving up the Parish,' he re-emphasized.[92] 'The School and the Parish are different entities and only the School is in question,' Trafford reminded the Prior, and 'I shall not allow any discussion about the Parish at all in the Chapter.'

The Downside Chapter met on 9 April and voted not to withdraw its commitment from Ealing's school. Abbot Trafford had been defeated. By this time, the Abbot's alleged autocratic manner had so annoyed Downside that he could not count on the support of the community for his plan concerning Ealing. He had, literally, lost or forfeited the trust of the community. The Ealing community had rushed to the Downside meeting, some armed with the proxy votes of the army chaplains, to save their school. These monks pointed out that the chaplains could supply the needed manpower. Their argument resonated with confidence: Ealing's school had survived an horrendous war and the future looked bright; and therefore there was no sound reason to close the school.

St Benet's, however, could not be allowed to exist in its present condition. The efficiency of Ealing's school must be improved and it must pass the inspection conducted by the Board of Education. A headmaster with a proper university degree, moreover, became an imperative, and consequently Abbot Trafford acted on a suggestion which Dom Rupert had voiced immediately after the school had failed the last inspection. And the Abbot informed the headmaster of his new plan. 'In spite of all the excellent work you have done in the past years, I see no solution but to replace you.'[93] Abbot Trafford announced that Dom Bernard Orchard would succeed him in the fall term, and he also informed Dom Rupert that Dom Bernard would arrive in Ealing as soon as possible in order to acquaint himself with St Benet's and the other Catholic schools in London. Abbot Trafford asked Dom Rupert to be discreet with the news of the new headmaster. Prior Chatterton was also informed, and he approved of the change in leadership.

The Prior's response revealed not only his keen agreement with the appointment, but also contained hints of another movement which several Downside monks had openly supported. 'Two or three communications from Downside have reached us here with regard to a proposition that Ealing should be made an independent foundation,' he noted.[94] Moreover, a Downside monk 'has told us that you have expressed yourself as willing to go into the matter should there be an actual request to you from several and individual members of the Conventus as to their willingness to throw in their lot with Ealing in this matter.' The Prior admitted that he had thought about this possibility for several years, but honestly believed it would never happen. But his excitement escalated with the news that other monks also supported the idea of an independent Ealing. 'In the first place I think one of the most meritorious works an Abbot of a Monastery can do is to found a daughter house,' he told his Abbot. Although he admitted he would be 'of no use to the school', Prior Chatterton emphatically volunteered to join the community if it became independent. Hearing confessions, choir duties, and retreats would be his contribution to an independent Ealing. He knew that Downside would experience great sacrifices, but he maintained that independence might offer 'the only real lasting and final solution to the whole Ealing problem'.

Abbot Trafford responded and confessed that 'it was not until a couple of days before the Chapter that I heard of any desire at Ealing for independence and it never occurred to me that there were sufficient numbers'.[95] Because of Prior Chatterton's letter and several others which urged a discussion dealing with Ealing's independence, the Abbot promised that he 'would go into it carefully'. He ended his letter with some guarded optimism. 'I need only add that if we can go forward with the independence of Ealing it would mean a heavy sacrifice on the part of Downside, but it would not be impossible as we could close some of the Missions and concentrate on vital points.' But the immediate problem still remained the recognition of the school by the Board of Education. Without this, the idea of an independent Ealing would be stillborn.

Abbot Trafford admitted that he felt 'anxious about this refusal of

October 1940

Prior Stanislaus Chatterton, in tin hat, inspects the damage

Prior Benedict Kuypers

*Prior Charles Pontifex, elected first
Abbot of Ealing Abbey in 1955*

The Ealing community at Independence, December 1947.

Standing: D.D. Casimir Wilkins, Gerard Hayes, Bernard Orchard, Kevin Horsey, George Brown, Gilbert Smith, Clement Hayes
Seated: D.D. Philip Clarke, Ambrose Agius, Dominic Young, Charles Pontifex, Basil Bolton, Rupert Hall, Matthew Kehoe

Ealing Abbey, Restored 1962. The church is built in the Perpendicular Gothic style

recognition,' and asked Dom Rupert to send him all the documentation dealing with the unsuccessful 1943 inspection.[96] With the arrival of Dom Bernard in early May, Ealing began to inch toward the precious treasure of recognition. Dom Bernard reported that he was 'absorbing and learning all I can about the place, and as soon as I can formulate my own ideas and plans I will lay them before you'.[97] He described the task before him as formidable, and he probably surprised Abbot Trafford by linking the school's fortunes with the independence of the priory. 'I do not think success is obtainable without the backing of an independent resident community,' he believed. 'Still I have seen enough to convince me that a great thing may be made of Ealing.'

While still at Downside, Dom Bernard had spoken in favour of maintaining the school at Ealing. Abbot Trafford informed Dom Bernard of his new job on the day of the Abbot's defeat at the Chapter concerning the school. Yet the new headmaster thought that he was being sent to Ealing to begin the liquidation of the property and to 'wind it up quickly'.[98] He believed that Abbot Trafford assigned him to Ealing to get the school recognized, and thus begin the process for another vote on the future of St Benet's sometime in the future; for recognition by the government would make a sale easier. But Dom Bernard also began to think about the possibility of independence: he believed that dependent priories had been used by superiors to rid themselves of troublesome monks. If he had to go to Ealing, he was keen that it should survive. And this meant independence from Downside. When it became certain that he would be the new headmaster, Dom Bernard wrote to a confrère at Ealing Priory and told him that 'you Ealing Fathers better get together if you want Ealing to survive'.

As soon as he arrived at Ealing, Dom Bernard began to improve the standing of the school. The change of the name to St Benedict's signalled the dawn of a new regime. His first victory came with the procurement of more space. After an interview, the National Fire Service agreed to return the majority of the school buildings used during the war at the beginning of the next term. Dom Bernard was also promised that the school could occupy the remaining buildings within a year. The new Ealing headmaster informed Abbot Trafford that he would visit Archbishop Bernard Griffin in the future and would also arrange a meeting with the local educational officer concerning recognition. The dream of independence never left Dom Bernard's thoughts, and he approached Abbot Trafford on the question. In May, he pointed out that the Abbot's backing and support of this proposal would represent 'the biggest chance Downside has ever had for bringing Benedictine and Gregorian influence to bear upon the conversion of London'.[99] 'This place in spite of its suburban site would become the chief spiritual centre for West London.' Independence was a necessity. 'There must be a monastery here for the scheme to succeed and bear fruit,' he concluded.

Abbot Trafford did bring the question of Ealing to the forum of a community meeting, and on 22 May, the Downside Chapter considered the question of Ealing's independence. Unlike the earlier Chapter on the future of the school, the mind of the Downside community divided on this issue. One member described the attitude of the meeting as 'indecisive'. Some thought that Abbot Trafford had no intention of pushing for Ealing's independence. Those opposed to this move took their cue from the Abbot who allegedly announced that if the Chapter ceded independence, he would not be responsible for the consequences. Others believed that Trafford was only 'testing the waters' to see how he stood after his defeat on Ealing in the April Chapter. Most monks, however, seriously maintained that Ealing was not ready for this step, while those who supported the separation from Downside argued that the London community could successfully manage its own affairs. Not surprisingly, the Downside Chapter rejected the proposal as inopportune and premature.

Regardless of his dubious intention towards Ealing, Abbot Trafford's zeal for government recognition of Ealing's school never faded. On 24 May 1945, the day he publicly announced his appointment of Dom Bernard as the new headmaster, the Abbot sent a letter to the parents which outlined his vision for the school's future. He noted that 'the new Educational Act makes fresh and heavy demands on schools, and energetic steps will have to be taken in order to get the schools officially recognized as fully efficient in all departments by the Ministry of Education'.[100] Efficiency and high academic standards also represented major goals in Archbishop Griffin's plan to reorganize the capital's Roman Catholic Grammar Schools. And Ealing wanted to participate in this diocesan programme. 'Though nothing final can yet be decided,' Abbot Trafford explained to the parents, 'it is very much hoped that we may take part in this scheme and that St Benedict's may play an important part in it by becoming the official Catholic Grammar School for the West London area'. Dom Bernard worked to bring this dream of excellence to fulfilment. In May, for example, he reported that the numbers for the new term had greatly increased: he counted 145 students already enrolled; and he told Trafford that he had set his aim at 200 boys. During the summer he continued to work toward the required recognition and his enrolment goal. September smiled on St Benedict's. The term opened with Dom Bernard greeting 223 students.

Changes also took place on the monastic side when Abbot Trafford announced a number of assignments from Downside which touched Ealing. Dom Rupert went to Beccles, and the Abbot named a new superior. Dom Ambrose Agius, who had been at Ealing earlier, returned from Liverpool to act as Prior and parish priest. Dom Stanislaus Chatterton, who had expressed some interest in remaining at an independent Ealing, went to Bungay. The new Prior began his tenure in office with a burst of enthusiasm. 'We are getting under way,' he told Abbot Trafford, 'the framework is fixed, now we have to keep the team up to the collar and pulling evenly'.[101] In October, he informed

Downside that the parish had been divided into districts and that all the church societies and clubs were functioning at full steam. Prior Agius confessed to Abbot Trafford that the change to a post-war world might have been too abrupt and sudden for some members of the community. 'There is a good keen community here, but naturally the present regime is very different from the wartime laissez-faire.'[102] 'I think it may be some time before the War Chaplains really settle down,' he continued.

The parallel movements of academic recognition and independence for the priory, however, dwarfed all other activities at Ealing. During his first months as headmaster, Dom Bernard had already written to the Ministry of Education and requested an inspection for the spring of 1946. In May of that year, he informed Downside that the inspection had been scheduled for the first week of June. The anxious headmaster also commented on the personality of the inspector in charge. Noting that he had met her in the past, he told his Abbot that 'though she looks formidable she proved to be very kind and helpful'.[103] Time and effort paid off; St Benedict's, Ealing, passed the required inspection and received the treasured recognition by the Ministry of Education a year later. Public-school status, therefore, became the next goal for the Benedictine school. Also, the campaign for an independent monastic house at Ealing seemed to have picked up speed and support.

A change in the leadership at Downside pushed Ealing further down the road to independence. In September 1946, the Downside community elected Christopher Butler as its new Abbot. The change surprised very few. By 1946, Abbot Trafford had offended or irritated a number of his monks. In the opinion of some, the Abbot had become despotic, autocratic, and acted the role of a *grand seigneur*. Consequently, the need for fresh blood became obvious. Christopher Butler, the headmaster of Downside School, appeared the obvious successor, and he brought to the abbatial office a refreshing and positive policy towards Ealing. Trafford, many believed, had viewed Ealing Priory as a troublesome and costly place which drained needed manpower from Downside, and the history of his reign showed a desire to trim the sails at the London priory. For Abbot Trafford, Ealing represented all the evils, attractions, and allurements of suburbia, which he saw as not conducive to the monastic schedule. But Ealing did serve a purpose. In the minds of many, it represented a monastic Siberia. One monk thought that Trafford related to Ealing with a touch of snobbery because of its size, lack of resources, and its extensive parochial involvements; it was certainly not Downside with its country atmosphere, proper monastic routine, and prestigious school. And, many believed, if Trafford were elected to another term, he would have used it as a mandate to close down Ealing.

Abbot Christopher Butler's new Ealing policy also reflected the thinking of some Downside monks about the existence of dependent priories. In general, many were not happy with these anomalies. The past policy of some superiors who transferred monks in and out of these priories seemed unmonastic. And the new Abbot believed that a priory dependent on the mother house for nearly forty-six years represented a Benedictine aberration. Ealing, therefore, should receive a fair hearing at the Chapter and be granted independence. Abbot Butler's first actions towards Ealing revealed his concern and also a positive interest. Due to reasons of health, the Abbot quickly replaced Dom Ambrose Agius as Prior. Dom Charles Pontifex became the new superior, but Dom Ambrose soon returned as a member of the community. In other matters, some also believed that Abbot Butler began to treat Ealing as an independent house before the Downside Chapter voted on the issue.

But Abbot Butler had to prove to his community that Ealing should become an independent monastery. Convinced that he was right, and encouraged by other monks, the Abbot started the constitutional machinery rolling. In spring 1947, therefore, the Downside Chapter met to consider the independence of Ealing Priory. The spirit of the Chapter reflected a consensus that Ealing had grown to a point where it should enjoy the rights and privileges associated with an independent Benedictine house. A majority of the Ealing monks went to Downside determined to fight for their independence, and they found and were encouraged by others who felt the same way. Along with Abbot Butler, this group argued that long-term dependent priories harmed the true spirit of Benedictinism. Ealing, for example, should be given the freedom to run its own affairs and to shoulder the responsibilities like any other monastery. Some addressed the harmful effects of the so-called 'autumn manoeuvre' when past superiors had re-assigned monks indiscriminately, without concern for the person or the needs of the priory. Some grew to like life at Ealing; others abhorred the idea of going to the suburb and were never happy there. Others pointed out that Ealing had become too large and too important to remain dependent on a distant Downside; a stability of policy and manpower could only be guaranteed by an independent status. Another group of monks thought Downside should not be responsible for the workings of its sizeable and complex foundation, and they tried to convince the Chapter to grant monastic freedom. Arguing for independence, but in a negative manner, some Downside monks believed that Ealing would always remain problematic, and voted to free Downside of this burden.

Those opposed to independence also voiced strong reasons for keeping the London priory tied to Downside. It was impossible to live a proper monastic life according to the English Benedictine tradition in a town; city life tended to tarnish the Benedictine ideal. Benedict's *fuga mundi* or 'flight from the world' always implied seclusion and withdrawal. Some believed that Ealing was deserting and taking valuable manpower and capital with it, and they maintained that the interests of the mother house required Ealing to remain dependent on it. Downside still needed a safety valve, some argued, to absorb the monk who had problems living at Downside. And some monks appealed to a more mundane reason for rejecting Ealing's bid for independence: Ealing had no money, little capital, and therefore would flounder.

Ealing's financial health and prospect for the future became a major subject for the Chapter. The outlook looked good: surplus assets of £2,826, substantial land and property, modest capital, 'the healthy state of the parish and the loyalty of a wide circle of friends'.[104] Moreover, this memorandum written by Abbot Butler pointed out that 'there are no debts or charges on the property, and the Priory will have no obligations of any sort or kind at the inception of its independence'. The Chapter also discussed the sources of revenue, and the future of the parish and school. The average surplus before the war stood at approximately £100, but 1946 saw a deficit of £520. But, Butler explained, 'the Downside Conventual Chapter has agreed to meet any Revenue deficits, as [the] General Chapter may consider proper, for the period covered by the next three ordinary General Chapters'. An auditors' report shed more light on Ealing's finances. This report drew attention to the £2,261 received from the National Fire Service for rent of the school buildings.[105] With this increment, the auditors estimated Ealing's excess income for 1946 at approximately £240, but they also warned against any false optimism or security. 'It is difficult to say whether the stream of expenditure has now dried up, but it seems clear that no substantial profits can be expected at Ealing unless receipts, especially from the school, can be increased.' Consequently, the report singled out another source of income: 'A start has been made in this direction by raising the Fees'.

The result of these deliberations shocked no one. The Chapter of Downside voted decisively in favour of Ealing's independence and 'passed a proposal to erect Ealing Priory into an independent house with the rank of a Conventual Priory'.[106] Consequently, Abbot Butler wrote to the other monasteries of the English Benedictine Congregation and explained that, according to their constitution, 'each house of the Congregation has to express its opinion of this proposal'. Butler sent them a summary of Ealing's financial records, which had been examined by the Downside Chapter. And the favourable replies trickled in during the summer.

Abbot Christopher Butler then sought the approval of Rome for Downside's decision to make Ealing an independent Benedictine priory. He also sent a letter to the monks of his monastery asking for volunteers to join an independent Ealing. But before Butler took the proposal to the General Chapter, he adopted a suggestion by the auditors concerning the economic health of the school. The parents were informed that the Benedictines 'have decided to raise the fees to a figure sufficient to maintain the education of the boys at the highest possible level'.[107] This letter announced the new tuition scale: Upper School, twenty guineas (£21) a term, and fifteen guineas (£15.15s.0d) a term for the Junior School. With the approval of the Downside

Chapter secured and the additional financial safeguard of increased fees, the question of Ealing's independence at the next congregational chapter appeared straightforward.

In the early autumn, the Abbot President of the English Benedictine Congregation, Abbot Herbert Byrne, announced that an Extraordinary General Chapter would be held at Downside Abbey on 9 October. Two items were placed on the agenda, and the one which was concerned with Ealing read: 'To receive, consider and vote in accordance with Constitution 177 on the petition of the Abbot of Downside that the dependent Priory of St Benedict's Ealing, be granted that status of an independent conventual Priory in our Congregation'.[108] The General Chapter reviewed the decision reached by the Downside Chapter, discussed the memorandum which outlined Ealing's economic stability, and was told that Ealing Priory expected to realize a profit during the current year. The General Chapter, naturally, gave its consent. A week after this meeting, Abbot Butler officially announced the outcome, namely, 'a proposal for the independence of Ealing was passed'.[109] But the General Chapter altered one of the conditions suggested by Downside: 'Owing to an amendment of the resolution originally proposed, Downside is not required to guarantee Ealing against revenue deficits'. While awaiting for approval from Rome, Abbot Butler also revealed that he would shortly 'inform fourteen of those who volunteered to join the new community that they have been selected to do so'.

Roman sanction, the membership of the new priory, and its canonical establishment constituted the next step in Ealing's history. On 15 November 1947, Abbot Butler received the rescript from the Sacred Congregation of Religious which declared Ealing an independent priory under the jurisdiction of the English Benedictine Congregation. Dom Philip Langdon, the English Benedictine procurator in Rome, sent Butler the document and remarked that this 'closes the procedure'.[110] Soon after, Abbot President Herbert Byrne accepted the rescript in the name of the Congregation and told Abbot Butler that he planned to be present at a ceremony when the new members would transfer their vows of stability to Ealing Priory. And on 19 December 1947, in the presence of the Abbot President and Abbot Christopher Butler, Ealing was constituted an independent Benedictine priory. The following monks volunteered to make up the new independent priory: Dominic Young, Basil Bolton, Ambrose Agius, Rupert Hall, Philip Clarke, Matthew Kehoe, Clement Hayes, Gilbert Smith, Bernard Orchard, Gerard Hayes, Casimir Wilkins, George Brown, and Kevin Horsey. The Roman rescript gave Abbot Butler the authority to select Ealing's first Prior, and he appointed Charles Pontifex to an eight-year term. The monks then renewed their vows to their new superior.

On the following Sunday, 21 December, Cardinal Griffin presided at the public celebration. He began by emphasizing that 'the establishment of the Benedictine community here at Ealing as an independent priory marks a further development in Benedictine life in this country'.[111] The Archbishop thanked Abbot Butler for the great sacrifices Downside had made for the Ealing foundation, and then praised the work done by the London Benedictines in educating the Catholic youth of the area. After taking his audience on a journey through pages of English Benedictine history, he invoked the power and the protection of the saints and martyrs of the order 'on the . . . monks of Ealing Priory in their future work for the conversion of this great country'.[112]

Abbot Butler also spoke a few words. Taking the theme from *Hebrews*, 'Let the charity of the brotherhood abide in you', he told the congregation that the 'social principle of our whole religion, the principle of the family, that principle of corporate life bound together in the bonds of charity, is a principle which St Benedict incorporated into his rule for monks'.[113] Comparing the independence of a monastery to the action of a mature adult who leaves his father's house to start a new family and becomes a father himself, the Abbot stated that 'it is just that moment which we hope and trust has been reached in the life of your own Priory of Ealing'.[114] 'It is a wonderful moment in the life of human beings when they set up home for themselves,' he continued, 'and it is a natural instinct, I may say it is a supernatural instinct, that we should flock to their assistance, and encourage them with help and affection in the great moment in their lives.'[115]

Joy, enthusiasm, and a sense of accomplishment coloured this event. *The Priorian* explained that 'we are a monastery in our right. . .'[116] 'The beginnings are still small,' the author pointed out, 'but with confidence we can look to the future and picture the stately Church, the cloistered abbey and the dignified School buildings that will one day arise around us.' The *Downside Review* told its readers about the new status of Ealing and stated that 'this step realized a hope that was expressed some thirty years ago, and that present conditions at Ealing, where parish and school are both thriving and vigorous, make possible'.[117]

Numerous letters of congratulations and wishes of good luck and support poured in to the new independent monastery from old friends of the community, secular priests, and members of Downside. Several individuals who had enjoyed close connections with Ealing expressed their happiness. The former Abbot of Downside, Bruno Hicks, sent his best wishes to Prior Charles and told his friends that he would 'follow the fortunes of the Ealing Community with interest and with my prayers, such as they are'.[118] Stationed at Bungay, the war-time Prior, Stanislaus Chatterton, wrote to Dom Basil Bolton, the 'old man of Ealing', and expressed his feelings of joy, but a touch of sadness also emerged. 'I cannot tell you how happy I am personally at this day and its events,' he revealed, 'but at the same time my happiness is tempered with a gnawing inside that I have not been allowed to be one of you.'[119] He acknowledged that his advanced years would 'saddle [Ealing] . . . with a more or less Passenger'. After reminiscing about his various experiences at Ealing, he wished Dom Basil much success. Abbot Butler also sent a personal letter 'before the ship is launched'.[120] 'We shall watch with the proud anxiety of a parent,' he wrote to Prior Charles, 'the fortunes and achievements of Downside's progeny.' He also expressed a 'hope and trust that the links of charity and affection between the daughter and the mother community will be uniquely strong'.

Epilogue

ovices soon arrived at the London monastery. On 13 September 1948, Prior Charles Pontifex clothed four postulants 'with the full monastic habit as the first novices of the new foundation, the first independent monastery in London since the suppression of Westminster Abbey by Queen Elizabeth.'[1] The monastic community slowly began to grow, parish work increased, and the school became recognized as a first-rate educational institution.

Less than a decade after its independence, Rome recognized Ealing Priory's monastic maturity and stability, and raised the London Benedictine community to the rank of an abbey. The papal brief which announced this honour, *Londinii in Urbe*, was issued in Rome on 26 May 1955. The Roman document stated that 'it was only at the close of the last century that monastic life according to the Rule of St Benedict began to flourish again in the busy and populous city of London, from which place England, caught up on the tide of new opinions, had fallen away from the ancient ancestral faith'. The brief then traced the early history of Ealing, emphasized the trials the young community suffered during the 1939–45 war, and noted that when peace was restored 'this house of religion and divine service was not only brought back to its former flourishing state, but developed so much that in 1947 it was granted by this same Apostolic See the title and rights of a Conventual Priory'. This document made references to the proud heritage of English Roman Catholicism, and monasticism in particular:

> It has accordingly seemed expedient that this London house of the Order of St Benedict, after so many vicissitudes, should be honoured by the Abbatial dignity, so that at no greater distance from the monastery of Westminster, once the celebrated abode of these monks and the ancient centre of their Congregation, an important religious foundation should be constituted in London.

In July, the twenty-four Ealing monks elected their Prior, Dom Charles Pontifex, as their first Abbot. In a few weeks, however, he sustained a serious injury is a car accident, and resigned. The monks then elected the former headmaster and Prior, Dom Rupert Hall, and he immediately began to repair

189

the damages suffered by the abbey church during the war. Abbot Rupert resigned in 1967, and he was succeeded by Francis Rossiter. Growth seemed to mark the 1960s and 1970s: a parish centre and a new monastery extension graced the 'island site'. With the completion of this extension, the houses formerly occupied by the monks became a guest house and prayer centre.

Currently, Benedictine monasticism is thriving in Ealing. The three schools have a combined enrolment of approximately eight hundred students. The Prayer Centre offer the opportunity for private and group meditation, and the Retreat Centre carries on an active programme of personal and directed retreats during the year. In 1977, Ealing Abbey established a foundation in Montreal, Canada, at the request of the local Archbishop. A place where one can experience prayer and meditation, it has been affiliated with the American monastery, Mount Saviour. St Benedict's parish offers extensive religious and social programmes for its congregation. Staffed by four priests, who are assisted by other members of the monastery, the parish numbered over 5,000 in 1987. At Ealing itself the monastic life continues to grow stronger. The membership of the abbey reached twenty-six in 1987. Because of the spirit and success of these urban monks, the ominous warnings and prophesies about the sterility and fruitlessness of the Benedictine life in a city have been proved groundless.

Appendixes

APPENDIX 1

Archbishops of Westminster who had contact with Ealing Abbey

Cardinal Herbert Vaughan (1893–1903)

Cardinal Francis Bourne (1903–35)

Cardinal Arthur Hinsley (1935–43)

Cardinal Bernard Griffin (1945–56)

Cardinal William Godfrey (1956–63)

APPENDIX 2

Superiors at Downside associated with Ealing Abbey

Prior Hugh Edmund Ford (1885–8); (1894–1900); as Abbot Ford, 1900–06.

Abbot Cuthbert Butler (1906–22)

Abbot Leander Ramsey (1922–29)

Abbot John Chapman (1929–33)

Abbot Bruno Hicks (1933–38)

Abbot Sigebert Trafford (1938–46)

Abbot Christopher Butler (1946–66)

APPENDIX 3

Ealing Priors and Abbots

Prior Wulstan Pearson (1916–25)

Prior Benedict Kuypers (1925–35)

Prior Edward Green (1935–38)

Prior Mark Pontifex (1938)

Prior Stanislaus Chatterton (1938–45)

Prior Ambrose Agius (1945–46)

Prior Charles Pontifex (1946–55)

Abbot Charles Pontifex (1955–56)

Abbot Rupert Hall (1956–67)

Abbot Francis Rossiter (1967-

Notes to the Text

List of Abbreviations used (see also Bibliography)

AAW	Archives of the Archdiocese of Westminster
DAA	Downside Abbey Archives
DR	Downside Review
EAA	Ealing Abbey Archives
MCT	*Middlesex County Times*
MH	Mill Hill Fathers Archives
Butler	Butler Papers, Downside Abbey Archives
Butler EAA	Butler Papers, Ealing Abbey Archives
Cave	Cave Papers, Ealing Abbey Archives
Corney	Corney Papers, Ealing Abbey Archives
Dolan	Dolan Papers, Ealing Abbey Archives
Ealing DAA	Ealing Abbey Papers, Downside Abbey Archives
Ford	Ford Papers, Ealing Abbey Archives
Gasquet	Gasquet Papers, Downside Abbey Archives
Pearson	Pearson Papers, Ealing Abbey Archives
Ramsey	Ramsey Papers, Downside Abbey Archives

CHAPTER I

A NEW WESTMINSTER CATHEDRAL
AND BENEDICTINE MONKS (pages 1–22)

1 O. Chadwick, *The Victorian Church*, Part II (London: Adam and Charles Black, 1972), p. 242.

2 E.S. Purcell, *Life of Cardinal Manning, Archbishop of Westminster* (London: MacMillan Co., 1896), p. 353.

3 Quoted in S.L. Leslie, *Henry Edward Manning: His Life and Labour* (London: Burns and Oates, 1921), p. 171.

4 Ibid., pp. 171–2.

5 E.S. Purcell, *Life of Cardinal Manning, Archbishop of Westminster*, p. 354.

6 For biographies of Cardinal Vaughan see: A Mill Hill Father, *Remembered in Blessing: The Courtfield Story* (London: Sands Co., 1969); and J.G. Snead-Cox, *The Life of Cardinal Vaughan* 2 vols. (London: Herbert and David, 1910).

7 J.D. Holmes, *More Roman than Rome: English Catholicism in the Nineteenth Century* (London: Burns and Oates, 1978), p. 201.

8 Ibid.

9 J.G. Snead-Cox, *The Life of Cardinal Vaughan*, vol. ii, pp. 319–20.

10 *The Tablet*, 6 July 1895.

11 Ibid. The Cardinal's brother, Jerome, died on 9 September 1896.

12 M.A. Hicks, 'Ealing and Brentford,' *The Victorian History of the Counties of England: A History of Middlesex*, vol. vii (Oxford: Oxford University Press, 1982), p. 106.

13 M. Robbins, *Middlesex* (London: Collins, 1953), p. 238.

14 A. Jahn, *Railroads and Suburban Development: Outer West London 1850–1900*, University of London unpublished M. Phil. thesis, 1970, pp. 59–60.

15 Ibid., p. 10.

16 *Middlesex County Times*, 1 June 1872.

17 MCT, 27 September 1879.

18 A. Jahn, *Railroads and Suburban Development*, p. 92.

19 M.A. Hicks, 'Ealing and Brentford', p. 111.

20 E. Jackson, *Annals of Ealing: From the Twelfth Century to the Present Time* (London: Phillimore, 1890), p. 297.

21 Ibid., pp. 297–8.

22 M.A. Hicks, 'Ealing and Brentford', p. 100.

23 M. Robbins, *Middlesex*, pp. 238–42.

24 C. Jones, *From Village to Corporate Town or Forty Years of Municipal Life* (Ealing: S.B. Spaull, 1902), p. 8.

25 *Ealing: A County Town Near London*, 1904, p. 1. No author, place of publication or publisher given.

26 M. Timms, 'Brentham, A Pioneer Garden Suburb,' *Local Historian*, 1964, p. 39. *Local Historian* was a publication of the Ealing Local Historical Society.

27 M.A. Hicks, 'Ealing and Brentford,' p. 137.

28 Ibid., p. 111.

29 A. Jahn, *Railroads and Suburban Development*, p. 156.

30 *Ealing Illustrated*, p. 3, quoted in M.A. Hicks, 'Ealing and Brentford', p. 111.

31 *Ealing: A County Town Near London*, p. 19.

32 Ibid., p. 15.

33 Ibid.

34 E. Jackson, *Annals of Ealing*, p. 291.

35 C. Jones, *Ealing: From Village to Corporate Town*, p. 147

36 'Memorandum,' *Liber Baptizatorum*, 1897–1919, Ealing Abbey Archives, Charlbury Grove, London.

37 Ibid.

38 J.G. Snead-Cox, *The Life of Cardinal Vaughan*, vol. ii, p. 347.

39 Ibid.

40 Ibid., p. 348.

41 For a history of the English Benedictines in the nineteenth century see British Museum, *The Benedictines in Britain* (London: The British Library, 1980); E. Cruise, 'Development of the Religious Orders', in *The English Catholics 1850–1950* (London: Burns and Oates, 1950); and B. Green, *The English Benedictine Congregation* (London: Catholic Truth Society. 1980).

42 For a biography of Hugh Edmund Ford, see B. Hicks, *Hugh Edmund Ford* (London: Sands, Co., 1947).

43 Vaughan to Ford, 5 May 1896, Ford Papers, EAA (*Ford*)

44 Ford to Vaughan, 6 May 1896, *Ford*.

45 See 'In Memoriam: Abbot Snow,' *Downside Review* Spring, 1905, pp. 1–18. Snow was the titular Abbot of Glastonbury.

46 Ford to Snow, 6 May 1896, *Ford*.

47 B. Hicks, *Hugh Edmund Ford*, p. 57.

48 Ibid., p. 93.

49 Ibid., pp. 121–2.

50 'In Memoriam: Abbot Snow,' *DR*, Spring 1905, p. 6. See also H.N. Birt, *Obit Book of the English Benedictines From 1600 to 1912* (Edinburgh: Mercat Press, 1923), p. 200.

51 Ibid., p. 7.

52 Snow to Ford, 12 May 1896, *Ford*.

53 See Chapter Two for the early history of the relationship between Fr O'Halloran and the Ealing monks.

54 Sister Mary Frances to Ford, 17 May 1896, *Ford.*

55 Sister Mary Frances to Ford, 3 June 1896, *Ford.*

56 Snow to Ford, 3 June 1896, *Ford.*

57 Ford to Vaughan, 6 May 1896, *Ford.*

58 B. Hicks, *Hugh Edmund Ford*, p. 73

59 Ford to Vaughan, 5 June 1896, *Ford.*

60 Ibid.

61 Vaughan to Ford, 10 June 1896, *Ford.*

62 Vaughan to Ford, 17 June 1896, *Ford.*

63 'Notes: Ealing,' 28 June 1896, *Ford.*

64 B. Hicks, *Hugh Edmund Ford*, pp. 76–7.

65 'Notes: Ealing,' 28 June 1896, *Ford.*

66 Handwritten Note on Vaughan's Original 1896 Proposal, *Ford.*

67 Ford to Snow, 6 July 1896, *Ford.*

68 Snow to Ford, 7 July 1896, *Ford.*

69 Tidmarsh to Ford, 23 July 1896, *Ford.*

70 Richards to Ford, July 1896, *Ford.*

71 Sister Mary Frances to Ford, 21 June 1896, *Ford.*

72 Sister Mary Frances to Ford, 8 July 1896, *Ford.*

73 Ford to Sister Mary Frances, 13 July 1896, *Ford.*

74 For a description of the governance of the English Benedictine Congregation during this period, see B. Hicks, *Hugh Edmund Ford*, pp. 100–37.

75 Ford to O'Gorman, 17 August 1896, *Ford.*

76 Ford to Benedictine Fathers, 18 August 1896, *Ford.*

77 Ford to O'Gorman, 21 August 1896, Ford Papers in Downside Abbey Archives, Downside Abbey, Bath.

78 Morrall to O'Gorman, 23 August 1896, Ealing Abbey Papers, DAA (*Ealing DAA*).

79 O'Gorman to Wood, 26 August 1896, *Ealing, DAA.*

80 Two small Benedictine houses had been opened in East Dulwich and at Great Ormond Street.

81 Wood to O'Gorman, 28 August 1896, *Ealing DAA.*

82 Doyle to O'Gorman, 1 September 1896, *Ealing DAA.*

83 O'Gorman to Ford, 3 September 1896, *Ford.*

84 O'Gorman to Ford, 9 September 1896, *Ford.*

85 O'Gorman to Ford, 29 September 1896, *Ford.*

86 Snow to Ford, 15 September 1896, *Ford.*

87 Snow to Ford, 23 September 1896, *Ford.*

88 Ford to Snow, 30 September 1896, *Ford.*

89 Ford to Vaughan, 1 October 1896, *Ford*.

90 Ford to Snow, 30 September 1896, *Ford*.

91 Ford to O'Gorman, 12 September 1896, *Ford*.

92 Ford to O'Gorman, 25 September 1896, *Ford*.

93 Petition of Prior Ford to the Holy See, *Ford*.

94 A copy of the Rescript is among the Ford Papers at Ealing Abbey.

95 Vaughan to Ford, 28 October 1896, *Ford*.

96 'Notes Extracted from the Agenda of the Chapter of Westminster,' 6 November 1896, *Ford*.

97 Johnson to Ford, 2 November 1896, *Ford*.

98 Johnson to Ford, 7 December 1896, *Ford*.

99 'Odds and Ends,' *DR*, December 1896, p. 314.

100 'Obituary of Reverend Dom Bernard Bulbeck,' *DR*, December 1901, p. 343.

101 Vaughan to Ford, 1 February 1897, *Ford*.

102 *Catholic Times*, 23 July 1897.

103 *Universe*, 31 July 1897.

104 *MCT*, 3 September 1897.

105 Bulbeck to Ford, 11 October 1897, *Ford*.

106 *Spiritualia Ministeria*, 1897, EAA.

107 'General Balance, 11.18.97,' EAA.

108 Johnson to Ford, 19 December 1898, *Ford*.

109 Gasquet to Ford, 28 June 1898, *Ford*.

110 Ford to O'Gorman, 21 December 1898, *Ford*.

111 'Obituary,' *DR*, 1901, p. 343.

112 'Odds and Ends,' *DR*, March 1899, p. 111.

113 Annual Account of the Mission of St Benedict's Ealing, 1898, EAA.

114 *Spiritualia Ministeria*, 1898, EAA.

115 Ford to Weld-Blundell, 30 November 1898, *Ford*.

116 Snow to Ford, 30 September 1897, *Ford*.

117 Snow to Ford, 16 September 1898, *Ford*.

118 Gasquet to Ford, 18 August 1897, *Ford*.

119 Gasquet to Ford, 17 September 1898, *Ford*.

120 Ford to O'Gorman and members of the Regimen, 19 September 1898, *Ford*.

CHAPTER II

FATHER O'HALLORAN AND THE MONKS OF EALING ABBEY (pages 23–49)

1 Personal File: Richard O'Halloran, Mill Hill Archives, Mill Hill, London (MH).

2 O'Halloran to Benoit, 2 December 1880, MH.

3 Verrey to O'Halloran, 7 December 1880, MH.

4 O'Connell to Benoit, December 1880, MH.

5 Log Book, MH.

6 O'Halloran to Benoit, 28 December 1880, MH.

7 J.G. Snead-Cox, *The Life of Cardinal Vaughan*, vol. i. p. 162.

8 Ibid., p. 165.

9 J.D. Holmes, *More Roman than Rome*, p. 174.

10 O'Halloran to Vaughan, 19 February 1881, printed in *Cardinal Vaughan and Father O'Halloran: The Rights of the Secular Priests Vindicated*, 1901. Printed by Father O'Halloran, this pamphlet detailed the history of the relationship between the two clerics and also contains some of the early correspondence.

11 O'Halloran to Benoit, 6 September 1881, MH.

12 Benoit to Vaughan, 7 September 1881, MH.

13 O'Halloran to Vaughan, 28 January 1882, MH.

14 Bagshawe to Vaughan, 3 February 1882, MH.

15 *Cardinal Vaughan and Father O'Halloran.*

16 Ibid.

17 Ibid.

18 Bagshawe to O'Halloran, 8 May 1882, MH. The period was later extended to a month.

19 O'Halloran to Vaughan, 11 May 1882, MH.

20 O'Halloran to Vaughan, 13 May 1882, MH.

21 Douglas to Benoit, 29 December 1882, MH.

22 O'Halloran to Benoit, 21 February 1884, MH.

23 Ibid.

24 Benoit to O'Halloran, 5 March 1884, MH.

25 O'Halloran to Benoit, 27 March 1884, MH.

26 *Daily Chronicle*, 26 July 1897.

27 Great Britain, Parliament, Sessional Papers (Commons) *1887 York East Riding Election* vol. LXVI.

28 *Daily Chronicle*, 27 July 1897, printed in *MCT*, 7 August 1897.

29 Lacy to O'Halloran, 17 November 1886, printed in *MCT*, 7 August 1897.

30 Printed in *MCT*, 7 August 1897.

31 Vassall to *Daily Chronicle*, printed in *MCT*, 7 August 1897.

32 Lacy to O'Halloran, 20 March 1888, printed in *Cardinal Vaughan and Father O'Halloran.*

33 *Cardinal Vaughan and Father O'Halloran.*

34 *MCT*, 15 July 1905.

35 *Cardinal Vaughan and Father O'Halloran.*

36 Ibid.

37 Herbert Cardinal Vaughan, 'Notification to the Catholics Living in Ealing and the Neighbourhood,' 1897, EAA.

38 Ledochowski to Vaughan, 4 May 1894, Vaughan Papers, Archives of the Archdiocese of Westminster, 16 Abingdon Road, London.

39 O'Halloran Statement, 4 June 1894, O'Halloran File, AAW.

40 *Cardinal Vaughan and Father O'Halloran.*

41 O'Halloran to Ford, 20 December 1898, *Ford.*

42 Vaughan, 'Notification to the Catholics Living in Ealing and the Neighbourhood.'

43 O'Halloran Statement, 13 July 1894, O'Halloran File, AAW.

44 In reality the debt was £17.17s.4d.

45 *Daily Chronicle*, 26 July 1897.

46 *Cardinal Vaughan and Father O'Halloran.*

47 *The Tablet*, 28 November 1896.

48 *Daily Chronicle*, 24 July 1897.

49 Clipping Book, EAA.

50 *MCT*, 23 September 1899.

51 *MCT*, 16 September 1899.

52 Vaughan, 'Notification to the Catholics Living in Ealing and the Neighbourhood'.

53 O'Halloran to Ford, 17 June 1896, printed in *Daily Chronicle*, 28 July 1897.

54 *Cardinal Vaughan and Father O'Halloran.*

55 Barry to O'Halloran, 25 August 1896, printed in *Cardinal Vaughan and Father O'Halloran.*

56 Barry to O'Halloran, 27 August 1896, printed in *Cardinal Vaughan and Father O'Halloran.*

57 Barry to O'Halloran, 16 September 1896, printed in *MCT*.

58 Vaughan to O'Halloran, 27 August 1896, printed in *MCT*.

59 Vaughan, 'Notification to the Catholics Living in Ealing and the Neighbourhood'.

60 Johnson to Ford, 30 January 1897, *Ford.*

61 Vaughan to Ford, 11 March 1897, *Ford.*

62 Vaughan, 'Notification to the Catholics Living in Ealing and the Neighbourhood'.

63 O'Halloran to Brenan (a Dean of the Archdiocese of Westminster), 22 March 1897, *Ford*.

64 Ford to O'Halloran, 2 April 1897, printed in *MCT*, 30 September 1899.

65 Barry to O'Halloran, 8 April 1897, *Ford*.

66 Vaughan to Bulbeck, 9 April 1987, *Ford*.

67 Vaughan, 'Notification to the Catholics Living in Ealing and the Neighbourhood'.

68 Ledochowski to Vaughan, 19 May 1897, Vaughan Papers, AAW.

69 Ledochowski to O'Halloran, 20 May 1897, Vaughan Papers, AAW.

70 O'Halloran to Ledochowski, 31 May 1897, printed in *Catholic Times*, 6 August 1897.

71 *Universe*, 31 July 1897.

72 *Daily Chronicle*, 27 July 1897.

73 *Westminster Gazette*, 20 July 1897.

74 Barry to Bulbeck, 5 June 1897, *Ford*.

75 Vaughan, 'Notification to the Catholics Living in Ealing and the Neighbourhood'.

76 O'Halloran to Vaughan, 23 July 1897, *Ford*.

77 Brenan to Bulbeck, 24 July 1897, *Ford*.

78 Snow to Ford, 20 April 1897, *Ford*.

79 O'Halloran to Ford, 3 April 1897, printed in *MCT*, 16 September 1899.

80 Snow to Ford, 2 July 1897, *Ford*.

81 Barry to Bulbeck, 26 August 1897, *Ford*.

82 Bulbeck to Ford, 11 October 1897, *Ford*.

83 *MCT*, 19 June 1897.

84 *MCT*, 10 July 1897.

85 *MCT*, 17 July 1897.

86 *MCT*, 24 July 1897.

87 Ibid.

88 *Daily Chronicle*, 23 July 1897.

89 *Daily Chronicle*, 24 July 1897.

90 *Daily Chronicle*, 26 July 1897.

91 Ibid.

92 *Daily Chronicle*, 27 July 1897.

93 Ibid.

94 *Daily Chronicle*, 28 July 1897.

95 Ibid.

96 *Daily Mail*, 19 July 1897.

97 *Daily Mail*, 20 July 1897.

98 *Catholic Herald*, 23 July 1897.

99 *Catholic Herald*, 30 July 1897.

100 *Universe*, 24 July 1897.

101 *Universe*, 14 August 1897.

102 *Catholic Times*, 1 October 1897.

103 *Catholic Times*, 8 October 1897.

104 *Catholic Times*, 15 October 1897.

105 *Daily Chronicle*, 27 July 1897.

106 *MCT*, 7 August 1897.

107 *MCT*, 3 September 1897.

108 *MCT*, 18 September 1897.

109 *MCT*, 6 October 1897.

110 *MCT*, 28 October 1897.

111 *MCT*, 18 December 1897.

112 *MCT*, 1 January 1898.

113 *MCT*, 5 March 1898.

114 *MCT*, 8 May 1898.

115 *MCT*, 22 October 1898.

116 O'Halloran to Ford, 20 December 1898, *Ford*.

117 *Ealing Gazette*, 19 December 1898.

118 Ibid.

119 *MCT*, 19 November 1898.

120 Dolan to Ford, 10 October 1899, Dolan Papers, EAA (*Dolan*).

121 Ford to Corney, 21 December 1898, *Ford*.

122 Ford to Corney, 22 December 1898, *Ford*.

123 Bulbeck to Ford, 10 March 1899, *Ford*.

CHAPTER III

CONSOLIDATION AND EXPANSION: THE EALING BENEDICTINES AT THE TURN OF THE CENTURY (pages 50–82)

1 'In Memoriam: Dom Gilbert Dolan,' *DR*, 1914, pp. 252–254.

2 Ford to Dolan, 28 February 1899, *Ford*.

3 Ford to Corney, 22 December 1898, *Ford*.

4 *MCT*, 14 January 1899.

5 *MCT*, 21 March 1899.

6 *MCT*, 8 April 1899.

7 *MCT*, 8 July 1899.

8 Ford to Weld-Blundell, 27 August 1897, *Ford.*

9 Snow to Ford, 25 July 1897, *Ford.*

10 Knight to Ford, 24 March 1898, *Ford.*

11 Knight to Ford, 1 April 1898, *Ford.*

12 Ford to Knight, 3 April 1898, *Ford.*

13 Knight to Ford, 14 April 1898, *Ford.*

14 Morrall to Ford, 20 April 1898, *Ford.*

15 Knight to Ford, 14 April 1898, *Ford.*

16 Snow to Ford, June 1899, *Ford.*

17 Snow to Ford, 28 June 1898, *Ford.*

18 Gasquet to Ford, 28 June 1898, *Ford.*

19 Ford to Members of the Council, 27 June 1898, *Ford.*

20 To the Right Reverend Father President, and the Very Reverend Fathers of the Regimen: Church at Ealing, June 1898, *Ford.*

21 *MCT*, 28 January 1899.

22 Dolan to Ford, 11 January 1899, *Dolan.*

23 Dolan to Ford, 19 February 1899, *Dolan.*

24 *MCT*, 18 February 1899.

25 *The Tablet*, 8 July 1899.

26 Dolan to Ford, 26 September 1899, *Ford.*

27 'Odds and Ends,' *DR*, December 1899, p. 314.

28 Dolan to Ford, 9 August 1901, *Dolan.*

29 Dolan to Ford, 16 February 1899, *Dolan.*

30 Dolan to Ford, 10 June 1899, *Dolan.*

31 Dolan to Ford, 26 September 1899, *Dolan.*

32 Dolan to Ford, 18 December 1899, *Dolan.*

33 Dolan to Ford, 30 December 1899, *Dolan.*

34 Missionary Statistics, 31 December 1899, EAA.

35 Dolan to Ford, 6 April 1900, *Dolan.*

36 Dolan to Ford, 17 April 1900, *Dolan.*

37 *MCT*, 16 February 1901.

38 *Ealing Gazette*, 16 February 1901.

39 *MCT*, 2 February 1901.

40 Dolan to Ford, 21 August 1901, *Dolan.*

41 Dolan to Ford, 7 March 1902, *Dolan.*

42 Dolan to Ford, 17 May 1903, *Dolan.*

43 Dolan to Ford, 16 June 1904, *Dolan.*

44 *Spiritualia Ministeria*, 1902, 1903, 1904, EAA.

45 Dolan to Ford, 27 February 1899, *Dolan.*

46 Dolan to Ford, 22 April 1901, *Dolan.*

47 Dolan to Ford, 2 March 1899, *Dolan.*

48 Dolan to Ford, 21 May 1902, *Dolan.*

49 Dolan to Ford, 5 January 1905, *Dolan.*

50 Dolan to Ford, 5 December 1900, *Dolan.*

51 Mission Statement, 31 December 1899, EAA.

52 Ford to Penny, 10 September 1900, *Ford.*

53 Dolan to Ford, 19 March 1899, *Ford.*

54 Dolan to Ford, 26 September 1899, *Dolan.*

55 Dolan to Ford, 6 October 1899, *Dolan.*

56 Dolan to Ford, 10 October 1899, *Dolan.*

57 Dolan to Ford, 23 October 1899, *Dolan.*

58 Dolan to Ford, 30 December 1899, *Dolan.*

59 Ibid.

60 Annual Account of the Mission of St Benedict, 1899, EAA.

61 Dolan to Ford, 16 February 1899, *Dolan.*

62 Dolan to Ford, 10 June 1899, *Dolan.*

63 Dolan to Ford, 19 June 1899, *Dolan.*

64 Dolan to Ford, 23 June 1899, *Dolan.*

65 Dolan to Ford, 30 July 1899, *Dolan.*

66 Sr. Aloysius to Ford, 8 July 1899, *Ford.*

67 Dolan to Ford, July 1899, *Ford.*

68 Dolan to Ford, 18 July 1899, *Dolan.*

69 Dolan to Ford, 28 August 1899, *Dolan.*

70 Dolan to Ford, 20 October 1899, *Dolan.*

71 Dolan to Ford, 5 January 1900, *Dolan.*

72 Mother Angelica to Ford, 6 February 1900, *Ford.*

73 Ford to Mother Angelica, 8 February 1900, *Ford.*

74 Sister to F.B., 10 & 12 February 1900, *Ford.*

75 Sister Angelica to Ford, 4 April 1900, *Ford.*

76 Dolan to Ford, 30 April 1900, *Ford.*

77 Dolan to Ford, 5 May 1900, *Ford.*

78 Russell to Ford, 31 May 1900, *Ford.*

79 Dolan to Ford, 3 June 1900, *Ford.*

80 Ford to Russell, 3 June 1900, *Ford.*

81 Russell to Ford, 5 June 1900, *Ford.*

82 Russell to Ford, 14 June 1900, *Ford.*

83 Ford to Russell, 24 July 1900, *Ford.*

84 Mother Angelica to Ford, 24 July 1900, *Ford.*

85 Russell to Ford, 25 July 1900, *Ford.*

86 Dolan to Ford, 28 July 1900, *Ford.*

87 Dolan to Ford, 18 August 1900, *Ford.*

88 Dolan to Ford, 15 September 1900, *Ford.*

89 Ford to Snow, 19 October 1900, *Ford.*

90 Ford to Russell, 11 September 1900, *Ford.*

91 Ford to Dolan, 18 February 1901, *Dolan.*

92 Dolan to Ford, 2 July 1901, *Dolan.*

93 Dolan to Ford, 21 August 1901, *Dolan.*

94 Dolan to Ford, 5 March 1900, *Dolan.*

95 The distance is about two miles. Corney to Ford, 25 January 1900, Corney Papers, EAA (*Corney*).

96 Corney to Ford, 2 March 1900, *Corney.*

97 W. Corney to Ford, 2 March 1900, *Corney.*

98 Dolan to Ford, 5 March 1900, *Dolan.*

99 Ford to Dolan, 15 March 1900, *Ford.*

100 Dolan to Ford, 10 March 1900, *Dolan.*

101 Ford to Dolan, 16 March 1900, *Ford.*

102 Ford to Snow, 15 March 1900, *Ford.*

103 Dolan to Ford, 5 November 1900, *Dolan.*

104 Annual Account of the Mission of St Benedict's Ealing, 31 December 1900, EAA.

105 Dolan to Ford, 5 February 1901, *Ford.*

106 Ibid.

107 Dolan to Ford, 22 April 1901, *Ford.*

108 Dolan to Ford, 7 October 1901, *Ford.*

109 Dolan to Ford, 28 October 1901, *Ford.*

110 Annual Account for the Mission of Ealing, 31 December 1891, EAA.

111 Abbot Ford's Report to Chapter, 1901, EAA.

112 *Ealing Gazette*, 16 February 1901.

113 J.G. Snead-Cox, *The Life of Cardinal Vaughan*, vol. ii, p. 349.

114 *The Tablet*, 1 June 1901. R. Kollar's *Westminster Cathedral: From Dream to Reality* tells the story of Cardinal Vaughan's attempt to staff his cathedral with Benedictine monks from England and France and the failure of this romantic vision.

115 Dolan to Ford, 7 February 1902, *Dolan*.

116 Dolan to Ford, 20 February 1902, *Dolan*.

117 Dolan to Ford, 22 February 1902, *Dolan*.

118 Mother Superior to Ford, 10 March 1902, *Ford*.

119 Ford to Mother Superior, 15 March 1902, *Ford*.

120 Mother Superior to Ford, 14 April 1902, *Ford*.

121 Ford to Mother Superior, 17 April 1902, *Ford*.

122 Mother Superior to Ford, 22 May 1902, *Ford*.
123 Ford to Mother Superior, 27 May 1902, *Ford*.

124 Dolan to Ford, 25 May 1902, *Dolan*.

125 Dolan to Ford, 14 July 1902, *Dolan*.

126 Dolan to Ford, 16 July 1902, *Dolan*.

127 Corney to Ford, 3 November 1902, *Ford*.

128 Dolan to Ford, 16 February 1899, *Dolan*.

129 Dolan to Ford, 19 February 1899, *Dolan*.

130 O'Halloran to O'Gorman, 8 March 1889, *Dolan*.

131 Note by Gilbert Dolan, 13 March 1899, *Dolan*.

132 Dolan to O'Gorman, 13 March 1889, *Dolan*.

133 O'Halloran to Vaughan, 10 July 1899, printed in *MCT*, 15 July 1899.

134 *The Universe*, July 1899.

135 Dolan to Ford, 18 July 1899, *Dolan*.

136 Vaughan to the *MCT*, printed in the *MCT*, 22 July 1899.

137 *MCT*, 15 July 1899.

138 O'Halloran to Vaughan, 24 July 1899, printed in *MCT*, 29 July 1899.

139 *MCT*, 5 August 1899.

140 *MCT*, 12 August 1899.

141 *MCT*, 26 August 1899.

142 *MCT*, 29 July 1899.

143 *MCT*, 12 August 1899.

144 *MCT*, 26 August 1899.

145 Dolan to Ford, 11 September 1899, *Dolan*.

146 *MCT*, 16 September 1899.

147 O'Halloran to Prior, St. Dominic's, London, 22 November 1899, *Dolan*.

148 O'Halloran to O'Gorman, 28 March 1900, O'Gorman Papers, DAA.

149 O'Halloran to Vaughan, 28 March 1900, O'Gorman Papers, DAA.

150 Dolan to Ford, 30 March 1900, *Dolan*.

151 O'Halloran to Dolan, 25 June 1900, *Ford*.

152 O'Halloran to Vaughan, 25 June 1900, *Ford*.

153 O'Halloran to Vaughan, 3 July 1900, *Ford*.

154 O'Halloran to Mother Superior, 15 December 1900, *Dolan*.

155 *Cardinal Vaughan and Father O'Halloran*

156 Ibid.

157 Ibid.

158 *Irish Catholic*, 24 July 1901.

159 *Freedmans Journal*, 25 March 190

CHAPTER IV:

CONSOLIDATION AND GROWTH: THE EARLY TWENTIETH CENTURY (pages 83–124)

1 Dolan to Ford, 19 June 1899, *Dolan*.

2 Dolan to Ford, 18 December 1899, *Dolan*.

3 Dolan to Ford, 21 August 1901, *Dolan*.

4 Ford to Dolan, 2 April 1902, *Ford*.

5 Quoted in B. Hicks, *Hugh Edmund Ford*, p. 93.

6 Corney to Ford, 6 April 1902, *Ford*.

7 'Report,' 1902, EAA.

8 Butler to Ford, 16 May 1902, *Ford*.

9 Ford to Butler, 20 May 1902, *Ford*.

10 Ford to Gasquet, 28 September 1902, *Ford*.

11 'Odds and Ends,' *DR*, 1902, p. 313.

12 'Obituary,' *DR*, July 1938, pp. 10–14.

13 *MCT*, 4 October 1904.

14 *Prospectus of Ealing Catholic Day School* 1902, EAA.

15 Cave to Ford, 7 November 1902, Cave Papers, EAA. (*Cave*).

16 Ford to Cave, 9 November 1902, *Ford*.

17 Cave to Ford, 20 November 1902, *Cave*.

18 Cave to Ford, 5 February 1903, *Cave*.

19 Ford to Cave, 11 February 1903, *Ford*.

20 Cave to Ford, 2 March 1903, *Cave*.

21 Cave to Ford, 27 October 1903, *Cave*.

22 Ford to Cave, 2 November 1903, *Ford*.

23 Cave to Ford, 5 February 1903, *Cave.*

24 Cave to Ford, 12 February 1903, *Cave.*

25 Cave to Ford, 14 March 1903, *Cave.*

26 *Ealing School Prospectus*, 1904, EAA.

27 Cave, 'Memorandum: Re Ealing,' *Cave.*

28 Ford to Cave, 28 September 1903, *Ford.*

29 Ford to Cave, 2 November 1903, *Ford.*

30 Cave to Ford, 14 March 1903, *Cave.*

31 Ford to Dolan, 7 April 1903, *Ford.*

32 Ford to Dolan, 8 June 1903, *Ford.*

33 Ford to Dolan, 9 June 1903, *Ford.*

34 Dolan to Ford, 5 October 1903, *Ford.*

35 Cave to Ford, 15 November 1903, *Cave.*

36 Dolan to Ford, 5 October 1903, *Ford.*

37 *Catholic Weekly*, 16 December 1904.

38 *Spiritualia Ministeria*, 1903, St Benedict's Ealing, EAA.

39 Ibid. R. Mudie-Smith, *The Religious Life of London* (London: Hodder and Stoughton, 1904), a random census of Sunday church attendance in the nation's capital, confirmed Dom Gilbert's estimation.

40 Dolan to Ford, 28 September 1903, *Dolan.*

41 Ford to Dolan, 3 September 1904, *Ford.*

42 Ford to Dolan, 17 July 1904, *Dolan.*

43 Cave to Ford, 15 November 1903, *Cave.*

44 Cave to Ford, 1 September 1904, *Cave.*

45 Annual Account of the Mission of Ealing, 1902, EAA.

46 Annual Account of the Mission of Ealing, 1903, EAA.

47 Annual Account of the Mission of Ealing, 1904, EAA.

48 Annual Account of the Mission of Ealing, 1906, EAA.

49 St Benedict's Church: Debt Fund, EAA.

50 Cave to Ford, 14 December 1902, *Cave.*

51 Ford to Dolan, 27 February 1903, *Ford.*

52 Circular, 1903, EAA.

53 Ford to Corney, 7 June 1903, *Ford.*

54 Ford to Cave, 29 September 1903, *Ford.*

55 Ford to Corney, 1 October 1903, *Ford.*

56 See pp. 93–6.

57 Dolan to Ford, 5 October 1903, *Ford.*

58 Dolan to Ford, 10 December 1903, *Ford*.

59 Circular, 1904.

60 Circular, 1905.

61 *The Tablet*, 2 April 1904.

62 *MCT*, 27 June 1903.

63 *Ealing Gazette*, 27 June 1903.

64 Dolan to Ford, 22 March 1904, *Ford*.

65 *Ealing Gazette*, 26 March 1904.

66 Dolan to Ford, 22 March 1904, *Ford*.

67 *Daily Chronicle*, 21 March 1904; *Universe*, 26 March 1904.

68 *Ealing Gazette*, 26 March 1904.

69 Dolan to Ford, 22 March 1904, *Ford*.

70 B. Hicks, *Hugh Edmund Ford*, p. 97.

71 Ford to Gasquet, 10 August 1906, printed in B. Hicks, *Hugh Edmund Ford*, p. 97.

72 Gasquet to Ford, 11 August 1906, printed in B. Hicks, *Hugh Edmund Ford*, p. 97.

73 See pp. 86–8.

74 Quoted in B. Hicks, *Hugh Edmund Ford*, p. 99.

75 'Odds and Ends,' *DR*, July 1907, p. 207.

76 'Dom Leo Almond,' *DR*, May 1926, p. 197.

77 Butler to Chambers, 29 March 1907, *Ford*.

78 *Spiritualia Ministeria*, 1904, EAA.

79 Visitation Report, Diocese of Westminster, 1905, AAW.

80 Johnson to Ford, 5 May 1907, *Ford*.

81 Cox to Ford, 3 January 1908, *Ford*.

82 Memo, 21 January 1908, *Ford*.

83 Ibid.

84 Visitation Report, Diocese of Westminster, 1907, AAW.

85 Memo, 21 January 1908, EAA.

86 B. Hicks, *Hugh Edmund Ford*, p. 138.

87 *The Tablet*, 27 March 1909.

88 Butler to Gasquet, 24 September 1907, Gasquet Papers, DAA. (*Gasquet*).

89 Butler to Gasquet, 27 September 1907, *Gasquet*.

90 Butler to Almond, 7 April 1909, Almond Papers, EAA.

91 Butler to Almond, 14 April 1909, Almond Papers, EAA.

92 B. Hicks, *Hugh Edmund Ford*, p. 138.

93 Ibid., pp. 138–9.

94 Ealing Mission and School: Abstract of Accounts, 1911–1915, EAA.

95 Third Triennial Visitation, 1911, Finance, EAA.

96 Ealing Mission and School: Abstract of Accounts, 1911–1915, EAA.

97 Cave to Butler, 9 January 1911, *Cave.*

98 'Odds and Ends,' *DR*, December 1913, p. 364.

99 Ford to Butler, 4 August 1914, *Ford.*

100 Butler to Ford, 12 December 1912, *Butler.*

101 Butler to Cave and Kuypers, 16 January 1913, *Cave.*

102 Second Triennial Visitation Return, Archdiocese of Westminster, 1908, AAW.

103 Ford, 'Notes on Ealing 26.1.08,' EAA.

104 Second Triennial Visitation Return, Archdiocese of Westminster, 1908, AAW.

105 Third Triennial Visitation Return, Archdiocese of Westminster, 1911, AAW.

106 Fourth Triennial Visitation Return, Archdiocese of Westminster, 1911, AAW.

107 *Catholic Weekly*, 16 December 1904.

108 Ford to Cave, 10 April 1904, *Ford.*

109 Ford to Cave, 3 September 1904, *Ford.*

110 Cave to Ford, 16 October 1904, *Cave.*

111 Ford to Borzoli, 17 October 1904, *Ford.*

112 J.B. Bicknell, 'In the Beginning,' *The Priorian*, 1977–78, p. 25.

113 B. Bolton, 'Fifty Years: St. Benedict's School, 1902–1952,' *The Priorian*, Summer 1952, p. 553.

114 'Odds and Ends,' *DR*, July 1907, p. 218.

115 Butler to Cave, 8 March 1907, *Cave.*

116 Butler to Cave, 13 March 1907, *Cave.*

117 *MCT*, 8 July 1905.

118 *MCT*, 11 July 1914.

119 'Education: St. Benedict's Ealing,' *The Whitehall Review*, 7 March 1908.

120 'Odds and Ends,' *DR*, December 1913, p. 364.

121 Cave to Butler, 18 June 1911, *Ford.*

122 Sr Maria to Ford, 2 September 1904, *Ford.*

123 Ford to Sr Maria, 3 September 1904, *Ford.*

124 Ford to Cave, 3 September 1904, *Ford.*

125 Ford to Dolan, 3 September 1904, *Ford.*

126 Sr Maria to Ford, 5 September 1904, *Ford.*

127 Ford to Sr Maria, 10 September 1904, *Ford.*

128 Mother Mary Frances to Butler, 10 March 1910, *Ford.*

129 Mother Mary Clara to Bolton, 19 December 1955, Bolton Papers, EAA.

130 Butler to Mother Mary Frances, 13 March 1910, *Ford.*

131 O'Halloran to Rev Mother, 1910, O'Halloran Papers, EAA.

132 R. Mudie-Smith, *The Religious Life of London*.

133 *Daily Chronicle*, 23 March 1903.

134 *MCT*, 25 April 1903.

135 *MCT*, 1 July 1905.

136 O'Halloran to Ferriera, 22 January 1903, O'Halloran Papers, EAA.

137 Sass and Young to O'Halloran, 23 January 1903, O'Halloran Papers, EAA.

138 Sass and Young to Webb, 23 January 1903, O'Halloran Papers, EAA.

139 O'Halloran to Sass and Young, 23 January 1903, O'Halloran Papers, EAA.

140 O'Halloran to Sass and Young, 24 January 1903, O'Halloran Papers, EAA.

141 Sass and Young to O'Halloran, 26 January 1903, O'Halloran Papers, EAA.

142 Dunn to Sass and Young, 27 January 1903, O'Halloran Papers, EAA.

143 O'Halloran to Sass and Young, 27 January 1903, O'Halloran Papers, EAA.

144 Corney to Ford, 28 August 1903, *Corney*.

145 O'Halloran to Gasquet, 21 August 1903, *Gasquet*.

146 O'Halloran to Gasquet, 14 September 1903, *Gasquet*.

147 Gasquet to O'Halloran, September 1903, *Gasquet*.

148 O'Halloran to Gasquet, 16 September 1903, *Gasquet*.

149 Gasquet to O'Halloran, 29 October 1903, *Gasquet*.

150 O'Halloran to Gasquet, 18 October 1903, *Gasquet*.

151 O'Halloran to Fenton, 17 October 1903, *Gasquet*.

152 Fenton to O'Halloran, 29 October 1903, printed in *MCT*, 27 October 1904.

153 O'Halloran to Gasquet, 18 October 1903, *Gasquet*.

154 O'Halloran to Merry Del Val, 21 March 1904, printed in *MCT*, 26 March 1904.

155 Dolan to Ford, 27 March 1904, *Dolan*.

156 Bourne to Dolan, 28 March 1904, *Dolan*.

157 *MCT*, 2 April 1904.

158 O'Halloran to ?, 10 April 1904, O'Halloran Papers, EAA.

159 S. Congregazione de Propaganda Fide to Bourne, 2 April 1907, Roman Letters VII, AAW.

160 O'Halloran to Gasquet, 27 May 1907, *Gasquet*.

161 *MCT*, 2 March 1904.

162 *MCT*, 5 February 1910

163 *MCT*, 8 October 1910.

164 *MCT*, 5 November 1910.

165 *MCT*, 26 November 1910.

166 *The Tablet*, 12 November 1910.

167 *Catholic Herald*, 28 January 1911.

168 *Catholic Herald*, 4 February 1911.

169 Sacred Congregation of the Council to Bourne, 6 December 1910, Roman Letters VII, AAW.

170 *MCT*, 30 September 1911.

171 *MCT*, 7 October 1911.

172 *Ealing Gazette*, 26 October 1913.

173 O'Halloran to Butler, December 1913, *Butler*.

174 Notificatio, 16 April 1914, Roman Letters VIII, AAW.

CHAPTER V:

BETWEEN THE WARS: A DEPENDENT OR INDEPENDENT EALING PRIORY?
(pages 125–156)

1 'The Reception of His Eminence Cardinal Gasquet,' *Ealing Catholic School Magazine*, July 1914, p. 5. Publication of this magazine was suspended during the First World War. It reappeared in December 1927 under the name of *The Priorian*.

2 Ibid., p. 19.

3 Fourth Triennial Visitation Returns, Diocese of Westminster, 1914, AAW.

4 Ealing Comprehensive Statement, 1916, *Ford*.

5 The Economus was a monk in charge of the finances of the parishes and missions of Downside.

6 Ealing Comprehensive Statement.

7 'Odds and Ends,' *DR*, December 1914, p. 303.

8 'Odds and Ends,' *DR*, December 1915, p. 243.

9 'The Late Dom Gilbert Dolan,' *Ealing Catholic School Magazine*, July 1914, p. 7.

10 Almond to Butler, 3 April 1909, Butler Papers, EAA (*Butler EAA*).

11 B. Hicks, *Hugh Edmund Ford*, p. 139.

12 Almond to Butler, 13 April 1909, *Butler EAA*.

13 See F.W. Scouse, ed., *Ealing 1901–1951* (Ealing: Ealing Town Council, 1951), pp. 93–6.

14 'The War Memorial,' *The Priorian*, December 1927, p. 9. Pages 9 and 10 contain the list of those who died in action. A War Memorial was later dedicated in November 1928.

15 B. Hicks, *Hugh Edmund Ford*, p. 139.

16 Ealing Comprehensive Statement.

17 Abbot Ford, Notes on Abbot Butler's Report of July, *Ford.*.

18 Ealing Comprehensive Statement.

19 Abbot Ford, Notes on Abbot Butler's Report.

20 Report of the Ealing Committee, 1916, Ealing Papers, DAA.

21 Ealing Comprehensive Statement.

22 Suggestions Re Ealing Priory and School, 1916, **Ford.**

23 Hudleston to Butler, 17 July 1916, *Butler.*

24 Cave to Butler, 26 June 1916, *Butler.*

25 Butler to the Ealing Benedictines, 28 July 1916, *Butler EAA.*

26 Green to Butler, 29 July 1916, *Butler EAA.*

27 Rylance to Butler, 29 July 1916, *Butler EAA.*

28 Goolden to Butler, July 1916, *Butler EAA.*

29 Butler to Pearson, 7 August 1916, *Butler EAA.*

30 Pearson to Butler, 8 August 1916, Pearson Papers EAA (*Pearson*).

31 Pearson to Butler, 9 August 1916, *Pearson.*

32 Butler to Pearson, 11 August 1916, *Butler EAA.*

33 Pearson to Butler, 12 August 1916, *Pearson.*

34 Butler to Pearson, 13 August 1916, *Butler EAA.*

35 Pearson to Butler, 14 August 1916, *Pearson.*

36 'Odds and Ends,' *DR*, July 1916, p. 161.

37 'Obituary: Dom Wulstan Pearson,' *DR*, January 1939, p. 1.

38 'Dom Sebastian Cave,' *The Priorian*, July 1938, p. 231.

39 Butler to Bourne, 17 August 1916, *Butler.*

40 Bourne to Butler, 19 August 1916, *Butler.*

41 Butler to Bourne, 3 November 1916, Bourne Papers, Bo. 5/48d, AAW.

42 Butler to Bourne, 8 November 1916, Bourne Papers, Bo. 5/48d, AAW.

43 C. Butler, 'On Dependent and Independent Priories,' 8 November 1916, Bourne Papers, Bo. 5/48d, AAW.

44 Butler to Pearson, 18 December 1916, *Butler.*

45 Hudleston to Butler, 21 December 1916, *Butler.*

46 Hudleston to Butler, 30 December 1916, *Butler.*

47 The notes were written by Cardinal Bourne on a letter from Abbot Butler, Butler to Bourne, 29 October 1918, Bourne Papers, Bo. 5/48d, AAW.

48 Hudleston to Butler, 21 December 1916, *Butler.*

49 Hudleston to Butler, 2 March 1917, *Butler EAA.*

50 Butler to Pearson, 3 April 1917, *Butler EAA.*

51 Pearson to Butler, April 1917, *Butler.*

52 Hudleston to Butler, 16 April 1917, *Butler EAA*.

53 Butler to Pearson, 24 June 1917, *Butler EAA*.

54 Pearson to Butler, June 1917, *Pearson*.

55 Butler to Ephrem Seddon, 4 January 1918, *Butler*.

56 Hudleston to Butler, 7 April 1918, *Butler EAA*.

57 Hudleston, Open Letter, 4 September 1918, *Pearson*.

58 Pearson to Butler, 5 January 1917, *Butler*.

59 Hudleston to Butler, 2 March 1917, *Butler EAA*.

60 Butler to Pearson, 24 June 1917, *Butler*.

61 Butler to Pearson, 22 August 1917, *Butler EAA*.

62 Pearson to Butler, August 1917, *Pearson*.

63 Pearson to Butler, 9 December 1917, *Pearson*.

64 Pearson to Butler, 22 January 1918, *Butler*.

65 Butler to Pearson, 7 January 1918, *Butler*.

66 Pearson to Butler, 8 January 1918, *Butler*.

67 Butler to Pearson, 11 December 1918, *Butler*.

68 Butler to Cox, 29 March 1917, *Butler EAA*.

69 'Ealing Abbey Appeal,' February 1917, EAA.

70 Butler to Kuypers, 5 May 1918, *Butler EAA*.

71 Butler to Kuypers, 4 December 1919, *Butler EAA*.

72 Hudleston to Butler, 7 April 1918, *Butler EAA*.

73 Pontifex to Butler, 2 March 1919, *Butler EAA*.

74 Diocese of Westminster Visitation Returns, 1918, EAA.

75 D. Knowles, 'Abbot Butler: A Memoir,' *DR*, July 1934, p. 404.

76 Ibid., p. 405.

77 Ibid., p. 406.

78 Ibid., p. 414.

79 Butler to Bourne, 12 November 1922, *Butler EAA*.

80 Butler, 'Conventual Chapter,' September 1926, *Butler*.

81 Butler, 'Ealing Priory,' 1927, *Butler EAA*.

82 'The First Bishop of Lancaster,' *DR*, May 1925, p. 85.

83 Pearson to Ramsey, 26 December 1924, Ramsey Papers, DAA (*Ramsey*).

84 Ramsey to Pearson, 13 December 1924, *Ramsey*.

85 Pearson to Ramsey, 20 December 1924, *Ramsey*.

86 Pearson to Ramsey, December 1924, *Ramsey*.

87 *MCT*, 17 October 1925.

88 B. Kuypers, Memo on Fr O'Halloran, EAA.

89 Diocese of Westminster Visitation Returns, 1923, EAA.

90 Diocese of Westminster Visitation Returns, 1928, EAA.

91 Butler, Ealing Priory, 1927, *Butler EAA*.

92 'Ealing Priory, 1898–1938,' *The Priorian*, 1938, p. 225.

93 'The Church Extension,' *The Priorian*, December 1932, p. 110.
94 *MCT*, 27 August 1932.

95 'Odds and Ends,' *DR*, July 1934, p. 17.

96 'Odds and Ends,' *DR*, October 1930, p. 355.

97 'The School Extension,' *The Priorian*, Spring 1936, p. 88.

98 *MCT*, 13 February 1937.

99 'Odds and Ends,' *The Priorian*, October 1929, p. 146.

100 'Prior Kuypers,' *The Priorian*, October 1935, p. 41.

101 Secretary to Evans, 13 July 1932, *Ealing DAA*.

102 Secretary to Evans, 20 July 1932, *Ealing DAA*.

103 Bolton to Chapman, 15 August 1932, *Ealing DAA*.

104 Bolton, 'The Ealing Question,' 15 August 1932, *Ealing DAA*.

105 Hicks to Kuypers, 8 March 1934, *Ealing DAA*.

106 'Editorial,' *The Priorian*, July 1938, p. 219.

CHAPTER VI

ANOTHER WAR, AND INDEPENDENCE
(pages 157–188)

1 'Ealing Priory, 1898–1938, An Historical Sketch,' *The Priorian*, 1938, p. 229.

2 Morey to Hicks, 24 March 1938, Ealing 1930–38, DAA.

3 Interview with Dom Adrian Morey, August 1983, St Benet's, Cambridge, EAA.

4 Morey to Hicks, 24 March 1938, Ealing 1930–38, DAA.

5 Morey to Hicks, 5 May 1938, Ealing 1930–38, DAA.

6 Morey, 'Ealing School,' 7 June 1938, Ealing 1930–38, DAA.

7 Morey to Hicks, 26 July 1938, Ealing 1930–38, DAA.

8 Morey to Hicks, 18 September 1938, Ealing 1930–38, DAA.

9 Morey to Hicks, 28 September 1938, Ealing 1930–38, DAA.

10 Pontifex to Hicks, 27 September 1938, Ealing 1930–38, DAA.

11 Morey to Hicks, 28 September 1938, Ealing 1930–38, DAA.

12 Chatterton to Trafford, 18 January 1939, Ealing 1939–40, DAA.

13 Morey to Trafford, 29 March 1939, Ealing 1939–40, DAA.

14 Noonan to Trafford, 17 May 1939, Ealing 1939–40, DAA.

15 Trafford to Noonan, 19 May 1939, Ealing 1939–40, DAA.

16 Trafford to Morey, 3 June 1939, Ealing 1939–40, DAA.

17 Morey to Trafford, June 1939, Ealing 1939–40, DAA.

18 Morey to Trafford, 4 July 1939, Ealing 1939–40, DAA.

19 Thierry to Trafford, 2 September 1939, Ealing 1939–40, DAA.

20 Trafford to Thierry, 4 September 1939, Ealing 1939–40, DAA.

21 McNabb to Trafford, 4 September 1939, Ealing 1939–40, DAA.

22 Shuldham to Trafford, 4 September 1939, Ealing 1939–40, DAA.

23 Trafford to McNabb, 5 September 1939, Ealing 1939–40, DAA.

24 Trafford to Wood, 7 September 1939, Ealing 1939–40, DAA.

25 Trafford to Shuldham, 7 September 1939, Ealing 1939–40, DAA.

26 Morey to Trafford, 7 September 1939, Ealing 1939–40, DAA.

27 Chatterton to Trafford, 24 September 1939, Ealing 1939–40, DAA.

28 'Circular,' September 1939, Ealing 1939–40, DAA.

29 N. Longmate, *How We Lived Then: A History of Everyday Life during the Second World War* (London: Hutchinson, 1971), p. 61.

30 Hall to Trafford, 1 November 1939, Ealing 1939–40, DAA.

31 Trafford to Hall, 3 November 1939, Ealing 1939–40, DAA.

32 Chatterton to Trafford, 5 March 1940, Ealing 1939–40, DAA.

33 Trafford to Chatterton, 28 March 1940, Ealing 1939–40, DAA.

34 Trafford to Chatterton, April 1940, Ealing 1939–40, DAA.

35 'Dom Gervase Hobson-Matthews, C.F.,' *The Priorian*, January 1941, p. 137.

36 Matthews to Chatterton, 15 May 1940, Chatterton Papers, EAA.

37 N. Longmate, *How We Lived Then*, p. 61.

38 Hinsley to Chatterton, 11 June 1940, Chatterton Papers, EAA.

39 Trafford to Hall, 5 July 1940, Ealing 1939–40, DAA.

40 Hall to Trafford, 12 July 1940, Ealing 1939–40, DAA.

41 Trafford to Hall, 13 July 1940, Ealing 1939–40, DAA.

42 Trafford to Hall, 19 July 1940, Ealing 1939–40, DAA.

43 Hall to Trafford, 21 July 1940, Ealing 1939–40, DAA.

44 C.R. Wallis, 'Ealing at War,' in F.W. Scouse, *Ealing 1901–1951*, p. 94.

45 *MCT*, 12 October 1940.

46 C.R. Wallis, 'Ealing at War,' p. 94.

47 Ibid., p. 95.

48 Hall to Trafford, 21 September 1940, Ealing 1939–40, DAA.

49 Chatterton to Trafford, 21 September 1940, Ealing 1939–40, DAA.

50 Chatterton to Trafford, 26 September 1940, Ealing 1939–40, DAA.

51 Chatterton to Trafford, October 1940, Ealing 1939–40, DAA.

52 'Editorial,' *The Priorian*, January 1941, p. 133.

53 Hall to Trafford, 21 September 1940, Ealing 1939–40, DAA.

54 Chatterton to Trafford, 21 September 1940, Ealing 1939–40, DAA.

55 Chatterton to Trafford, 26 September 1940, Ealing 1939–40, DAA.

56 Chatterton to Trafford, 27 September 1940, Ealing 1939–40, DAA.

57 Chatterton to Trafford, 29 September 1940, Ealing 1939–40, DAA.

58 Chatterton to Trafford, October 1940, Ealing 1939–40, DAA.

59 *MCT*, 12 October 1940.

60 Chatterton to Trafford, 22 October 1940, Ealing 1939–40, DAA.

61 Chatterton to Trafford, 3 December 1940, Ealing 1939–40, DAA.

62 Chatterton to Trafford, 21 September 1940, Ealing 1939–40, DAA.

63 Chatterton to Trafford, 26 September 1940, Ealing 1939–40, DAA.

64 'Fifty Years, St Benedict's School, 1902–1952,' *The Priorian*, Summer, 1952, p. 571.

65 Ibid.

66 Chatterton to Trafford, 26 September 1940, Ealing 1939–40, DAA.

67 'Fifty Years, St Benedict's School, 1902–1952,' p. 571.

68 Chatterton to Trafford, 27 September 1940, Ealing 1939–40, DAA.

69 Chatterton to Trafford, October 1940, Ealing 1939–40, DAA.

70 Chatterton to Trafford, 26 September 1940, Ealing 1939–40, DAA.

71 Chatterton to Trafford, October 1940, Ealing 1939–40, DAA.

72 Chatterton to Trafford, October 1940, Ealing 1939–40, DAA.

73 Chatterton to Trafford, October 1940, Ealing 1939–40, DAA.

74 Chatterton to Trafford, 22 October 1940, Ealing 1939–40, DAA.

75 Chatterton to Trafford, 3 September 1940, Ealing 1939–40, DAA.

76 Ibid.

77 Visitation Report, 1948, EAA.

78 Chatterton to Trafford, 5 December 1940, Ealing 1939–40, DAA.

79 Chatterton to Trafford, 9 January 1941, Ealing 1939–40, DAA.

80 'Odds and Ends,' *The Priorian*, May 1942, p. 129.

81 Chatterton to Trafford, 10 April 1941, Ealing 1941–44, DAA.

82 Chatterton to Trafford, 17 May 1943, Ealing 1941–44, DAA.

83 Hall to Trafford, 28 May 1943, Ealing 1941–44, DAA.

84 Browne to Hall, 27 July 1943, Ealing 1941–44, DAA.

85 'Ealing Priory School: Recommendations Made by H.M. Inspectors at Full Inspection,' May 1943, Ealing 1941–44, DAA.

86 Chatterton to Trafford, 23 February 1944, Ealing 1941–44, DAA.

87 Chatterton to Trafford, February 1944, Ealing 1941–44, DAA.

88 Trafford to Chatterton, 3 July 1944, Ealing 1941–44, DAA.

89 Trafford to Fathers, 6 March 1945, Ealing 1945-Independence, DAA.

90 Hall to Trafford, 9 March 1945, Ealing 1945-Independence, DAA.

91 Trafford to Hall, 12 March 1945, Ealing 1945–Independence, DAA.

92 Trafford to Hall, 19 March 1945, Ealing 1945–Independence, DAA.

93 Trafford to Hall, 16 April 1945, Ealing 1945-Independence, DAA.

94 Chatterton to Trafford, 18 April 1945, Ealing 1945–Independence, DAA.

95 Trafford to Chatterton, 19 April 1945, Ealing 1945–Independence, DAA.

96 Trafford to Hall, 5 May 1945, Ealing 1945–Independence, DAA.

97 Orchard to Trafford, 7 May 1945, Ealing 1945–Independence, DAA.

98 Interview with Dom Bernard Orchard, August 1983, Ealing Abbey, EAA.

99 Orchard to Trafford, 15 May 1945, Ealing 1945–Independence, DAA.

100 Abbot Trafford, 'Circular Letter,' 24 May 1945, Ealing 1945–Independence DAA.

101 Agius to Trafford, 25 September 1945, Agius Papers, EAA.

102 Agius to Trafford, 8 October 1945, Agius Papers, EAA.

103 Orchard to Trafford, 6 May 1945, Ealing 1945–Independence, DAA.

104 Butler to Fathers, 10 July 1947, Independence File, DAA.

105 'Ealing Priory: Auditors' Report on Accounts for 1946,' Ealing 1945–Independence, DAA.

106 Butler to Fathers, 10 July 1947, Independence File, DAA.

107 Circular Letter, 21 August 1947, Independence File, DAA.

108 'Announcement of General Chapter,' Abbot Herbert Byrne, Autumn 1947, Independence File, DAA.

109 Butler to Fathers, 15 October 1947, Independence File, DAA.

110 Langdon to Butler, 15 November 1947, Independence File, DAA.

111 'Cardinal Griffin's Sermon,' *The Priorian*, March 1948, p. 221.

112 Ibid., p. 222.

113 'Sermon of the Abbot of Downside,' *The Priorian*, March 1948, p. 224.

114 Ibid., p. 225

115 Ibid., p. 227.

116 'Editorial,' *The Priorian*, March 1948, p. 217.

117 'Downside News,' *DR*, January 1948, p. 2.

118 Hicks to Pontifex, 14 December 1947, Independence File, EAA.

119 Chatterton to Bolton, 18 December 1947, Independence File, EAA.

120 Butler to Pontifex, 2 December 1947, Independence File, EAA.

EPILOGUE Pages 189–92

1 'Priory Chronicle,' *The Priorian*, September 1948, p. 276.
2 Pontifex to Butler, 19 January 1949, Pontifex Papers, EAA.
3 Memo: Overton, 25 February 1949, Pontifex Papers, EAA.
4 Pontifex to Butler, 25 March 1949, Pontifex Papers, EAA.
5 *Londinii in Urbe*, 26 May 1955, EAA.

Bibliography

A. MANUSCRIPT COLLECTIONS

Leo Almond Papers, Ealing Abbey Archives.

Ambrose Agius Papers, Ealing Abbey Archives.

Basil Bolton Papers, Ealing Abbey Archives.

Francis Bourne Papers, Archives of the Archdiocese of Westminster.

Cuthbert Butler Papers, Downside Abbey Archives, Ealing Abbey Archives.

Sebastian Cave Papers, Ealing Abbey Archives.

Stanislaus Chatterton Papers, Ealing Abbey Archives.

Vincent Corney Papers, Ealing Abbey Archives.

Gilbert Dolan Papers, Ealing Abbey Archives.

Edmund Ford Papers, Downside Abbey Archives, Ealing Abbey Archives.

Aidan Gasquet Papers, Downside Abbey Archives, Ealing Abbey Archives.

Anselm O'Gorman Papers, Downside Abbey Archives, Ealing Abbey Archives.

Richard O'Halloran Papers, Downside Abbey Archives, Ealing Abbey Archives, Mill Hill Archives.

Wulstan Pearson Papers, Ealing Abbey Archives.

Charles Pontifex Papers, Ealing Abbey Archives.

Leander Ramsey Papers, Downside Abbey Archives.

Herbert Vaughan Papers, Archives of the Archdiocese of Westminster, Ealing Abbey Archives.

The papers of Christopher Butler, Stanislaus Chatterton, Rupert Hall, Roger Hudleston, Adrian Morey, Bernard Orchard, Wulstan Pearson and Siegebert Trafford are located at Downside Abbey Archives. They are filed under Ealing Abbey Papers, which are arranged in chronological order: Ealing Papers, Foundation to 1929; Ealing Papers, 1930–1938; Ealing Papers, 1939–1940; Ealing Papers, 1941–1944; Ealing Papers, 1945–Independence; and Ealing Papers, Independence.

B. NEWSPAPERS AND PERIODICALS.

Catholic Herald

Catholic Times

Catholic Weekly

Daily Chronicle

Daily Mail

Downside Review

Ealing Catholic School Magazine

Ealing Gazette

Freedman's Journal

Irish Catholic

Middlesex County Times

The Priorian

The Tablet

The Whitehall Review

Universe

Westminster Gazette

C. PRINTED BOOKS.

A Mill Hill Father, *Remembered in Blessing: The Courtfield Story*, London, 1969.

Beck, G. (ed.), *The English Catholics: 1850–1950*, London, 1950.

Birt, H., *Obit Book of the English Benedictines from 1600 to 1912*, Edinburgh, 1923.

———. *History of Downside School*, London, 1902.

British Museum, *The Benedictines in Britain*, London, 1969.

Chadwick, O., *The Victorian Church*, Part I, London, 1972.

Ealing: A County Town Near London, 1904. No author or place of publication given.

Green, B., *The English Benedictine Congregation*, London, 1980.

Hastings, A. (ed.), *Bishops and Writers: Aspects of the Evolution of Modern English Catholicism*, Wheathampstead, 1977.

Heenan, J., *Cardinal Hinsley*, London, 1944.

Hicks, B., *Hugh Edmund Ford*, London, 1947.

Hicks, M.A., 'Ealing and Brentford,' in *The Victorian History of the Counties of England: A History of Middlesex* vol. vii, Oxford, 1982.

Holmes, J.D., *More Roman than Rome: English Catholicism in the Nineteenth Century*, London, 1978.

Jackson, E., *Annals of Ealing: From the Twelfth Century to the Present Time*, London, 1890.

Jahn, A., *Railroads and Suburban Development: Outer West London 1850– 1900* (University of London M. Phil. thesis, 1970; University of London Library).

Jones, C., *From Village to Corporate Town or Forty Years of Municipal Life*, Ealing, 1903.

Kollar, R., *Westminster Cathedral: From Dream to Reality*, Edinburgh, 1987.

Longmate, N., *How We Lived Then: A History of Everyday Life During the Second World War*, London, 1971.

Mudie-Smith, R., *The Religious Life of London*, London, 1904.

Norman, E., *Roman Catholicism in England from the Elizabethan Settlement to the Second Vatican Council*, Oxford, 1985.

———. *The English Catholic Church in the Nineteenth Century*, Oxford, 1984.

O'Halloran, R., *Cardinal Vaughan and Father O'Halloran: the Rights of the Secular Priests Vindicated*, Ealing, 1901.

Oldmeadow, E., *Francis Cardinal Bourne* 2 vols., London, 1940.

Pearce, D., *Ealing Abbey*, Ealing, 1980.

Leslie, S., *Henry Edward Manning: His Life and Labour*, London, 1921.

Purcell, E.S., *Life of Cardinal Manning, Archbishop of Westminster* 2 vols., London, 1896.

Reynolds, E.E., *The Roman Catholic Church in England and Wales*, Wheathampstead, 1973.

Robbins, M., *Middlesex*, London, 1953.

Scouse, F.W. (ed.), *Ealing 1901–1951*, Ealing, 1951.

Snead-Cox, J.G., *The Life of Cardinal Vaughan* 2 vols., London, 1910.

Timms, M., 'Brentham, A Pioneer Garden Suburb,' in *Local Historian* (1964).

Watkin, E.J., *Roman Catholicism in England from the Reformation to 1950*, London, 1957.

Whelan, B., *The Annals of the English Congregation of the Black Monks of St Benedict* (1850–1900), 1971.

Index

Books of general Christian interest as well as books on theology,
scripture, spirituality and mysticism are available from the pub-
lishers Burns and Oates and Search Press Limited. A catalogue
will be sent free on request.

Burns and Oates
Search Press Limited
Wellwood, North Farm Road, Tunbridge Wells, Kent TN2 3DR
Tel. (0892) 510850